CORRUPTION FROM A REGULATORY PERSPECTIVE

This book seeks to enrich and, in some cases, reverse current ideas on corruption and its prevention. It is a long-held belief that sanctions are the best guard against corrupt practice. This innovative work argues that in some cases sanctions may paradoxically increase corruption and that controls provide opportunities for corrupt transactions. Instead, this book suggests that better regulation and responsive enforcement, not sanctions, offer the most effective response to corruption. Taking both a theoretical and applied approach, it examines the question from a regulatory perspective, drawing particularly on regulatory effectiveness, to provide a model for tackling corrupt practices.

Corruption from a Regulatory Perspective

Maria De Benedetto

·HART·
OXFORD · LONDON · NEW YORK · NEW DELHI · SYDNEY

HART PUBLISHING

Bloomsbury Publishing Plc

Kemp House, Chawley Park, Cumnor Hill, Oxford, OX2 9PH, UK

1385 Broadway, New York, NY 10018, USA

29 Earlsfort Terrace, Dublin 2, Ireland

HART PUBLISHING, the Hart/Stag logo, BLOOMSBURY and the Diana logo are trademarks of Bloomsbury Publishing Plc

First published in Great Britain 2021

First published in hardback, 2021

Paperback edition, 2023

Copyright © Maria De Benedetto, 2021

Maria De Benedetto has asserted her right under the Copyright, Designs and Patents Act 1988 to be identified as Author of this work.

All rights reserved. No part of this publication may be reproduced or transmitted in any form or by any means, electronic or mechanical, including photocopying, recording, or any information storage or retrieval system, without prior permission in writing from the publishers.

While every care has been taken to ensure the accuracy of this work, no responsibility for loss or damage occasioned to any person acting or refraining from action as a result of any statement in it can be accepted by the authors, editors or publishers.

All UK Government legislation and other public sector information used in the work is Crown Copyright ©. All House of Lords and House of Commons information used in the work is Parliamentary Copyright ©. This information is reused under the terms of the Open Government Licence v3.0 (http://www.nationalarchives.gov.uk/doc/open-government-licence/version/3) except where otherwise stated.

All Eur-lex material used in the work is © European Union, http://eur-lex.europa.eu/, 1998–2023.

A catalogue record for this book is available from the British Library.

Library of Congress Cataloging-in-Publication data

Names: De Benedetto, Maria, author.
Title: Corruption from a regulatory perspective / Maria De Benedetto.
Description: Oxford, UK ; New York, NY : Hart Publishing, an imprint of Bloomsbury Publishing, 2021. | Includes bibliographical references and index.
Identifiers: LCCN 2021021406 (print) | LCCN 2021021407 (ebook) | ISBN 9781509929214 (hardback) | ISBN 9781509953257 (paperback) | ISBN 9781509929238 (pdf) | ISBN 9781509929221 (Epub)
Subjects: LCSH: Corruption—Law and legislation. | Corruption—Prevention. | Sanctions, Administrative. | Sanctions (Law)
Classification: LCC K5261 .D43 2021 (print) | LCC K5261 (ebook) | DDC 345/.02323—dc23
LC record available at https://lccn.loc.gov/2021021406
LC ebook record available at https://lccn.loc.gov/2021021407

ISBN: PB: 978-1-50995-325-7
ePDF: 978-1-50992-923-8
ePub: 978-1-50992-922-1

Typeset by Compuscript Ltd, Shannon

To find out more about our authors and books visit www.hartpublishing.co.uk. Here you will find extracts, author information, details of forthcoming events and the option to sign up for our newsletters.

to my children

ACKNOWLEDGEMENTS

Nobody writes a book alone. I would like to express my gratitude to a long list of persons who generously helped me during these years.

I met the three topics of *regulation, controls* and *corruption* thanks to the mentoring of Marco D'Alberti, so my debt of gratitude to him is particularly great. During the course of twenty years, I have reflected on many aspects of these topics together with Nicoletta Rangone, by developing an academic and human partnership.

More recently, I have had the opportunity to discuss the table of contents with colleagues and friends, and I received suggestions on many of the issues analysed in the book: among others, Edoardo Chiti, Guido Corso, Jose Esteve Pardo, Juli Ponce Solé, Claudio Maria Radaelli, Helen Xanthaki. I would also like to remember an important conversation with Adam Greycar, at Flinders University in 2014; the academic dialogue with Cary Coglianese and Bertrand du Marais; as well as the long-standing cooperation with Giuseppe Busia, current President of the Italian Anticorruption Authority.

Three prominent colleagues and friends have been extraordinarily generous and patient in reading chapters, giving me valuable comments and suggestions. I am thoroughly grateful to Jean-Bernard Auby, Robert Baldwin and Florentin Blanc.

I also owe a debt of recognition with a number of Librarians who supported my research: in the Libraries of the London School of Economics and of the Institute of Advanced Legal Studies in London; in the Biblioteca "Antonino De Stefano" of the Italian Corte dei Conti; and overall in my Department of Political Science, Roma Tre University, in the Biblioteca "Pietro Grilli di Cortona" where Simona Battisti, Antonella Silvestri and Raffaella Stimato have found for me practically whatever I wanted to read.

A final thanks goes to Simon Jolley, who helped me fall in love with written English by patiently teaching, revising it and supporting my job.

I would like to remember many persons outside of the academic world, who have encouraged and supported me while writing. The list would be too long, family and friends. I want to mention especially my children, *Francesco, Teresa* and *Cecilia*, to whom the book is dedicated. Thanks to them and together with them I have come to understand that as humans, we wish well but sometimes behave badly. I have learned that this is not a problem but a fundamental feature of our nature, and that we can help to develop a common strategy for managing our lives by reflecting together on its origins and how best to react. Rather, I have experienced thanks to and together with my children that we can do good and beautiful things only starting from our own human condition.

All opinions expressed are my own, and any errors or omissions are entirely my responsibility.

CONTENTS

Acknowledgements .... *vii*
List of Figures .... *xiii*
List of Tables .... *xv*

1. **Rules, Corruption and Controls: Setting the Scene** 1
   1.1. Preliminary Remarks 1
   1.2. Rules 5
      1.2.1. Definition 5
      1.2.2. Law is More than Legislation 6
      1.2.3. Does Legislation Threaten the Law? 7
      1.2.4. Regulation and Rules as Key Concepts 10
   1.3. Rules and Behaviour 16
      1.3.1. Decisions about Compliance with Rules as
             an Individual Problem 16
      1.3.2. Generating Compliance with Rules as
             an Institutional Problem 18
      1.3.3. Certifying Compliance with Rules as a
             Company's Interest (and Cost) 20
   1.4. Functioning of Rules and their Dysfunction 23
      1.4.1. How Rules Work 24
      1.4.2. When Rules Do Not Work 27
      1.4.3. Trust: The Intangible Factor of Rules' Effectiveness 29
   1.5. Corruption 32
      1.5.1. Definition 32
      1.5.2. A Basic Definition for a Complex Issue:
             (Simple) Corruption 33
      1.5.3. A Slightly Complex Definition: Corruption as a Regulatory
             Issue 34
   1.6. Corruption and Conflict of Interest 36
      1.6.1. Corruption as 'Actuality', Conflicts of Interest
             as 'Possibility' 37
      1.6.2. Criticisms and Paradoxes in Overregulating
             Conflicts of Interest 38
   1.7. Corruption and Corruptibility 40
      1.7.1. Corruption as 'Actuality', Corruptibility as 'Probability' 40
      1.7.2. Objective Corruption and Corruptibility:
             Type AP (Administrative Powers) and Type C (Controls) 41

x Contents

    1.8. Controls 44
        1.8.1. Definition 44
        1.8.2. The Notion of Control from an Anticorruption Perspective 45
        1.8.3. Criticism, Paradoxes and Dilemmas of Controlling 47
    1.9. Controlling Administrative Activities 49
        1.9.1. External Controls 50
        1.9.2. Internal Controls 53
        1.9.3. Criticisms and Paradoxes in Controlling
             Administrative Activities 54
    1.10. Controlling Private Activities 55
        1.10.1. 'Desk-Based' Controls 57
        1.10.2. 'Field-Based' Controls 58
        1.10.3. Criticisms and Paradoxes in Controlling
             Private Activities 59

2. **Anticorruption: Strategies and Risks** 61
    2.1. Preventing Corruption: A Contemporary Issue 61
        2.1.1. The Great Temptation: Justifying 63
        2.1.2. The Right Choice: Combating 64
    2.2. Anticorruption between Global Stance and Domestic Strategies 66
        2.2.1. Global Anticorruption Policies 66
        2.2.2. Domestic Administrative Strategies 70
    2.3. Anticorruption: Conventional, Behavioural and Beyond 72
        2.3.1. Conventional Anticorruption 72
        2.3.2. Behavioural Anticorruption 73
        2.3.3. Towards Regulatory Anticorruption 76
    2.4. Risks of Anticorruption 77
        2.4.1. Backfire 79
        2.4.2. Perception vs Reality 79
        2.4.3. Metastatic Bureaucracy 81
        2.4.4. Defensive Administration 82
        2.4.5. Difficulty in Recruitment of Honest and Expert People 83
    2.5. Feasible Objectives of Anticorruption 84

3. **Anticorruption: Rules (Can Good Rules Reduce Opportunities for Corruption?)** 87
    3.1. As with Corruption, Anticorruption Starts from Rules 87
        3.1.1. No Rules, No Corruption? 88
        3.1.2. Rules, their Market and their Profit 90
    3.2. Managing Rules, Combating Corruption 92
    3.3. Regulatory Stock 95

Contents   xi

        3.3.1. Simplification 95
              3.3.1.1. Simplification and Good Quality
                       Regulation Per Se 96
              3.3.1.2. Simplification and Anticorruption 98
        3.3.2. Advocacy Powers 100
              3.3.2.1. In Competition Law 101
              3.3.2.2. In Anticorruption 102
   3.4. Regulatory Flow 105
        3.4.1. Anticorruption Assessment of Legislation 105
              3.4.1.1. A First Step: Good Quality Regulation Per Se 106
              3.4.1.2. A Second Step: Highly Focused
                       Anticorruption Tools 107
        3.4.2. Tracing Interests 111
              3.4.2.1. Lobbying and Consultation 112
              3.4.2.2. Collecting Interests: The Good and the Bad 114
              3.4.2.3. Regulating Lobbying is not Necessarily
                       the Solution 116

4. **Anticorruption: Controls (Can Controls Help in Reducing
Corruption?)** 122
   4.1. Controls from a Theoretical Perspective 122
        4.1.1. The Mythology (and Threatening Practice)
              of Efficient Controls 124
        4.1.2. Controls in Regulatory Theory 127
        4.1.3. Controls and Theory of 'Policing' 130
        4.1.4. Controlling is Governing, No More and No Less 133
   4.2. Controls from a Practical Perspective: Warnings 135
        4.2.1. Controls have a Hybrid Nature 136
        4.2.2. Controlling Includes Administrative Tolerance 137
        4.2.3. Controls are a Cost 138
        4.2.4. Administrative Capacity of Control is Limited 140
        4.2.5. Planning Controls is not a Simple Task 141
        4.2.6. Sanctions Following Controls Must be Effective
              in Order to Deter 143
   4.3. Controls from a Practical Perspective: Suggestions 145
        4.3.1. Information 146
        4.3.2. Regulation 151
        4.3.3. Privacy and Data Protection 153
        4.3.4. Planning 156
        4.3.5. Enforcement 158
        4.3.6. Communication 159
        4.3.7. Reform 162

xii *Contents*

5. **Combating Corruption via Regulation and Controls: Which Formula?** **167**
    5.1. Corruption (and Anticorruption) from a Regulatory Perspective: A Recap 167
    5.2. Combating Corruption: Why? 169
    5.3. Combating Corruption: How? 170
        5.3.1. Regulatory Anticorruption: From Alternative Theoretical Approaches to an Integrated Strategy 170
        5.3.2. Regulatory Anticorruption Toolkit (Corruptibility Assessment) 174
            5.3.2.1. Incentives or the Genetics of Corruption 174
            5.3.2.2. A Protocol to Identify and Assess Corruptibility 176
            5.3.2.3. Criminal Databases Should Talk Administrative Language 180
        5.3.3. Regulatory Anticorruption in Practice 182
    5.4. Combating Corruption: Who? 187
        5.4.1. Legislators and Regulators 187
        5.4.2. Public Agents and Enforcement Officers (in General) 188
        5.4.3. Anticorruption Bodies (in Particular) 190
    5.5. Trust vs Corruption: Governing the Intangible 191

Index *195*

LIST OF FIGURES

Figure 1.1	Regulatory Effectiveness	4
Figure 1.2	Effectiveness of Rules	26
Figure 1.3	Principal-Agent-Client Model: Infringements	35
Figure 1.4	Principal-Agent-Client Model: Controls	48
Figure 4.1	The Panopticon	125
Figure 4.2	Ayres and Braithwaite's Pyramid of Enforcement	128
Figure 4.3	Graduated Invasiveness of Privacy Protection and Data Regulation	154
Figure 5.1	Corruptibility Assessment: Assessing a Piece of Primary Corruptible Legislation	185
Figure 5.2	Corruptibility Assessment in short	186

LIST OF TABLES

Table 1.1	Analysis of Rules when Functioning and when Dysfunctional	28
Table 1.2	Objective Corruption/Corruptibility	44
Table 2.1	Types of Anticorruption Strategies	78
Table 2.2	Regulatory Anticorruption: Risks and Objectives	86
Table 3.1	Rules Under Scrutiny I – Which (Sensitive) Rules Should Be Monitored	110
Table 3.2	Rules Under Scrutiny II – Tool-Kit: Summarising the Conceptual Framework	120
Table 4.1	The Role of Controls	123
Table 4.2	How to Control to Prevent Corruption: Synoptic Table of Remedies	164
Table 5.1	How Authorisations May Contribute to Facilitating Corruption	177
Table 5.2	Lexical Table	178
Table 5.3	Anticorruption Preventive Responses in Cases of Infringements and Corruption Related to Authorisations	179
Table 5.4	Evidence which may come from Queries to Criminal Databases	181
Table 5.5	Regulatory Anticorruption (a Recap)	191

1

Rules, Corruption and Controls: Setting the Scene

1.1. Preliminary Remarks

The central idea of the book is that administrative corruption, like other kinds of illicit behaviour, presupposes both the existence and the ineffectiveness of rules, and it follows that a regulatory perspective may therefore help in preventing both corruption and infringements. The book builds upon research into rules, controls and corruption, topics which are usually studied in parallel, as distinct issues, by different epistemic communities. This parallel approach is still the prevalent feature of current academic contributions, at national as well as at international level, all over the world: there is a huge quantity of literature on legislation, drafting and quality of regulation;[1] a further abundance of publications regarding

---

[1] Among the numerous contributions on *rules, regulation and the regulatory state*: William Twining and David Miers, *How to Do Things with Rules* (Cambridge University Press, 2010; first published 1976); Colin S Diver, 'The Optimal Precision of Administrative Rules' (1983) 93(1) *Yale Law Journal* 65; Robert Baldwin, *Rules and Government* (Clarendon Press, 1995); Stephen G Breyer and Richard B Stewart, *Administrative Law and Regulatory Policy* (Little, Brown and Company, 1992); Peter Grabosky, 'Counterproductive regulation' (1995) 23(4) *International Journal of the Sociology of Law* 347; Anthony Ogus, *Regulation. Legal Form and Economic Theory* (Hart Publishing, 2004); Robert Baldwin, Martin Cave and Martin Lodge, *Understanding Regulation. Theory, Strategy and Practice* (Oxford University Press, 2012); Cary Coglianese and Robert Kagan (eds), *Regulation and Regulatory Processes* (Ashgate, 2007); Cary Coglianese (ed), *Regulatory Breakdown: The Crisis of Confidence in U.S. Regulation* (University of Pennsylvania Press, 2012); see also Mercur Olson, *The Logic of Collective Action. Public Goods and the Theory of Group* (Harvard University Press, 1965) and Richard H.Thaler and Cass R Sunstein, *Nudge: Improving Decisions about Health, Wealth, and Happiness* (Yale University Press, 2008). Regarding *legislation and drafting*, see Ulrich Karpen and Helen Xanthaki (eds), *Legislation in Europe: A Comprehensive Guide For Scholars and Practitioners* (Hart, 2017) and Ulrich Karpen and Helen Xanthaki (eds), *Legislation in Europe: A country by country guide* (Hart, 2020); see also Helen Xanthaki, *Drafting Legislation: Art and Technology of Rules for Regulation* (Hart, 2014). Regarding the specific literature on *quality of regulation*, among other titles, see: Claudio M Radaelli 'The diffusion of Regulatory Impact Analysis in OECD countries: best practices or lesson-drawing?' (2004) 43(5) *European Journal of Political Research* 723; Claudio M Radaelli and Oliver Fritsch, *Measuring Regulatory Performance, Evaluating Regulatory Management Tools and Programs* (OECD Expert Papers n 2, 2012); Cary Coglianese, *Measuring Regulatory Performance, Evaluating the Impact of Regulation and Regulatory Policy* (OECD Expert Paper n 1, 2012); Jean-Bernard Auby and Thomas Perroud (eds), *Regulatory Impact Assessment/La evaluación de impacto regulatorio* (Global Law Press/Inap, 2013); Nicoletta Rangone, 'The Quality of Regulation. The Myth and Reality of Good Regulation Tools' (2012) 4(1) *Italian Journal of Public Law*.

enforcement, inspection and administrative controls;[2] and an exponential number of books and articles from many fields of research, finally, concern corruption and anticorruption.[3]

---

[2] Literature on *controls* in English is especially related to inspections in the more general framework of regulatory enforcement and theories of compliance. Important contributions have been carried out (even recently), among them: Gary S Becker, 'Crime and Punishment: An Economic Approach' (1968) 76(2) *Journal of Political Economy* 169; about implementation in general, see Jeffrey L Pressman and Aaron Wildavsky, *Implementation. How Great Expectations in Washington Are Dashed in Oakland; Or, Why It's Amazing that Federal Programs Work at All, This Being a Saga of the Economic Development Administration as Told by Two Sympathetic Observers Who Seek to Build Morals on a Foundation* (University of California Press, 1973); George J Stigler, 'The Optimum enforcement of Law', in Gary S Becker and William M Landes (eds), *Essays in the Economics of Crime and Punishment* (NBER, 1974); Eugene Bardach and Robert A Kagan, *Going by the Book: The Problem of Regulatory Unreasonableness* (Transaction Publishers, 2010; originally published in 1982 by Temple University Press); Keith Hawkins and John M Thomas, *Enforcing Regulation* (Kluwer-Nijhoff Publishing, 1984); Robert A Kagan, 'Understanding Regulatory Enforcement' (1989) 11(2) *Law and Policy* 91; Tom R Tyler, *Why People Obey to the Law* (Yale University Press, 1990); Ian Ayres and John Braithwaite, *Responsive Regulation. Transcending the Deregulation Debate* (Oxford University Press, 1992); John Braithwaite, *Improving Compliance: Strategies and Practical Applications in OECD Countries* (Organization for Economic Cooperation and Development, 1993); Florentin Blanc, *Inspection Reforms: Why, How and with what Results* (OECD, 2012); Wim Voermans, 'Motive-based Enforcement', in Luzius Mader and Sergey Kabyshev (eds), *Regulatory Reform. Implementation and compliance* (Nomos, 2014) 41; Lawrence M Friedman, *Impact. How Law Affects Behaviour* (Harvard University Press, 2016); Florentin Blanc, *From Chasing Violations to Managing Risks* (Edward Elgar, 2018); Graham Russell and Christopher Hodges, *Regulatory Delivery* (Hart/Beck, 2019). See also OECD, *Reducing the Risk of Policy Failure: Challenges for Regulatory Compliance* (OECD, 2000) and OECD, *Regulatory Enforcement and Inspections*, (OECD, 2014). On controls as costs, HM Treasury, *Hampton Report, Reducing administrative burdens: effective inspection and enforcement* (2005).

[3] The literature on *corruption* is enormous and adopts different perspectives (criminal, economic, sociological and so on). Among others, the following titles have been especially relevant for this book: Nathaniel Leff, 'Economic Development Through Bureaucratic Corruption', *American Behavioural Scientist*, 8 November 1964; Joseph Samuel Nye, 'Corruption and Political Development: a Cost-Benefit Analysis' (1967) 61(2) *American Political Science Review* 417; John A Gardiner, *The Politics of Corruption* (Russel Sage Foundation, 1970); Edward C Banfield, 'Corruption as a Feature of Government Organization' (1975) XBIII *Journal of Law and Economics* 587; Susan Rose-Ackerman, *Corruption. A Study in Political Economy* (Russel Sage, 1978); John A Gardiner, 'Controlling official corruption and fraud: Bureaucratic incentives and disincentives' (1986) 1 *Corruption and Reform* 33; Arnold J Heidenheimer, Michael Johnston and Victor T Levine (eds), *Political Corruption. A Handbook*, 3rd edn (Transaction Publishers, 1993); Andrei Shleifer and Robert W Vishny, 'Corruption' (1993) 108(3) *Quarterly Journal of Economics* 599; Paolo Mauro, 'Corruption and Growth' (1995) 110(3) *Quarterly Journal of Economics*, 681; Pranab Bardhan, 'Corruption and Development: A Review of Issues' (1997) XXXV *Journal of Economic Literature* 1320; Gary S Becker, 'Want to Squelch Corruption? Try Passing Out Raises' [1997] in *Business Week*, No. 3551, 3 November, 26; Vito Tanzi, *Corruption Around the World: Causes, Consequences, Scope, and Cures* (1998) 45(4) IMF Staff Papers; Susan Rose Ackerman, *Corruption and Government: Causes, Consequences and Reform* (Cambridge University Press, 1999); Roger Bowles, 'Corruption', in Boudewijn Bouckaert and Gerrit De Geest (eds), *Encyclopedia of Law and Economics*, Vol V The Economics of Crime and Litigation (Edward Elgar 2000), 460; Johann Graf Lambsdorff, 'Corruption and Rent-seeking' (2002) 113 *Public Choice*, Vol 113, 97; Mark Robinson (ed), *Corruption and Development* (Routledge 2004); Nuno Garoupa and Daniel Klerman, 'Corruption and the optimal use of nonmonetary sanctions' (2004) in *International Review of Law and Economics*, 24, 219; Colin Nicholls, Tim Daniel, Martin Polaine and John Hatchard, *Corruption and Misuse of Public Office* (Oxford University Press 2006); Monique Nuijten and Gehrard Anders (eds), *Corruption and the Secret of law. A Legal Anthropological Perspective* (Ashgate Publishing, 2007); Adam Greycar and Russel G Smith (eds), *Handbook of Global Research and practice in Corruption* (Edward Elgar, 2011); Donatella Della Porta and Alberto Vannucci, *The hidden order of corruption. An institutional approach* (Ashgate Publishing, 2012); Manuel Villoria Mendeita, Gregg Van Ryzin and Cecilia Lavena,

However, in each of these fields of research, literature is multidisciplinary more than interdisciplinary[4] and not so frequently have scholars and academics in all the three fields of research integrated their sectorial knowledge.[5]

The book builds upon a legal, administrative law background and has been written from a regulatory perspective – a perspective which takes into consideration rules and regulation during their whole life-cycle, from their proposal to their delivery, especially focusing on compliance and enforcement as drivers of regulatory effectiveness, because when rules are effective there is very limited space for infringements and administrative corruption. The novelty of the book is in systematic application[6] of such a perspective to corruption and in the consideration of its

---

'Social consequences of government corruption: A study of institutional disaffection in Spain' (2013) 73(1) *Public Administration Review* 85; Jean-Bernard Auby, Emmanuel Breen and Thomas Perroud (eds), *Corruption and Conflicts of interest. A comparative Law Approach* (Edward Elgar, 2014); Agustí Cerillo-I-Martinez A and Juli Ponce (eds), *Preventing Corruption and Promoting Good Government and Public Integrity* (Bruylant, 2017). See also, Christopher Hodges and Ruth Steinholtz, *Ethical Business Practice and Regulation. A Behavioural and Values-Based Approach to Compliance and Enforcement* (Hart, 2017). See finally Adam Graycar (ed), *Handbook on Corruption, Ethics and Integrity in Public Administration* (Edward Elgar, 2020).

[4] On this topic see Marilyn Stember, 'Advancing the social sciences through the interdisciplinary enterprise' (1991) 28(1) *Social Science Journal* 1; see also Julie Thompson Klein, 'Typologies of Interdisciplinarity: the Boundary Work of Definition', in Robert Frodeman (ed), *Oxford Handbook of Interdisciplinarity* 2nd edn (Oxford University Press, 2017) 22.

[5] There are only a few titles which concern the relationship between *corruption and controls*. Among the most important works, Robert Klitgaard, Controlling Corruption (University of California Press 1988); John A Gardiner and Theodore R Lyman, 'The logic of corruption control', in Arnold J Heidenheimer, Michael Johnston and Victor T Levine (eds), *Political Corruption. A Handbook* 3rd edn (Transaction Publishers, 1993) 837; Frank Anechiarico and James B Jacobs, *The Pursuit of Absolute Integrity. How Corruption Control Makes Government Ineffective* (The University of Chicago Press, 1996); Adam Graycar and Aiden Sidebottom, 'Corruption and control: a corruption reduction approach' (2012) 19(4) *Journal of Financial Crime* 384; finally see Maria De Benedetto, 'Corruption and controls' (2015) 4 *European Journal of Law Reform* 47; Florentin Blanc, *From Chasing Violations to Managing Risks*, 125 et seq, 'Regulations, inspections and corruption'; and Marco D'Alberti (ed), *Corruzione e pubblica amministrazione* (Jovene, 2017), especially the section devoted to 'corruption and controls'. Some authors have analysed the relationship between *rules and corruption*. The most important titles in this field are: Anthony Ogus, 'Corruption and regulatory structures' (2004) 26 *Law & Policy* 329. Other titles worthy of mention are Gary S Becker and George J Stigler, 'Law Enforcement, Malfeasance, and Compensation of Enforcers' (1974) III *Journal of Legal Studies* 1; Giorgio Barbieri and Francesco Giavazzi, *Corruzione a norma di legge. La lobby delle grandi opere che affonda l'Italia* (Rizzoli, 2014); George RG Clarke, 'Does over-regulation lead to corruption? Evidence from a multi-country survey' (2014) 14(1) *Southwestern Business Administration Journal* 28; and again Peter Grabosky, 'Counterproductive regulation'. On the specific topic of *Corruption Impact Assessment*, Jeremy Pope, *Parliament and Anticorruption legislation*, in Rick Stapenhurst, Niall Johnston and Riccardo Pelizzo (eds), *The role of Parliament in curbing corruption* (WBI Development Studies, 2006); Luca Di Donato, 'The Quality of Regulation in the Service of Preventing Corruption' (2016) 2 *European Journal of Law Reform*. Finally, see Claudio M Radaelli, Claire A Dunlop, Jonathan Kamkhaji, Gaia Taffoni and Claudius Wagemann, 'Does consultations count for corruption?' (2020) 27(11) *Journal of European Public Policy*, 1718.

[6] The regulatory perspective has been adopted by Anthony Ogus, *Corruption and Regulatory Structures*. Other scholars have contributed to focus on some aspects, Johann Graf Lambsdorff, 'Corruption and Rent-seeking' (2002) 113 *Public Choice* 97 and *The Institutional Economics of Corruption and Reform: Theory, Evidence, and Policy* (Cambridge University Press, 2007), esp 10 (Corruption and regulatory quality). See also Tom Vander Beken and Annelies Balcaen, 'Crime Opportunities Provided by Legislation in Market Sectors: Mobile Phones, Waste Disposal, Banking, Pharmaceuticals' (2006) 12(3-4) *European Journal on Criminal Policy and Research* 299. See finally Maria De Benedetto,

important operational consequences. In fact, it aims to expand the logic of current anticorruption policies, which now focus on corruption (the symptom) and which should be reoriented to include rules, determinants of any corruption processes: in a state of law, without rules no public power is established, no public agents can be in charge of competences in any administrative procedures, and consequently no corruption can be carried out, at all. For this reason, from a regulatory perspective, rules can even be used to enrich the anticorruption toolkit, by affirming the centrality of the way in which rules are adopted, how the interests which move their adoption are considered during procedures, and how rules are implemented and enforced, via controls.

In short, rules, corruption and controls – which apparently are separate fields of research – will be considered as being strictly linked, as a whole system, as though they were the three points of a triangle: if we focus on one of them, we will unavoidably meet the others, because the three topics cannot be fully understood without keeping the others in mind. This quality of being interlinked is more easily understood in terms of regulatory effectiveness, which represents a point of unity, as the apex of a tetrahedron: rules need to be effective; controls are needed in order to make effective rules and they must in turn be effective to do so; corruption constitutes a special kind of side-effect and/or ineffectiveness of rules based very often on ineffective controls; finally, legal systems in which rules and controls are not so effective, and where corruption flourishes, are ineffective themselves and risk collapse.

Figure 1.1 Regulatory Effectiveness

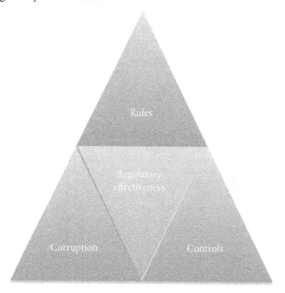

In the light of effectiveness, concrete anticorruption policies may vary and have to be tailored to the context of individual countries and cultures.[7] For this reason, the analysis will be developed with limited references to national anticorruption legislations by giving preference to a comprehensive analysis of the phenomenon (corruption) and of the regulatory environment in which it occurs. Therefore, this is not a book on the Italian anticorruption system.[8] However, Italy is the paradigmatic case in the backstage of my research, being a sort of 'perfect storm' from a regulatory perspective: not only long-standing distrust in institutions[9] and a wide presence of criminal organisations,[10] but also legislative inflation, bad quality regulation, too rigid controlling, administrative tolerance and a tendency towards overwhelming bureaucracy have all together nurtured systemic corruption. On the other hand, Italy seems to be the country in which everything and its opposite are always possible: the National Recovery and Resilience Plan adopted in April 2021 in the framework of the Next Generation EU, introduced a very relevant Regulatory Anticorruption measure: in fact, among other 'enabling reforms', the Plan has required the repeal and revision of rules that fuel corruption.

Definitions are indispensable before moving deeper into the topic: it is crucial to agree about the notion and scope of *rules*, *controls* and *corruption* in a way in which the definition of each concept helps in preparing the ground for the understanding of the others.

1.2. Rules

1.2.1. Definition

Literature on legal normativity is huge and multidisciplinary. This is the reason way it is impossible to begin any reasoning without some preliminary clarifications. When people say 'rules', 'norms' or 'legislation' they refer to concepts

---

'Understanding and preventing corruption: a regulatory approach', in A Cerrillo-i-Martínez, J Ponce (eds), *Preventing Corruption and Promoting good Government and Public Integrity* (Bruylant, 2017).

[7] Claudio M Radaelli, Claire A Dunlop, Jonathan Kamkhaji, Gaia Taffoni and Claudius Wagemann, 'Does consultation count for corruption?' (2020) 27(11) in *Journal of European Public Policy* 1729: 'Accordingly, there can be more than one solution path (equifinality) – this is important for our analysis since we do not expect causal patterns to be equal in all countries.'

[8] On this point see the relevant contribution of Francesco Merloni, *Corruption and Public Administration. The Italian Case in a Comparative Perspective* (Routledge, 2018). See also Enrico Carloni, 'Italian Anticorruption and Transparency Policies. Trends and Tools in Combating Administrative Corruption', in Alexander Grasse, Markus Grimm and Jan Labitzke (eds), *Italien zwischen Krise und Aufbruch. Reformen und Reformversuche der Regierung Renzi* (Springer, 2018), 365.

[9] On this aspect, see the notion of *amoral familism* in Edward C Banfield, *The Moral Basis of Backward Society* (Free Press, 1958), and the notion of *social capital* in Robert Putnam, *Making Democracy Work: Civic Traditions in Modern Italy* (Princeton University Press, 1993).

[10] On this point, see Giacomo Di Gennaro and Antonio La Spina (eds), *Mafia-type Organisations and Extortion in Italy. The Camorra in Campania* (Routledge, 2018) and Sabrina Cavatorto and Antonio La Spina, *The Politics of Public Administration Reform in Italy* (Palgrave Macmillan, 2020), especially La Spina's chapter on 'Fighting Corruption', 75 onwards.

6 *Rules, Corruption and Controls: Setting the Scene*

perceived as connected with (or in the field of) 'law'. However, distinctions among these terms are significant and their overlapping is limited. In order to make the whole discourse fit for the purpose of understanding and preventing corruption, the book has adopted a regulatory perspective which focuses on how rules can be concretely used to steer behaviour, achieve desired results and avoid unwanted side-effects (such as corruption) and how they work in practice, by briefly analysing their functioning and dysfunctions (such as when they produce occasions for infringements and corruption).

1.2.2. Law is More than Legislation

Despite the pervasive presence of *law* in everyone's daily life, defining it is far from a simple task.[11] It will suffice to say, in this context, that law is a social institution[12] which simultaneously expresses an individual and a collective stance, being both the idea of 'a binding custom or practice of a community' and also 'the whole body of such customs, practices, or rules'.[13] In any case, law is deeply ingrained in society (*ubi societas, ibi ius*), indispensable to the organisation of social life and to the limitation of social conflicts,[14] being characterised by coercion.

On the other hand, the concept of *legislation* requires the introduction of the question of the 'great machine of legislation'[15] because legislation is not only a product but also the factory,[16] not only the final act but the whole procedure which prepares it. In any case, it constitutes the prevalent way to produce written law and to place it in the context of a formalised hierarchy of sources. Each single legislative act is qualified by the level of the 'machine' at which it has been produced, according to established procedures. However, the prevailing opinions of scholars

---

[11] Herbert Lionel Adolphus Hart, *The Concept of Law* (Oxford University Press, 2012; 1st edn 1961), 1: 'few questions concerning human society have been asked with such persistence and answered by serious thinkers in so many diverse, strange, and even paradoxical ways as the question "What is law?"'.

[12] On this point see John Rawls, *A Theory of Justice* (Harvard University Press, 1971; revd edn 1999) 6; see also Douglass C North, *Institutions, Institutional Change and Economic Performance* (Cambridge University Press, 1990) 5: 'Institutions are a creation of human beings. They evolve and are altered by human beings; hence our theory must begin with the individual. At the same time, the constraints that institutions impose on individual choices are pervasive. Integrating individual choices with the constraints institutions impose on choice set is a major step towards unifying social science research'. See finally Hamish Ross, *Law as a Social Institution* (Hart Publishing, 2001).

[13] See *Merriam-Webster's Dictionary of Synonyms: A Dictionary of Discriminated Synonyms with Antonyms and Analogous and Contrasted Words*, Merriam-Webster Inc, Springfield, MA: 'a rule of conduct or action prescribed or formally recognized as binding or enforced by a controlling authority'.

[14] See Lawrence M Friedman, *The Legal System. A Social Science Perspective* (Russel Sage, 1975) 18: 'a basic legal function is to offer machinery and a place where people can go to resolve their conflicts and settle their disputes'.

[15] Gaetano Filangieri, *La scienza della legislazione (1780-1785). Benjamin Constant, Comento sulla scienza della legislazione* (IPZS, 1984) 27: 'Noi cominceremo dunque a scomporre la gran macchina della legislazione' ('Therefore, we will begin to deconstruct the great machine of legislation').

[16] The formula 'factory of law' is devoted to Filippo Patroni Griffi, 'La "fabbrica delle leggi" e la qualità della normazione in Italia' (2000) 1 *Diritto amministrativo* 97.

and academics suggest that legislation should be considered in a broader sense, as a system[17] including: constitutions; primary sources of law (such as statute law enacted by parliaments); sources of law enacted together by the parliament and the government or by the government (defined as regulation); multi-level legislation (such as EU legislation and legislation adopted by sub-national levels of government, for instance, *Länder* or regions).

In view of this, *law is more than legislation*:[18] for instance, law may even take the form of customary (unwritten) law, which is a source of law especially relevant in some legal systems;[19] law is constituted not only by rules but also by legal principles;[20] moreover, law is also the product of regulation adopted by independent authorities (which are non-majoritarian institutions);[21] law may take the form of soft regulation (which is written but outside – or at the boundary of – the sources of law).[22] In other words, legislation is a very significant element in the contemporary discourse on law, but not the only one.

Alongside law and legislation, the term *norm* expresses a wider connotation, by evoking in general standardisation of something, not necessarily in the legal field. There are, in fact, technical standards or even social and ethical norms which operate without coercion, as legal norms usually do.[23]

1.2.3. Does Legislation Threaten the Law?

The relationship between *law and legislation* (to be intended in the above-mentioned wide sense) is characterised by a structural dialectic.

On one side, legislation is the most powerful driver for law because contemporary law is produced mainly via legislation, at different levels of government.

---

[17] Ulrich Karpen, 'Introduction', in Ulrich Karpen and Helen Xantachi (eds), *Legislation and Legisprudence in Europe. A Comprehensive Guide* (Hart Publishing, 2017) 2.
[18] On this point see, Antony Alcott, 'The effectiveness of law' (1981) 15(2) *Valparaiso University Law Review* 229, esp 230 where he mentions the relevance of customary law for developing countries.
[19] See Chuma Himonga and Thandabantu Nhlapo (eds), *African Customary Law* (Oxford University Press, 2014).
[20] On this topic see Ronald Dworkin, *Taking rights seriously* (Harvard University Press, 1977), 22 et seq (*Rules, principles and policies*); see also Joseph Raz, 'Legal principles and the limit of law' (1972) *Yale Law Journal* 81. The topic is particularly relevant in French public law, see Jean-Marc Maillot, *La théorie administrativiste des principes généraux du droit* (Dalloz, 2003).
[21] Legislation is traditionally a product of majoritarian institutions, while independent authorities are non-majoritarian bodies; legislation is expected to be general and abstract, IA regulation is adopted for specific categories of enterprise; legislation is produced by typical sources of law, mentioned in a constitution, while IA regulation has a mere legislative basis and their regulation can also take the form of soft regulation. However, the two notions are undoubtedly related especially when 'quality of regulation' and 'quality of legislation' are very often used in a fungible way because they share the problem of their quality. See Cary Coglianese, *Measuring regulatory performance. Evaluating the impact of regulation and regulatory policy*, 8.
[22] See, on this point the French Conseil d'État, *Le droit souple* (Le rapports de le Conseil d'État 2013).
[23] On moral and social norms see Geoffrey Brennan, Lina Eriksson, Robert E Goodin, Nicholas Southwood, *Explaining Norms* (Oxford University Press, 2013), 57 et seq.

8 Rules, Corruption and Controls: Setting the Scene

Furthermore, legislation – long idolised in the past[24] – has been even considered to be the perfect 'box' for rational law, resulting in the Enlightenment's *legolatry*;[25] nowadays it has also been seen as the perfect tool for political communication; not rarely politicians used to refer to legislation as if merely proposing and adopting it were their own task, independently from any possible impact and result.

On the other side, paradoxically, legislation can represent even a menace for law, in more than one way.

1. When single legislative acts are adopted exclusively for symbolic purposes (*symbolic legislation*, 'in the worst sense of the word'[26]), producing 'distortions in the regulatory process'.[27]
2. When single legislative acts and regulations discipline human activities too intrusively, such as when they intervene by establishing the need for too strict ethical codes in some area of the public sector[28] so that legislation goes beyond its own scope by requiring inducements or coercion in fields in which behaviour should be free (*improper or intrusive legislation*).

---

[24] Regarding the limits of reasoning and knowledge and the question of unintentional consequences of human behaviour which affect even legislation, see John Rawls, *A Theory of Justice*, 315. The issue has also been developed by Friedrich Von Hayek, *The Counter-revolution of Science. Studies on the Abuse of Reason* (The Free Press, 1952). Regarding the aspect that the consequences of behaviour depend (in part) on what other individuals might choose, see Gerald P O'Driscoll and Mario J Rizzo, *The Economics of Time and Ignorance* (Routledge, 1996) 'Introduction' (fn 58). Regarding the fallibilist perspective which should be adopted by regulators, see Karl Popper, *The Open Society and Its Enemies*, vol II (Routledge & Kegan Paul, 1945) addendum: 'Every discovery of a mistake constitutes a real advance in our knowledge.' See also Ralf Dahrendorf, 'Economic Opportunity, Civil Society, and Political Liberty' (1996) 27(2) *Development and Change* 229.

[25] The expression 'legolatria' has been used by Paolo Grossi, *L'Europa del diritto* (Laterza, 2007) 134; see also Paolo Grossi, *A History of European Law* (Blackwell Publishing, 2010). See also Eduardo García de Enterría, *La lengua de los derechos. La formación del Derecho Público europeo tras la Revolución Francesa* (Madrid, 1994), 28, where he talks about the 'componente utópico de la Revolución'.

[26] Bart van Klink, 'Symbolic Legislation: An Essentially Political Concept', in Bart van Klink, Britta van Beers, Lonneke Poort (eds), *Symbolic Legislation. Theory and New Developments in Biolaw* (Springer, 2015), 19: 'Symbolic legislation commonly has a bad name. In critical sociological studies, it refers to instances of legislation that are to a large extent ineffective and that serve other political and social goals than the goals officially proclaimed' while in a 'more recent and more positive understanding, symbolic legislation is an alternative legislative technique that differs from the traditional top-down approach' (19–20); see also John P Dwyer, 'The Pathology of Symbolic Legislation' (1990) 17 *Ecology Law Quarterly*, 233, 234: 'The enactment of symbolic legislation reflects a breakdown of the legislative policymaking machinery, a system that all too frequently addresses real social problems in an unrealistic fashion'. See finally Florentin Blanc, 'Tools for effective Regulation; Is "More" always "Better"?' (2018) 9 *European Journal of Risk Regulation* 465.

[27] John P Dwyer, 'The Pathology of Symbolic Legislation' 234.

[28] On this point, see as an interesting example of intrusive standards, International Monetary Fund-IMF, *Code of Conduct for Staff*, 31 July 1998 ('The code outlines in one document the guidelines for staff conduct, which are prescribed in various Fund rules and regulations'), VII. Examples: 'Conduct within the IMF: 4. I am taking orders for Girl Scout cookies on behalf of my daughter. May I ask colleagues whether they wish to place an order? Yes, so long as there is no coercion or pressure placed on colleagues to make a purchase'. In general on this point see Oscar Capdeferro Villagrasa, 'La eficacia anticorrupción de los códigos éticos y conducta: el papel del Derecho Administrativo' (2020), in *Revista Geeral d Derecho Administrativo*, fn 54.

3. When legislation is too frequently bad quality, adopted on the basis of unclear objectives or without adequate gathering of evidence, consultation, indicators (necessary for ex post evaluation) and with insufficient assessment of different regulatory options, making it highly probable that the law will be ineffective (*bad quality legislation*).
4. When *legislative inflation* occurs: there is large agreement about the opinion that low quality associated with a high quantity of legislation (a condition which characterises many contemporary legal systems) impedes full achievement of the main purposes of law, by producing widespread legal uncertainty.[29]

However, law should never be used as a scapegoat[30] because it is indispensable to the organisation of social life, to the limitation of social conflicts[31] and to the delivery of social and economic objectives related to specific kinds of public policies, but law should be effective to do it.[32] Legislation when adopted is not yet effective law; rather it may even be counterproductive:[33] until becoming a fact, until implemented and (when necessary) until being enforced, it expresses an exclusively verbal, written imperative, sometime characterised by expressive[34] consistence. It is 'essentially a kind of persuasion'[35] waiting for the proof of facts.

In this perspective, the dialectic which characterises the relation between law and legislation can be considered a 'struggle for law'.[36] In such a struggle, *legis-executio* (implementation and enforcement oriented to the achievement of legislative objectives or, in other words, 'regulatory delivery'[37]) is no longer separable from or ancillary to *legis-latio*[38] (law-making and rule-making), as in the past: law, in fact, to be effective needs good legislation but in the same way needs 'concretising'[39] legislation.

---

[29] Which consists of clarity, accessibility and predictability of rules see Conseil d'Etat, *Rapport public 2006 – Sécurité juridique et complexité du droit* (La Documentation française, 2006).
[30] See Cary Coglianese, 'Law as Scapegoat', in Maria De Benedetto, Nicola Lupo and Nicoletta Rangone (eds), *The Crisis of Confidence in Legislation* (Hart/Nomos, 2020), 337 esp 344: 'when scapegoating law, facts do not matter'.
[31] See Lawrence M Friedman, *The Legal System. A Social Science Perspective* 18: 'a basic legal function is to offer machinery and a place where people can go to resolve their conflicts and settle their disputes'.
[32] On this point see the special issue of the *European Journal of Risk Regulation*, Symposium on Effective Law and Regulation, Vol 9, Issue 3, September 2018. Among other contributions, see Maria De Benedetto, *Effective Law from a Regulatory and Administrative Law Perspective*, 391.
[33] Peter Grabosky, *Counterproductive regulation* 347.
[34] See Robert Cooter, 'Expressive Law and Economics' (1998) 27(2) *Journal of Legal Studies* 585 and Cass R Sunstein, 'On the expressive function of law' (1996) 144 *University of Pennsylvania Law Review* 2021.
[35] On this point see Anthony Alcott, 'The effectiveness of law' 235.
[36] Rudolph von Jhering, *The Struggle For Law* (The Lawbook Exchange, 1997; 1st edn *Der Kampf um's Recht*, Wien, 1872).
[37] Graham Russell and Christopher Hodges, *Regulatory Delivery* (Hart/Beck, 2019).
[38] On this point, see Hans Kelsen, *General Theory of Law and State* (Harvard University Press, 1945) 255.
[39] On this aspect see Susan Rose-Ackerman, Peter L Lindseth and Blake Emerson (eds), *Comparative Administrative Law* 2nd edn (Edwar Elgar, 2017) 1: 'The Germans speak of administrative law as "concretized" constitutional law'. See also John P Dwyer, 'The Pathology of Symbolic Legislation' 234: 'The most significant problem with symbolic legislation, however, is not delay; it is the resulting distortions in the regulatory process. Symbolic legislation hobbles the regulatory process by polarizing public discussion in agency proceedings and legislative hearings … By making promises that cannot be kept,

1.2.4. Regulation and Rules as Key Concepts

It is time to examine the 'container concept' of *regulation* and its 'content concept' of *rules*, which are both of special relevance in the present context giving the fact that the book intends to analyse corruption by adopting a regulatory perspective (as we will see below, chapter 2.3.3).

Talking about *regulation* seems to be relatively simply in English-speaking academic and institutional cultures (ie in the UK, US, Australia but also in international organisations and the European Union) where regulation is a specific although vast and interdisciplinary[40] notion which has its roots in political economics.[41] From a legal perspective, two aspects are particularly relevant here.

On the one hand, the mentioned influence from economics determines a strong link between regulation and its consequences,[42] by stressing an instrumental perspective[43] and by making regulation 'law as a means to an end':[44] law structurally built to achieve its objectives, to solve effectively various kinds of problems[45] and to avoid (as far as possible) regulatory failures.[46] As a consequence, regulation expresses a substantive (economic) nature which requires a detailed examination of the 'factory of law'[47] (law-making and rules-making) as a comprehensive and

---

and by leaving no middle ground for accommodation, the legislature makes it more difficult to reach a political compromise (either in the agency or the legislature) that would produce a functional regulatory program.'

[40] See Christel Koop and Martin Lodge, 'What is regulation? An interdisciplinary concept analysis' (2017) 11(1) *Regulation & Governance* 95: 'First, there is a remarkable absence of explicit definitions. Second, the scope of the concept is vast, which requires us to talk about regulation in rather abstract terms. Third, scholars largely agree that 'prototype regulation' is characterised by interventions that are intentional and direct – involving binding standard-setting, monitoring, and sanctioning – and exercised by public-sector actors on the economic activities of private-sector actors'.

[41] George J Stigler, 'The Theory of Economic Regulation' (1971) 2(1) *Bell Journal of Economics and Management Science* 3. See also Anthony Ogus, *Regulation. Legal Form and Economic Theory* and Giandomenico Majone, *Regulating Europe* (Routledge, 1996).

[42] See Cary Coglianese and Robert A Kagan (eds), *Regulation and Regulatory Process* xi.

[43] On this aspect see Keith Hawkins, *Law as Last Resort: Prosecution Decision-making in a Regulatory Agency* (Oxford University Press, 2002) 3, 'Instrumental and other uses of law'.

[44] On this point, see Rudolf Von Jhering, *Law as a Means to an End* (The Lawbook Exchange, 1999; first English translation 1913). See also Wim Voermans, 'Legislation and Regulation', in Ulrich Karpen and Helen Xanthaki (eds), *Legislation in Europe. A Comprehensive Guide For Scholars and Pratictioners* (Hart, 2017), 17: 'not all regulation needs to be cast in the form of legislation ... and not all legislation is regulation'.

[45] See Stephen G Breyer and Richard B Stewart, *Administrative Law and Regulatory Policy* 5–6.

[46] See Robert Baldwin, Martin Cave, Martin Lodge, *Understanding Regulation. Theories, Strategies and Practice* 68. See also Peter Grabosky, *Counterproductive regulation* and (for an overview) Robert Baldwin, Colin D Scott, Christopher Hood, *A Reader on Regulation* (Oxford University Press, 1998). On this point see also European Commission, Communication *Strengthening the foundations of Smart regulation – improving evaluation*, COM(2013) 686 final, 3: 'Thorough evaluation also identifies unintended and unexpected consequences'.

[47] See Filippo Patroni Griffi, 'The crisis of confidence and the factory of laws' (2019) 205–206 *Studi Parlamentari e di Politica Costituzionale* 119.

articulate process starting with the diagnosis of economic and social problems up to and including regulatory delivery and evaluation.[48]

On the other hand, regulation is a resulting concept which should be understood as 'collection of rules'[49] in specific sectors (health service, food regulation, education, communications, financial regulation, transport, and so on) by including rules not only as written arrangements but also as interpreted and delivered. Rules,[50] in the wider framework of regulation, are specific provisions[51] which impose obligations (ie, commands) and affect in some way the activities and the organisation of their addressees.[52] A rule is such because it is linked to its consequences,[53] in this way expressing a regulatory content. In other words, the core element of rules is their prescriptive content which directly affects the end-users. For this reason, individual rules could be part of primary legislation but they may be also part of other kinds of regulation,[54] in the sense that they can express such regulatory content in any other formal 'box'[55] (government regulation, guidelines, instruction manuals, regulation adopted by independent agencies, and so on).

While talking about regulation seems to be simpler in Anglophone countries, the very current relevance of regulation (as argued in this book) is based also to a large degree on contributions developed in other languages, among others by French, German, Italian and Spanish authors, with special regard to literature in the field of public law.

Starting from the 1980s, international and European integration, advances in the sciences and technology, and the increase of social expectations about risk prevention, have forced *ab extra* states to accept pieces of legislation and to manage the stock of legislation according to the 'logic' of regulation (eg, liberalisation

---

[48] See Graham Russell and Christopher Hodges (eds), *Regulatory Delivery* (Hart/Beck, 2019); see also Florentin Blanc, 'Regulation, Regulatory Delivery, Trust and Distrust: Avoiding Vicious Circles', in Maria De Benedetto, Nicola Lupo, Nicoletta Rangone (eds), *The Crisis of Confidence in Legislation* (Nomos/Hart, 2020) 307. In general, see Ian Ayres and John Braithwaite, *Responsive Regulation. Transcending the Deregulation Debate*.

[49] Cary Coglianese, *Measuring Regulatory Performance. Evaluating the impact of regulation and regulatory policy* 8.

[50] On this topic, see Robert Baldwin, *Rules and Government*.

[51] See Ronald Dworkin, *Taking Rights Seriously* (Harvard University Press, 1978; 1st edn 1977) 24 et seq.

[52] The definition has been firstly provided in Italian, see Maria De Benedetto, Mario Martelli, Nicoletta Rangone, *La qualità delle regole* (Il Mulino, 2011) 12–13.

[53] See Cary Coglianese, Robert Kagan (eds), *Regulation and Regulatory Processes* xi; on this point, see Julia Black, *Enrolling Regulated Actors in Regulatory Systems: Examples from Uk Financial Service Regulation* (2003) 1 *Public Law* 63, 69.

[54] See Cary Coglianese, *Measuring regulatory performance. Evaluating the impact of regulation and regulatory policy* 8: 'Regulations can also derive from any number of institutional sources – parliaments or legislatures, ministries or agencies … Given their variety, regulations can be described using many different labels: constitutions, statutes, legislation, standards, rules, and so forth. What label one uses to refer to them will not matter for purposes of evaluation.'

[55] OECD, *The OECD Report on Regulatory Reform: Synthesis* (1997) 6: 'Regulation refers to the diverse set of instruments by which governments set requirements on enterprises and citizens. Regulations include laws, formal and informal orders and subordinate rules issued by all levels of government, and rules issued by non-governmental or self-regulatory bodies to whom governments have delegated regulatory powers.'

directives, regulation of public utilities, food safety regulation, reports on regulatory reform etc) even in those legal systems influenced by continental legal traditions. This has contributed to a very peculiar convergence between legal systems especially at EU level, whose implications have not been immediately understood. However, multilingual continental scholars and academics have tried to face this epochal change and the ongoing complex legal transplant[56] process. This has made it ever more clear that regulation is no longer only the Anglophone way to describe public intervention in the market or society. It, in fact, also constitutes a much wider key topic characterised by a special gravitational force for contemporary legal theory and practice by representing a solemn claim for less rigid and more intelligent (in the Latin sense of *intus-legere*, to read inside, to penetrate and understand) exercise of normative and administrative powers,[57] with strong implications for the architecture and the grammar of politics, economics and law.

A first aspect has been expressed and discussed by French scholars and academics. To make a long story short, while the modern state was born as a result of a transformation process from concrete law towards abstract law, the contemporary state is currently in the middle of an inverse passage, coming back to reality because abstract, disembodied law is no longer capable of managing post-modern complexity. It is not by chance that many French social sciences scholars have long focused on the hot topic of law effectiveness.[58] Although this process includes critical aspects,[59] contemporary societies and institutions require law which corresponds to reality, is close to individuals, and is adequate to the demands imposed on it by society.[60] Difficulties and ambiguities in the use of the words

---

[56] Alan Watson, *Legal Transplants An Approach to Comparative Law*, 2nd edn (U Ga Press, 1993).

[57] On this point, see Gérard Timsit, 'Le deux corps du droit. Essai sur la notion de régulation' (1996) 78 *Revue française d'administration publique*, 375, 394.

[58] See Jean Carbonnier, 'Effectivité et ineffectivité de la règle de droit' (1957) 9 *L'année sociologique* 3 and Raymond Boudon, *Effets pervers et ordre social* (PUF, 1977). See also the important book by François Jullien, *Traité de l'efficacité* (Editions Grasset & Fasquelle, 1996); François Rangeon, 'Réflexions sur l'effectivité du droit', in *Les usages sociaux du droit* (Colloque, Amiens, 12 Mai 1989), Centre universitaire de recherches administratives et politiques de Picardie-Curapp (PUF, 1989) vol 1, 126 ; Pierre Lascoumes and Évelyne Serverin, 'Théories et pratiques de l'effectivité du droit' (1986) 2 *Droit et société* 102; Alexandre Flückiger, 'Le droit administratif en mutation: l'émergence d'un principe d'efficacité' (2001) *Revue de droit administratif et fiscal* 95 ; and Yann Leroy, 'La notion d'effectivité du droit' (2011) 79(3) *Droit et société* 731.

[59] On this point, see Pascal Gonod, 'L'externalisation de la function législative' (2010) *AJDA* 697.

[60] Gérard Timsit, 'Le deux corps du droit. Essai sur la notion de régulation' 375, 377: 'un autre droit – actuellement en formation – qui se caractérise, au contraire, par son adaptation au concret, son rapprochement des individus, son adéquation au context exact des sociétés qu'il prétend régir'. See also Jean-Bernard Auby, 'Régulations et droit administratif', in *Mélanges offerts à Gérard Timsit* (Bruylant, 2005) 209. On this point, Jacques Caillosse, *La constitution imaginaire de l'administration* (PUF, 2008) 238: 'Cette function régulatrice est au plus haut point caractéristique de la pratique du droit'. See, finally, Jacques Chevallier, 'La régulation juridique en question' (2001) 49 *Droit et société* 827: 'Il convient de relever d'emblée les équivoques que recèle ce concept de régulation: la régulation n'est pas seulement en effet un paradigme scientifique, dont la place dans le champ des sciences sociales est allée en s'élargissant; c'est encore une représentation idéologique, qui évoque une conception nouvelle du rôle de l'État et des conditions de maintien de la cohésion sociale'.

'réglementation' (related to the abstract, 'mystic body' of law)[61] and 'régulation' (related to the concrete, 'natural body' of law) express the struggle in this paradigm shift. However, the absolute relevance of the theory of regulation, as analysed from a continental (and French) perspective, consists in being both comprehensive (by considering regulations in a global and transversal way) and realistic (working as a tool to open the 'boîte noire' – the black box – of general interest).[62]

A second relevant contribution comes from the German *Neue Verwaltungrechtswissenschaft* ('New Administrative Law Science') which (among other things) constitutes an effort to translate the policy question of 'effects' into administrative law terms: the problem at the centre of this vein of research is the steering function;[63] in other words, how rules (and the institutions in charge of implementing and enforcing them) may contribute to achieving desired results without producing side effects – unwanted or dysfunctional consequences – and how this changes administrative procedures and organisation.[64]

A further perspective has characterised the Italian debate. Starting from the public policy notion of the '*Stato Regolatore*' (the Regulatory State),[65] regulation has been long discussed as a notion mainly related to public intervention in the economy with special reference to changes in the legal regime of public utilities, according to European Directives.[66] Thanks to the idea that administrative powers (or at least part of them) may be interpreted as responses to market failures,[67] to a greater use of economic analysis in public law[68] but also to periodical OECD

---

[61] See again Gérard Timsit, 'Le deux corps du droit. Essai sur la notion de régulation' 375, 377. On the different idea of regulation as dilution of normativity, see Yves Gaudemet, 'La regulation économique ou la diluition des norms' (2017) 1 *Revue de droit public* (Dossier: Le désordre normatif) 23. See finally the work of Bertrand Du Marais, *Droit public de la régulation économique* (Presses de Sciences Po et Dalloz, 2004).

[62] On this aspects see the relevant already mentioned work of Jean-Bernard Auby, 'Régulations et droit administratif' 228: 'La theorie des regulations est un theorie d'ensemble de l'intervention publique: elle envisage les regulations de façon globale et transversal ... L'intérêt de la théorie des régulations tient également au fait qu'elle est une théorie réaliste de l'intervention publique'.

[63] See, in the context of the *Neue Verwaltungrechtswissenschaft*, Wolfgang Hoffmann-Riem, 'The potential impact of Social Sciences on Administrative Law' in Matthias Ruffert (ed), *The Transformation of Administrative Law in Europe/La mutation du droit administratif en Europe* (Sellier, 2007), 214.

[64] Ibid, 213: 'effects matter!'.

[65] Giandomenico Majone, 'From the Positive to the Regulatory State: Causes and Consequences of Changes in the Mode of Governance' (1997) 17 *Journal of Public Policy* 139. See, in Italian, Antonio La Spina and Giandomenico Majone, *Lo Stato regolatore* (il Mulino, 2000).

[66] On this topic there is huge literature in Italian. See Sabino Cassese, 'Regolazione e concorrenza', in Giuseppe Tesauro and Marco D'Alberti (eds), *Regolazione e concorrenza* (il Mulino, 2001) 12. See also, Marco D'Alberti, 'Poteri regolatori tra pubblico e privato' (2013) *Diritto amministrativo* 608 and Marco D'Alberti, *Poteri pubblici, mercati e globalizzazione* (il Mulino, 2008) 45. See finally Luca De Lucia, *La regolazione amministrativa dei servizi di pubblica utilità* (Giappichelli, 2002) and Nicoletta Rangone, entry *Regolazione*, in *Dizionario di diritto pubblico*, directed by Sabino Cassese, Vol V (Giuffré, 2006) 5057.

[67] Guido Corso, 'Attività amministrativa e mercato' (1999) 1 *Rivista giuridica quadrimestrale dei pubblici servizi* 7.

[68] On this point see the book of Giulio Napolitano and Michele Abrescia, *Analisi economica del diritto pubblico* (il Mulino, 2009).

reporting on Regulatory Reform in Italy, more recently research and studies have been focused on further aspects: among others, risks connected to legislation (which was defined as a 'trap'),[69] on the increasing relevance of regulation and its quality[70] and on effectiveness of legislation and regulation,[71] questions which have been identified as the real challenge for contemporary legal systems.

Finally, the Spanish approach to regulation has been characterised (more or less) by the same Italian path, moving from the European legal system's pressure (and from the pressure of international organisations) with reference to public services and economic regulation (at first),[72] passing through the increasing interest for quality of regulation[73] and (more in general) finalising the idea of a deep reconfiguration in the relationship between state and society, between the science and the law, between traditional administration and institutions devoted to prevent risks.[74] In this wider framework, the *regulacíon* has been progressively considered a contemporary distinctive legal concept[75] and a driver of state modernisation.[76]

---

[69] Bernardo Giorgio Mattarella, *La trappola delle leggi. Molte, oscure, complicate* (il Mulino, 2011).

[70] Maria De Benedetto, Mario Martelli and Nicoletta Rangone, *La qualità delle regole* (Il Mulino, 2011).

[71] On this point see in English, Maria De Benedetto, 'Effective law from a regulatory and administrative law perspective' (2018) 9 *European Journal of Risk Regulation* 391; a further contribution is in French, Maria De Benedetto and Nicoletta Rangone, 'L'effectivité des règles et des décisions administratives', in Jean-Bernard Auby (ed) with Émile Chevalier and Emmanuel Slautsky, *Le futur du droit administratif* (LexisNexis, 2019) 235 and (finally) a much longer article in Italian, Maria De Benedetto and Nicoletta Rangone, 'La questione amministrativa dell'effettività: regole, decisioni e fatti' (2019) 3 *Diritto pubblico* 747.

[72] On this topic see Elisenda Malaret I Garcia, 'Regulacíon económica; su instrumentación normativa (El lugar de la ley en el Estado regulador, la experiencia reciente española)' (2003) 17 *Derecho Privado y Constitución* 327 and Elisenda Malaret I Garcia, 'Administración pública y regulación económica', in *La Autonomía municipal, administración y regulación económica, títulos académicos y profesionale* (Aranzadi, 2007).

[73] See Agustí Cerillo Martínez and Juli Ponce Solé (eds), *Innovación en el ámbito del buen gobierno regulatorio: ciencias del comportamiento, transparencia y prevención de la corrupción* (Instituto Nacional de Administración Pública, 2017).

[74] On these aspects see José Esteve Pardo, 'Sobre la estabilidad de la regulación. Fórmulas de equilibrio y frentes de riesgos' (2012) 4 *Cuadernos – Círculo cívico de opinión, Regular en tiempos de crisis* 19; José Esteve Pardo, 'La recepción en la Europa continental del Derecho de la regulación de la economía' (2010) 183 *Revista de administración pública* 295; José Esteve Pardo, 'El encuadre de la regulación de la economía en la sistemática del Derecho público' (2009) 20 *Revista General de Derecho Administrativo* 1696.

[75] On this point see Juli Ponce Solé, 'La calidad en el desarrollo de la discrecionalidad reglamentaria. Teorías sobre la regulación y adopción de buenas decisiones normativas por los Gobiernos y las Administraciones' (2003) 162 *Revista de administración pública* 89. See also *Anuario del Buen Gobierno y de la Calidad de la Regulación 2019*, Nueva publicación periódica de la Fundación Democracia y Gobierno Local, www.gobiernolocal.org/anuario-del-buen-gobierno-y-de-la-calidad-de-la-regulacion-2019-2/. See finally José Carlos Laguna de Paz, 'Regulación, externalización de actividades administrativas y autorregulacón' (2011) 185 *Revista de administración pública* 89 and Iñigo del Guayo Castiella, *Regulación* (Marcial Pons, 2017).

[76] José Luis Carro Fernández-Valmayor, 'Una introducción a la idea de modernización administrativa', (2011) *Dereito*, special issue *Estudios sobre la modernización administrativa* 5: modernisation is considered a 'constante en los últimos años en todo programa de actuación o de regulación normativa referido a las Administraciones publicas'.

Therefore, rules and regulation may be currently configured as key concepts, for two main reasons.

Firstly, rules represent a minimum element in common, valid and usable in many fields of research and in all kinds of legal systems. In other words, thanks to the concept of regulation and rules as a whole, it is possible to approach in a comparative way and to integrate without great difficulty, studies on legal normativity, constitutional and parliamentary law, legislative studies and legal drafting (the traditional world of formal quality) with economics, administrative law, public policy, sociology, psychology, in other words fields of research concerned with both justification and impact of rules (the emerging world of substantial quality). Adopting the regulatory perspective allows, as a first result, mismatches and parallelisms to be overcome, and research categories to be reconciled.

Secondly, rules represent a very concrete object of work, which is simple to identify for legislators, regulators, public agencies and enforcement officers. They should consider each single rule (and regulation as a whole) throughout its lifecycle from planning to ex post evaluation: only in this way is it possible to ensure that rules have been appropriately adopted and that they can effectively achieve their objectives without producing undesirable side-effects or being counterproductive. Given the impossibility of optimal rules,[77] the purpose of making good rules,[78] rules which are at least clear, consistent, understandable and which work well[79] need implementation, enforcement at street level[80] and evaluation of their impact according to the concepts of better regulation,[81] smart regulation[82] and 'fit for purpose' regulation.[83] Therefore, the regulatory perspective contributes

---

[77] Colin S Diver, 'The Optimal Precision of Administrative Rules' (1983) 93(1) *Yale Law Journal* 65, where he talks about 'dissatisfaction with the precision of administrative rules, because of either administrative underprecision or excessive regulatory rigidity'; on this aspect, see also Robert Baldwin, *Rules and Government* 176 et seq.

[78] Rules are a part of legislation in a strict sense, but they are also elements of regulation, Cary Coglianese, *Measuring regulatory performance. Evaluating the impact of regulation and regulatory policy* 8. On this point, see Maria De Benedetto, 'Effective law from a regulatory and administrative law perspective' 391.

[79] See Robert Baldwin, *Rules and Government* esp 142 ('making rules work').

[80] Michael Lipsky, *Street-level Bureaucracy: Dilemmas of the Individual in Public Services* (Russell Sage Foundation, 1980).

[81] See OECD, *Overcoming Barriers to Administrative Simplification Strategies: Guidance for Policy Makers* (OECD Publishing, 2009), 44: 'better regulation means to adopt regulations that meet concrete quality standards, avoids unnecessary regulatory burdens and effectively meets clear objectives'; see also OECD, *Recommendation on Improving the Quality of Government Regulation* (OECD, 1995); OECD, *Report on Regulatory Reform Synthesis* (OECD, 1997) 8.

[82] European Commission, Communication *Smart Regulation in the European Union*, COM (2010) 0543 final, 3, where smart regulation is defined as regulation 'about the whole policy cycle – from the design of a piece of legislation to implementation, enforcement, evaluation and revision'). See also Robert Baldwin, 'Is Better Regulation Smarter Regulation?' (2005) *Public Law* 485.

[83] See European Commission Communication, *EU Regulatory Fitness*, COM (2012) 746 final, 3: because of 'the current economic situation demands the EU legislation be even more effective and efficient in achieving its public policy objectives … REFIT will identify burdens, inconsistencies, gaps and ineffective measures'; European Commission Communication, *Strengthening the Foundations of Smart Regulation – Improving Evaluation*, COM (2013) 686 final, 3.

16 *Rules, Corruption and Controls: Setting the Scene*

to a second result: integrating operational categories of legislators, regulators, public agencies and enforcement officers at every level of government.

1.3. Rules and Behaviour

Rules aim, or rather, they exist, to guide behaviour. Guiding behaviour (better, effectively guiding) is indispensable (once again) in order to organise common life, to limit social conflicts as well as to address various public policy objectives. However, rules are not always successful in achieving such results: they often produce side-effects or can be counterproductive, even operating as a catalyst for undesirable impacts: this diversity of outcomes (as we will see below) may sometimes result in corruption.

1.3.1. Decisions about Compliance with Rules as an Individual Problem

Individual decisions about compliance are crucial, as argued starting from the still influential traditional rational economic approach.[84]

These decisions were firstly considered to be economic evaluations influenced by the cost of compliance, the size of the penalty and the risk of incurring the penalty; a rational and informed choice would be the basis of citizens' decisions in matters such as urban parking, or whether firms decide to pay or evade taxes.

However, this idea has been criticised by further compliance models[85] and, more recently, by behavioural and cognitive arguments,[86] ie heuristics, biases, inertia and (in general) unconscious thinking which characterise everyday decisions of real people, for instance when evaluating risks or in calculating their own benefits.[87]

Thanks to wide experimental evidence, the idea that behaviour is rational and responds to economic incentives/disincentives can be today reformulated by

---

[84] See Gary S Becker, 'Crime and Punishment: An Economic Approach' 169. For further aspects see Anthony Ogus, 'Corruption and regulatory structures' 329; see also Johann Graf Lambsdorff, 'Corruption and rent-seeking' 97. See finally Keith Hawkins, John M Thomas (eds), *Enforcing Regulation*.

[85] See John T Scholz, 'Managing Regulatory Enforcement in the United States', 425 onwards. See also Florentin Blanc, *From Chasing Violations to Managing Risks* 140: 'Models of compliance have gradually moved away from a narrow, deterrence-based vision to a more complex, multi-factor model'.

[86] On this topic, Nicoletta Rangone, 'Making Law Effective: Behavioural Insights into Compliance' (2018) 9(3) *European Journal of Risk Regulation* 483.

[87] On this point see, Christine Jolls, Cass R Sunstein, Richard Thaler, 'A Behavioural Approach to Law and Economics' (1998) 50 *Stanford Law Review* 1471; see also George A Akerlof, Robert J Shille, *Animal Spirits. How Human Psychology Drives the Economy, and Why It Matters for Global Capitalism* (Princeton University Press, 2009).

considering all factors which impact on compliance and which may help in understanding regulation from its human perspective;[88] On one side, it is important to take into account different non-rational elements which influence normativity;[89] on the other side, all factors which may impact on compliance should be considered in an integrated way because they have to operate in harmony, as otherwise they may come into conflict, and the results of regulation would be unpredictable.[90]

The fundamental, apparently simple, individual question about compliance (to comply or not to comply?) presents highly complex implications.

People may simply comply with rules. As we have seen, they can, for different reasons, be motivated to do so: intimate persuasion, strong sense of morality, social pressures, fear of sanctions and so on.

Others may not comply. Non-compliance also arises from different motivations:[91] for instance, it can allow extra income by saving money; or to comply can be difficult; or people are not informed about rules; or, finally, people could see the rules or regulators as illegitimate.

This binary representation is definitely relevant in theory and works for individual responses to rules. However, practice is full of more nuanced situations and compliance policies should take into account the ambiguity which comes from the sum total of all individual responses to rules, as when compliance may be selective, or when 'people think they comply, even if they don't'.[92]

A first point is that the same people on the same day may comply with some rules and not with others.[93] For instance, a substantially compliant citizen may rebel against some regulation which is perceived as unjust and too oppressive, or a compliant entrepreneur may infringe the law due to concrete and contingent impossibility of complying.

Secondly, people may alternate periods of more extensive non-compliance with periods in which they attempt to regularise their positions (for instance with fiscal agencies), to start 'a new life' and to seek behaving more correctly, as in the logic of tax amnesties.[94]

---

[88] The idea has been mentioned in E Allan Lind, Christiane Arndt, *Perceived Fairness and Regulatory Policy*, OECD Regulatory Policy Working Papers No 6 (OECD, 2016) 3: 'the human side of regulation'.

[89] George A Akerlof, Robert J Shiller, *Animal Spirits: How Human Psychology Drives the Economy, and Why It Matters for Global Capitalism* (Princeton University Press, 2009) 12: 'animal spirits … beyond the rational'. See also Thierry Devos, Dario Spini and Shalom H Schwartz, 'Conflicts among Human Values and Trust in Institutions' (2002) 41 *British Journal of Social Psychology* 481.

[90] Lawrence M Friedman, *Impact. How Law Affects Behaviour* 240.

[91] See OECD, *Reducing the risk of policy failures. Challenges for regulatory compliance* (OECD, 2000) 73.

[92] Christopher Hodges and Ruth Steinholtz, *Ethical Business Practice and Regulation. A Behavioural and Values-Based Approach to Compliance and Enforcement* 11.

[93] See Florentin Blanc, *From Chasing Violations to Managing Risks* 147–48.

[94] Katherine Baer and Eric Le Borgne, *Tax Amnesties: Theory, Trends, and Some Alternatives* (International Monetary Fund, 2008) 27 'Compliance effect (a complex, yet crucial, dynamic effect). Tax amnesties can either increase compliance by enabling current tax evaders to regularise their situation or decrease it by increasing expectations of future tax amnesties and by discouraging current law-abiding citizens (who observe that previous tax evaders were not detected)'.

Finally, people have an additional possibility, facilitated by huge legislative inflation, especially in overregulated sectors: *creative compliance*.[95] Creative compliance is outside of the traditional logic adopted to induce compliance, based on binary modalities (compliance/non-compliance; incentives/disincentives). In this case, in fact, people – without breaking the formal terms of the rule – circumvent its scope and breach its spirit in order to achieve some kind of profit (or to avoid some kind of cost). Traditional sanctions do not work and new enforcement means, such as anti-avoidance rules[96] are required, in order to invalidate abusive results, for instance, in the case of tax regulation.[97]

1.3.2. Generating Compliance with Rules as an Institutional Problem

When a behaviour is considered good, opportune or convenient from a legitimate public interest perspective, public policy makers plan to persuade people to adopt it. Such behaviour may be desirable in itself (as in the case of prohibitions on smoking) or may represent a step in a process which will lead to a desired result (as in the case of a firm which has to conform to health and safety regulations established in order to limit the risk of a certain kind of incident). To this end, they can resort to non-legal means, such as a communications campaign, hoping – for instance – that it would be sufficient to reduce the number of smokers, or to increase the consumption of green fuels. Sometimes, if people are not easily convinced, or if results are particularly complex and difficult to achieve, policy makers have to resort to stronger policy tools, such as rules. These can be elements of soft regulation or encapsulated in legislation, for instance by establishing a smoking ban in indoor workplaces, public transport and other public places, or a tax incentive for green fuels: rules, in fact, can help in making a legitimate public interest in a certain behaviour also a concrete individual interest to behave in a way which will not determine adverse consequences (disincentives) or which will produce some desired effects (incentives).

Even though this reasoning seems to be apparently linear, analysing all of its implications has an incredible relevance in understanding mechanisms which

---

[95] Robert Baldwin, Martin Cave, Martin Lodge, *Understanding Regulation* 232.
[96] HM Revenue & Customs, *General Anti-Abuse Rule guidance* (28 March 2018), B3.1: 'The primary policy objective of the GAAR is to deter taxpayers from entering into abusive arrangements, and to deter would-be promoters from promoting such arrangements'.
[97] In general, see Christopher Hodges, *Ethical Business Regulation: Understanding the Evidence* (Department for Business Innovation & Skills, Better Regulation Delivery Office February 2016) 9: 'Where actions are immoral, or accountability as described above has not been observed, a proportionate response should be made. Enforcement policies should generally avoid the concept of deterrence, since it has limited effect on behaviour, conflicts with a learning-based performance culture, and is undemocratic'.

make possible infringements and corruption and – conversely – to realise how anticorruption policies could be more effective. In fact, the efficacy of rules, far from working automatically is, in a certain way, quite unpredictable.

What does a rule's success[98] in persuading people depend on? What are the reasons which concretely influence compliance with rules? 'Why do people obey the law'?[99] Literature in this regard has given many valuable contributions.[100]

Firstly, compliance with rules can be the result of an external force, mainly the fear of sanctions (eg criminal penalties, monetary fines but also disqualifications from public benefits or procurements). Compliance through deterrence is strictly linked to the enforcement of rules and on the idea of incentives and disincentives.

Secondly, compliance can be the result of internal forces, which operate in the absence of external coercion such as personal values and ethical reasons[101] which move people to behave spontaneously with regard to fiscal law (by paying taxes), to driving codes (by parking legally), to building regulations (by applying for building permits) and so on.[102]

Other motivations for compliance are placed at the intersection between external and internal motivations. For instance, procedural justice and the interaction with authorities are considered relevant for the decision about whether to comply, being neither exclusively internal nor operating through simple deterrence.[103] Furthermore, social imitation factors contribute to the choice about compliance, but they are neither entirely external motivations[104] nor internal forces alone.[105]

---

[98] On this point, see Robert Baldwin and Martin Cave, *Taming the corporation. How to regulate for success* (Oxford University Press, 2021).

[99] Tom R Tyler, *Why People Obey to the Law*.

[100] For a review and consolidation of compliance drivers, see Florentin Blanc, *From Chasing Violations to Managing Risks* 130 et seq, section devoted to 'Promoting compliance, improving outcomes: models, drivers, methods and issues'.

[101] Herbert Lionelus A Hart, *The concept of Law* esp 258 where he mentions the conformity of laws 'with substantive moral values or principles'; see also Peter Koslowski, *Principles of Ethical Economy* (Kluwer Academic Publishers, 2001).

[102] See Erich Kirchler and Erik Hoelzl, 'Modelling Taxpayers Behaviour as a Function of Interaction between Tax Authorities and Taxpayers', in Henk Elffers, Wim Huisman and Peter Verboon (eds), *Managing and Maintaining Compliance. Closing the gap between science and practice* (Boom Legal Publishers, 2006) and Eva Hofmann, Erik Hoelzl and Erich Kirchler, 'Preconditions of Voluntary Tax Compliance: Knowledge and Evaluation of Taxation, Norms, Fairness, and Motivation to Cooperate' (2008) 216(4) *Zeitschrift für Psychologie* 209.

[103] On 'procedural injustice' as source of non-compliance see John Braithwaite, *Improving Compliance: Strategies and Practical Applications in OECD Countries* 9. See also Tom R Tyler, 'Procedural Justice, Legitimacy, and the Effective Rule of Law' (2003) 30 *Crime and Justice* 283.

[104] See Tom R. Tyler, 'The psychology of legitimacy: A relational perspective on voluntary deference to authorities' (1997) *Personality and Social Psychology Review*, 1(4), 323. See also Robert Cooter, 'Expressive Law and Economics' 585 and Cass R Sunstein, 'On the expressive function of Law' 2021.

[105] On this aspect, see James M Buchanan, 'Ethical rules, expected values and large numbers' (1965) LXXVI(1) *Ethics* 1.

20 Rules, Corruption and Controls: Setting the Scene

Early compliance models based on deterrence have presupposed people's rationality, while later models have integrated deterrence together with broader behavioural patterns following psychological and social drivers.[106]

Many institutional questions arise in this regard, especially relating to the 'enforcement style',[107] the choice between 'carrots and sticks'[108] (is it preferable to punish or to persuade?), the problem of limiting costs of enforcement,[109] and the use of behavioural and cognitive insights as a way to strengthen voluntary compliance.[110]

1.3.3. Certifying Compliance with Rules as a Company's Interest (and Cost)

Widespread non-compliance practices, complexity of controlling and regulatory failures have characterised many sectors of business regulation over the last 30 years, in this way generating the need for more effective compliance policies and the new paradigm of *regulatory compliance*.

Starting from the end of the 1980s, the 'concept of imposing responsibility on companies to establish internal controls to prevent corporate wrongdoing'[111] was introduced, first in the US. In the environmental sector, in occupational health and safety (OHS), or in financial services regulation, the risks of non-compliance were considered too high, and harmful consequences especially undesirable.[112] For this reason, alongside traditional public enforcement based on controls (too

---

[106] See John T Scholz, 'Managing Regulatory Enforcement in the United States', in David H Rosenbloom and Richard D Schwartz (eds), *Handbook of Regulation and Administrative Law* (Marcel Dekker, 1994) 423.

[107] Robert A Kagan, 'Understanding Regulatory Enforcement' (1989) 11 *Law and Policy* 89, 91.

[108] On this point, see Giuseppe Dari-Mattiacci, Gerrit De Geest, 'The Rise of Carrots and the Decline of Sticks' (2013) 80(1) *University of Chicago Law Review* 341, 346; regarding corruption, see Susan Rose-Ackerman, *Corruption and Government: Causes, Consequences and Reform* 78.

[109] See John T Scholz, 'Voluntary compliance and Regulatory enforcement' (1984) 6 *Law & Policy* 385: 'enforcement strategy that potentially can reduce both enforcement and compliance costs by encouraging cooperation rather than confrontation between agencies and regulated firms'.

[110] On this point see Christopher Hodges, 'Corporate Behaviour: Enforcement, Support or Ethical Culture?' (2015) *Oxford Legal Studies Research Paper* No 19/2015; see also Christopher Hodges and Ruth Steinholtz, *Ethical Business Practice and Regulation. A Behavioural and Values-Based Approach to Compliance and Enforcement*. See, among others, Richard H Thaler, Cass R Sunstein, *Nudge: Improving Decisions about Health, Wealth, and Happiness*; Robert Baldwin, 'From Regulation to Behaviour Change: Giving Nudge the Third Degree' (2014) 77(6) *Modern Law Review* 831; Alberto Alemanno and Anne-Lise Sibony (eds), *Nudge and the Law: A European Perspective* (Hart Publishing, 2015); Christine Jolls, Cass R Sunstein, Richard Thaler, 'A Behavioural Approach to Law and Economics'.

[111] Michael Josephson, 'History of the integrity, ethics and compliance movement: a cautionary tale for CEOs and corporate directors' (2014) *Ethikos*, 13. On the influence of the US experience in the field of regulatory compliance, see Bertrand Du Marais, 'Compliance et conformité', in *Dictionnaire des Régulations*, entrée n 20 (Lexis Nexis, 2016) 192.

[112] On this point, see Marius Aalders and Ton Wilthagen, 'Moving beyond command-and-control: Reflexivity in the regulation of occupational health and safety and the environment' (1997) 19(4) *Law & Policy* 415.

often ineffective), companies were increasingly required to adopt formal regulatory compliance systems[113] (or compliance programmes[114]) which combine management principles and regulatory instruments[115] and compel companies to develop a compliant organisational culture and to cooperate with public authorities in achieving regulatory objectives.[116]

Among other regulations belonging to this normative frame are European and member state regulation in matters of corporate social responsibility,[117] antitrust compliance,[118] banking conformity regulation,[119] compliance with data protection[120] and anti-money laundering regulation.[121]

Furthermore, the mechanism of compliance programmes has also been used to counter corruption because 'neither governments nor companies can fight corruption alone. The private and public sectors must work together in this effort'.[122] While private companies have been required to rigorously apply anticorruption regulation and standards – depending on the level of their business (national, European, international) – in the public sector, anticorruption

---

[113] Christine Parker, 'Compliance professionalism and regulatory community: The Australian trade practices regime' (1999) 26(2) *Journal of Law & Society* 215: 'Despite the dominance of organizational actors in contemporary social life, law is desperately short of doctrines, institutions, and regulatory techniques that adequately control corporate entities. The corporate veil frequently deflects the penetration of legal values into and, indeed, the imposition of legal sanctions upon the corporate entities'; Nancy Reichman, 'Moving backstage: Uncovering the role of compliance practices in shaping regulatory policy', in Kip Schlegel and David Weisburd (eds), *White Collar Crime Reconsidered* (Northeastern University Press, 1992) 244 et seq.

[114] OECD, *Reducing the risk of policy failure: challenges for regulatory compliance*.

[115] Bertrand Du Marais, 'Compliance et conformité' 196.

[116] Deborah DeMott, 'Organizational incentives to care about the law' (1997) 60(3) *Law & Contemporary Problems* 39, 40: 'While its control over individual actors is never perfect, the corporation establishes organizational rewards and sanctions for activity that shape how its agents interpret and otherwise respond to the instructions they are given'.

[117] Starting from the European Commission, Green paper, *Promoting a European framework for Corporate Social Responsibility*, 18 July 2001, COM(2001) 366 final.

[118] Stephen Calkins, 'Corporate compliance and the anti-trust agencies' bi-modal penalties' (1997) 60(3) *Law & Contemporary Problems* 127; Maria Luisa Stasi and Pierluigi Parcu, *Antitrust compliance programs in Europe Status quo and challenges ahead* (European University Institute, 2016). See https://ec.europa.eu/competition/antitrust/compliance/index_en.html: 'It is the prime responsibility of large, medium and small companies alike to comply with these rules. Companies need to be aware of the risks of infringing competition rules and how to develop a compliance strategy that best suits their needs. An effective compliance strategy enables a company to minimise the risk of involvement in competition law infringements, and the costs resulting from anti-competitive behaviour. The Commission welcomes and supports efforts by the business community to ensure compliance with EU competition rules. If an infringement is found, however, the mere existence of a compliance strategy will not be taken into consideration when setting the fine: the best reward for a good compliance strategy is not to infringe the law'.

[119] Directive 2004/39/EC of the European Parliament and of the Council on markets in financial instruments, art 13, Organisational requirements.

[120] Bertrand Du Marais, 'Compliance et conformité' 195.

[121] See Piero Pavone, Francesco Parisi, 'Compliance and corporate anti-money laundering regulation' (2018) 7(2) *Journal of Governance and Regulation* 7: 'The prevention system that, both at a national and an international level, was created leverages on the accountability of corporations, which, more or less knowingly, find themselves involved with criminality, during their normal course of business'.

[122] United Nation Office on Drugs and Crime (UNODC), *An Anticorruption Ethics and Compliance Programme for Business: A Practical Guide*, 2013, 2.

22 Rules, Corruption and Controls: Setting the Scene

legislation has established (among other measures) internal administrative controls and has regulated the activities of anticorruption bodies and anticorruption officers' tasks.

Compliance has been featured as an internal function of companies, expressed through procedures designed both to ensure the application of external rules and compliance with internal systems of control (introduced solely to attain the application of externally imposed rules), even in the presence of a movement for better and more ethical business.[123]

All this has quickly made clear, as in a mirror, that companies have an interest in certifying their effort for compliance, as confirmed by the global affirmation of 'compliance' as a dedicated, new company function in many areas of regulated business and by the incredible development of the professional sector ('compliance officer') and by the rise of regulatory technology (RegTech) as a help to solve regulatory and compliance challenges for business.[124] In fact, 'compliant' companies – in the sense of companies which have adopted compliance programmes or internalised a compliance function in their governance – would have (in different forms) the opportunity to limit their own responsibility, reduce possible sanctions and prevent reputational damage in the event of violations: procedural rules operate as signposted mountain trails, which, if followed, then a company can be reasonably confident that it will not be found to be in breach.[125]

Despite the importance of resorting to cooperative enforcement strategies which promote companies' values and ethical business, a compliance function in a company does not necessarily mean more regulatory effectiveness,[126] and does not avoid the risk of mere formal fulfilment (whereas outcome would be needed).[127] Moreover, the need for compliance programmes has dramatically revealed public enforcement and controls to be largely ineffective, but in any case,

---

[123] See again Christopher Hodges and Ruth Steinholtz, *Ethical Business Practice and Regulation. A Behavioural and Values-Based Approach to Compliance and Enforcement*. See also Colin Mayer, *Firm Commitment. Why the Corporation is Failing Us and How to Restore Trust in It* (Oxford University Press, 2012).

[124] See on this topic, Michael Becker, Kevin Merz and Rüdiger Buchkremer, 'RegTech the Application of Modern Information Technology Solutions in Regulatory Affairs: Areas of Interest in Research and Practice' (2020) 27(4) *Intelligent Systems in Accounting Finance & Management* 161: 'Concerning risk and compliance management activities of financial institutions (FIs), new technological solutions are referred to as regulatory technology, or RegTech'.

[125] On the topic, in general, see Christopher D Stone, *Where the Law Ends. The Social Control of Corporate Behaviour* (Harper & Row, 1975).

[126] OECD, *Reducing the risk of policy failure: challenges for regulatory compliance* 80: 'The implementation of corporate compliance programmes does not of itself necessarily represent an increase in compliance or in optimal regulatory outcomes. Indeed, it is possible that corporate compliance systems are an expensive response to unnecessarily complex laws. Indeed, one of the emerging themes of the research is the extent to which competitiveness and innovation is compatible with regulatory compliance'.

[127] On this point see Andrew Hopkins, 'Compliance with what? The Fundamental Regulatory Question' (1994) 34(4) *British Journal of Criminology* 431, 435, where he argue that occupational health safety regulation imposes a general duty on employers to safeguard their workers but, due to 'the problem

a compliance function produces relevant costs for companies, with the paradox that the perceived cost are especially high for those companies which would have complied in any case.

This is a very sensitive aspect: at the end of the day, the success of regulatory compliance systems corresponds to specific failures of public controls and to the need for new and more effective forms of administrative police[128] (see below, chapter four, section 4.1.3). Seeking this more effective policing, the power of control (which is public in nature) has been partially delegated to companies with the purpose of preventing infringements and corruption, as far as possible.[129]

However, together with the power of control, the cost of controlling too is shifted onto private companies because they have to internalise in their organisations a compliance function, and in their human resources, a certain number of compliance officers. There is no doubt that making regulatory compliance in a company's interest may definitely increase their commitment to legality and regulatory objectives. On the other hand, it is also necessary to be mindful of two aspects: firstly, compliance is a cost for companies and companies may very simply compare the possible sanctions and the costs of effective compliance programmes against the profits which might result from infringements and corruption;[130] secondly, when compliance is procedural based in the presence of substantive outcome regulation there is always the risk that 'compliance rhetoric will be used merely to *manage appearances*'.[131]

1.4. Functioning of Rules and their Dysfunction

Scholars and academics, politicians and public officers, practitioners and simple citizens have always faced the problem of how to make well-functioning rules.

According to an ideal vision, many rules work in a linear way: they prescribe or proscribe a certain behaviour and establish incentives or sanctions; people (almost automatically) behave according to rules because otherwise they will incur fines

---

of prosecuting for harm using procedural regulations', in practice employers need to comply with procedural standards in order to avoid punishment. See also Christine Parker, 'Reinventing Regulation within the Corporation: Compliance-Oriented Regulatory Innovation' (2000) 32(5) *Administration & Society* 529, 559-60: 'The paradox for business is that in one sense, compliance with a broad regulatory objective is much harder than even the toughest set of rules imposing the greatest paperwork burden because it requires thorough internalised commitment to showing regulatory responsibility in changing circumstances, not just ticking off a set of boxes'.

[128] Bertrand Du Marais, 'Compliance et conformité' 198; see also Peter N Grabosky, 'Using non-governmental resources to foster regulatory compliance' (1995) 8(4) *Governance: An International Journal of Policy and Administration* 527, 529: 'The paths to regulatory compliance are in practice diverse, and the traditional conception of government regulation has become obsolete'.

[129] See, in general, Robert Baldwin, 'Regulation after "command and control"', in Keith Hawkins, (ed) *Human Face of Law. Essays in honour of Donald Harris* (Clarendon Press, 1997) 65.

[130] Bertrand Du Marais, 'Compliance et conformité' 201.

[131] Christine Parker, 'Reinventing Regulation within the Corporation: Compliance-Oriented Regulatory Innovation' 560.

24 *Rules, Corruption and Controls: Setting the Scene*

or they will not gain the incentive. However, rules are different and not all rules work in same way. Moreover, in real life, where people and public officers live in the flesh, regulatory impact is rarely fully consistent with rules.[132]

1.4.1. How Rules Work

A first point is that rules are different and (as a consequence) they work differently.

Some rules consist of commands, prohibitions but also permissions.[133] They function thanks to obedience (compliance[134]), such as in cases of obligations to pay taxes or prohibitions of anti-competitive agreements. Moreover, when separating waste for recycling, not smoking in a restaurant or when applying for a building permit, citizens and firms cooperate with government in making law effective.

Some other rules establish sanctions[135] or confer certain powers upon administrations. Their effectiveness can be evaluated in terms of enforcement.[136] Normally these rules are strictly linked to the first ones, eg by establishing criminal or administrative penalties for fiscal evasion, competition infringements, smoking in a restaurant, not separating waste or building violations.

Moreover, there are rules which recognise freedoms and rights for individuals and which have some extent of utilisation.[137] In these cases, freedom means the possibility to 'act' as well as the possibility 'not to act':[138] for instance, legal provisions recognise the right to strike, which works even when not used, because its effectiveness consists in the fact that it is available for use.

---

[132] See Florentin Blanc, *From Chasing Violations to Managing Risks* 138.

[133] On the relationship between commands, prohibitions and permissions see Jeremy Bentham, *Collected Works*, Vol 2 in Herbert LA Hart (ed) *Principles of Legislation* (Athlone Press, 1945) in particular 111.

[134] On compliance, see Robert Baldwin, Martin Cave, Martin Lodge, *Understanding Regulation* 236 et seq. See also Tom R Tyler, *Why People Obey the Law*. See John T Scholz, 'Voluntary compliance and Regulatory enforcement' 385 and Gunther Teubner, 'After Legal Instrumentalism? Strategic Model of Post-Regulatory Law', in Gunther Teubner (ed), *Dilemmas of Law in the Welfare State* (Walter de Gruyter, 1988) 311: 'the law is ineffective because it creates no change in behaviour'.

[135] Monique Nuijten, Gerhard Anders (eds), *Corruption and the Secret of law. A Legal Anthropological Perspective* 12.

[136] On enforcement, George J Stigler, 'The Optimum enforcement of Law' 55: 'All prescriptions of behaviour for individuals require enforcement'. See also Keith Hawkins, John M Thomas, *Enforcing Regulation*. See also, OECD, *Reducing the Risk of Policy Failure: Challenges for Regulatory Compliance* cit. and John T Scholz, 'Enforcement policy and corporate misconduct: the changing perspective of deterrence theory' (1997) 60(3) *Law and Contemporary Problems* 254; Avlana Eisenberg, 'Expressive Enforcement' (2014) *UCLA Law Review* 858. See, finally, Geoffrey P Miller, *An Economic Analysis of Effective Compliance Programs* (New York University Law and Economics Working Papers, Paper 396, 2014).

[137] Alexandre Flückiger, 'Le droit administratif en mutation: l'émergence d'un principe d'efficacité' (2001) *Revue de droit administratif et fiscal* 93, 95.

[138] Jean Carbonnier, 'Effectivité et ineffectivité de la règle de droit' (2007) 57(2) *L'année sociologique* 6–7: 'L'effectivité de la loi qui consacre une liberté d'agir se situe non dans l'action, mais dans la liberté même, c'est-à-dire dans le pouvoir de choisir l'inaction aussi bien que l'action'.

Finally, there are rules which consist in persuasive measures (incentives), whose effectiveness has been considered dependent on the rate of usage by potential beneficiaries,[139] as in the case of subsidy programmes.

However, given this general framework, the effective functioning of rules has been developed by scholars and academics in three main steps.

The first is the legal normative step which considers rules as characterised by comprehensibility,[140] validity and binding force.[141] Rules have been studied and classified on the basis of their content or structure,[142] and their effectiveness is related to formal elements and to the existence inter alia of organised force.[143]

The second step focuses on compliance and on behaviour as a response to rules. In many fields of research in the social sciences, behaviour has been considered (firstly) rational and influenced by economic incentives – such as sanctions[144] – and (later) influenceable also by more complex explanations beyond rules.[145] On the basis of these insights, enforcement has been graduated[146] (as we will see later, in chapter four) according to the need for strategies which are more nuanced than in the compliance/deterrence binary model, and has become ever more oriented towards cooperative solutions[147] due to its own responsiveness also to non-economic incentives.

---

[139] Alexandre Flückiger, 'Le droit administratif en mutation: l'émergence d'un principe d'efficacité' 95.

[140] See recently on this topic, Wendy Wagner with Will Walker, *Incomprehensible! A Study of How Our Legal System Encourages Incomprehensibility, Why It Matters, and What We Can Do About It* (Cambridge University Press, 2019).

[141] On this point see Alf Ross, *On Law and Justice* (University of California Press, 1959) 38: 'valid law means both an order which is in fact effective and an order which possesses "binding force" derived from *a priori* principles; law is at the same time something factual in the world of reality and something valid in the world of ideas'.

[142] On this point, see Hans Kelsen, *General Theory of Law and State* 60 et seq where he analysed the 'secondary norm': 'the legal norm is split into two separate norms, two "ought" statements: one to the effect that a certain individual "ought" to observe certain conduct, and one to the effect that another individual ought to execute a sanction in case the first norm is violated'. See also Karl Olivecrona, *Law as Fact* (Oxford University Press, 1939) esp 130 et seq where he distinguished between primary and secondary rules ('the primary rules are those which lay down rights and duties for citizens ... The secondary rules are those concerning sanctions to be applied when the primary rules are violated'). See, finally, Herbert Lionel Adolphus Hart, *The Concept of Law* 97–98: secondary rules 'confer the power to make them "rules of adjudication" ... They provide the centralized official "sanctions" of the system'.

[143] See Karl Olivecrona, *Law as Fact* esp 136 ('the necessity of organized force').

[144] See Gary S Becker, 'Crime and Punishment: An Economic Approach' 169.

[145] On this point see, Neil Gunningham, 'Compliance, Deterrence and Beyond', in Lee Paddock (ed) *Compliance and Enforcement in Environmental Law* (2015 Edward Elgar).

[146] See the pyramid of enforcement, Ian Ayres and John Braithwaite, *Responsive Regulation. Transcending the Deregulation Debate* (Oxford University Press 1992), 35.

[147] See Tom R. Tyler, *Why people obey the law* cit. and John T. Scholz, 'Enforcement policy and corporate misconduct: The changing perspective of deterrence theory' 253. On this point, see also Richard Johnstone, Rick Sarre (eds), *Regulation: Enforcement and Compliance* (Australian Institute of Criminology, Research and Public Policy Serie No. 57, 2004). See, finally, Anthony G. Heyes, 'Making things stick: Enforcement and compliance' (1998) in *Oxford Review of Economic Policy*, Vol 14, issue 4, 50. See Erich Kirchler et al., 'Combining Psychology and Economics in the Analysis of Compliance: From Enforcement to Cooperation' (2012) in *Tulane Economics Working Paper Series* No. 1212.

26 Rules, Corruption and Controls: Setting the Scene

Figure 1.2 Effectiveness of Rules

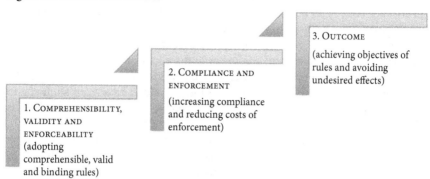

The last step is outcomes-based:[148] compliance in itself is not a value and is not enough. The idea is that a rule works when desired results are effectively achieved and the public interest which justifies the rule has been safeguarded.[149] A huge number of contributions from different academic disciplines can be considered as 'impact studies'[150] because 'impact deserves to be looked [at] as a whole'.[151] The outcomes of rules should be monitored and evaluated in order to avoid, as far as possible, perverse effects[152] and in order to catalyse effects which are compatible with the objectives of regulation.[153] This is, finally, the focus of 'positive regulation' in which context 'regulatory success is achieved when a regulator delivers the right outcome (for businesses, consumers and society) by acceptable procedures at the lowest feasible cost'.[154]

In conclusion, 'functioning rules' means rules which are clear, consistent, understandable, valid, enforceable and possibly applied (legal normativity);

---

[148] In general see, François Jullien, *Traité de l'efficacité* (Editions Grasset & Fasquelle 1996). With specific regard to regulation see Cary Coglianese, *Measuring regulatory performance. Evaluating the impact of regulation and regulatory policy* 8: 'Regulation is designed to work according to three main steps: 1. Regulation ... 2. The behaviour of individuals or entities targeted or affected by regulation ... 3. Outcomes ...'.

[149] Nicoletta Rangone, 'Making Law Effective: Behavioural Insights into Compliance' 485, where the first type 'formal' effectiveness and the second 'substantial' effectiveness are defined. On the 'importance of rules and rule designs in producing desired results', see Robert Baldwin, *Rules and Government* 142.

[150] On this point, see Lawrence M. Friedman, *Impact. How Law Affects Behaviour* 2: 'True, not too many studies explicitly label themselves 'impact studies' And there are only a few general discussion of impact, in one context or another'.

[151] Ibid, 249.

[152] Raymond Boudon, *Effets pervers et ordre social* (Puf, 1977).

[153] On this aspect, Yann Leroy, 'La notion d'effectivité du droit' (2011) 79(3) *Droit et societé* 715, 731.

[154] Robert Baldwin and Martin Cave, *Taming the corporation. How to regulate for success* 15.

rules characterised by high rates of compliance and few costs of enforcement (compliance and enforcement); rules whose results are consistent with regulatory objectives (outcomes). Effective rules – rules which work well[155] – consist in all these things together.

1.4.2. When Rules Do Not Work

What about the ways in which rules are dysfunctional? Rules currently present many problems, at each of the already mentioned levels.

At the first step (legal normativity) rules can be incomprehensible and even declared unlawful: unconstitutional by Constitutional Courts, when they consist in primary legislation; illegitimate by administrative courts, when rules consist in administrative regulations. Furthermore, rules can also be unenforceable, for instance because they establish no sanctions, because no public agency has been in charge of controls or because agencies in charge of control have not been provided with adequate resources.

At the second step (compliance and enforcement) rules may be disobeyed or enforcement may be too costly or difficult. This may even lead to 'administrative tolerance',[156] when administrations and their administrative officers tend not to apply certain rules or not to sanction their violation (see below, chapter four) and in so doing contribute to the reduction of deterrence and compliance.

At the third and last step (outcome), rules can produce results which are not consistent with or are even opposite to those intended; they can also cause side-effects which can be compatible with the rules' objectives to a greater or lesser degree.

Let us now consider rules as medicines, which are indispensable for treating patients.[157] Medicines should be well produced and their dosages should be well calibrated. In any case, patients have to cooperate in the treatment and to be observed after administering medications. More or less the same occurs for rules. They are needed to 'cure' some aspects of social life, protect people or prevent some kinds of risk, but to do it they have to be well produced and well dosed. The cooperation of citizens and firms is needed, and when administered the concrete application of rules must be accurately observed in order to check if it is producing the expected effects.

---

[155] Robert Baldwin, *Rules and Government* esp 142 ('making rules work').
[156] François Rangeon, 'Réflexions sur l'effectivité du droit', in Curapp, *Les usages sociaux du droit* (Colloque, Amiens, 12 May 1989, Presses Universitaire de France).
[157] On this point see Wim Voerman, 'De aspirinewerking van sancties', in L Loeber (ed), *Bruikbare wetgeving, preadviezen van Ph. Eijlander en P. Popelier aan de Vereniging voor wetgeving en wetgevingsbeleid* (Wolff Legal Publishers, 2007), 59, quoted by Florentin Blanc, *From Chasing Violations to Managing Risks* 169: 'the "aspirin-like effect of sanctions", suggesting that (just as for aspirin) many people will assert that 'it helps', without being able to explain why or how'.

Table 1.1 Analysis of Rules when Functioning and when Dysfunctional

	Rules	When functioning	When dysfunctional
Legal normativity	Comprehensibility	Rules are comprehensible	Rules are incomprehensible and generate problems, different interpretations and litigation
	Validity	Rules are valid and uncontested	Rules are not valid and are contested before Constitutional Courts or other kinds of courts (depending on the legal 'box' of the rule)
	Enforceability	Rules are enforceable when realistic (by considering the cost and complexity of compliance) – the *enforcement system* (including sanctions) has been properly considered and calibrated in the regulatory process – *enforcement officers* are adequate (in number, in expertise or in human skills required for effective supporting or deterring)	Rules are not enforceable when unrealistic (they do not consider the cost and complexity of compliance) – *no adequate enforcement and sanctions* are established – *enforcement officers are not adequate* (in number, in expertise or in human skills required for effective supporting or deterring)
Theories of compliance	Compliance	High rates of compliance – internal forces (personal values, ethical reasons) and external forces (fear of sanctions) converge, operating in harmony – procedural justice (good interaction with authorities) – social imitation factors	Low rates of compliance – internal forces (personal values, ethical reasons) and external forces (fear of sanctions) do not converge and conflict with each other – lack of procedural justice (bad interaction with authorities) – no social pressures for compliance (or social pressure for non-compliance)

(continued)

Table 1.1 *(Continued)*

	Rules	When functioning	When dysfunctional
		Regulatory compliance systems - Culture of compliance - Companies commitment - Regulatory effectiveness	Regulatory compliance systems - Formal compliance - Costs for companies which would have complied - Regulatory ineffectiveness
	Enforcement (and regulatory delivery)	Nuanced enforcement strategies, risk-based and focused on target of controls - Supporting compliance - Cooperative enforcement - Strict enforcement	- Rigid/ formalistic strategies (one-size-fits-all) - Administrative tolerance
IMPACT STUDIES	Impact	Effects consistent with objectives of rules	Effects not consistent with objectives of rules
		Side-effects not inconsistent with objectives of rules	Side-effects inconsistent with objectives of rules
		Limited creative compliance	Widespread creative compliance

1.4.3. Trust: The Intangible Factor of Rules' Effectiveness

Trust in institutions[158] is normally associated with higher degrees of compliant behaviour.[159] For this reason, a discourse on rules, compliance, law effectiveness and corruption (which will be intended as regulatory ineffectiveness, chapter two, section 2.3.3) necessarily includes trust.

Human relations, social groups, markets and institutions work by combining both trust and controls.[160] While 'trust implies confidence ... that some person or

---

[158] See Jacopo Domenicucci, 'Trusting Institutions'(2018) in *Rivista di estetica*, n. 68, 3.

[159] See, for example, European Commission Communication on *Improving the delivery of benefits from EU environment measures: building confidence through better knowledge and responsiveness* (2012) IP/12/220. On this point see John Braithwaite and Toni Makkai, 'Trust and compliance' (1994) 4 *Policing & Society* 1 and Christopher Hodges and Ruth Steinholtz, *Ethical Business Practice and Regulation. A Behavioural and Values-Based Approach to Compliance and Enforcement* 77–78.

[160] On this point, see Maria De Benedetto, 'The crisis of confidence in legislation: an overview', in Maria De Benedetto, Nicoletta Rangone, Nicola Lupo, *The Crisis of Confidence in legislation* (Nomos/Hart, 2020), 7.

institution will behave in an expected way', controls contribute to produce such confidence via coercive means by checking 'if' and 'how' people have complied with a certain rule and consequently by giving elements to impose sanctions, where appropriate. This dual-path approach to confidence (trust and rules/controls) is very strictly related to ordinary people's daily experience. For instance, even though I have no trust in my sister as a good driver, nonetheless I am confident that she will park legally in the city centre because otherwise (thanks to strict controls) she will surely be fined. In other words, confidence based on controls can be explained in terms of systems which provide sufficient and effective incentives to comply and behave according to rules.

From this perspective, even though trust can be configured as an alternative to controlling[161] and coercion a way to substitute trust,[162] the question is much more complex and requires to better focus on three aspects.

First, we should consider 'the importance of *institutions* for trust'.[163] Institutions produce and protect trust, they provide conditions for trust which are indispensable not only for cooperation but also for competition, both in the market and in political competition.[164] Furthermore, institutions scrutinise trust in order to verify if underlying interests effectively deserve protection.[165] For instance, trust is a 'motive for cooperation'[166] but it characterises agreements among private interests also when they carry out illicit infringements such as cartels or other monopolisation infringements in antitrust law[167] as well as criminal association[168] even corruption: in these cases, institutions operate

---

[161] Guido Möllering, 'The Trust/Control Duality An Integrative Perspective on Positive Expectations of Others' (2005) 20(3) *International Sociology* 283.

[162] Diego Gambetta, 'Can we trust trust?', in Diego Gambetta (ed), *Trust: Making and breaking cooperative relations* (Basil Blackwell, 1988) 220.

[163] Jacopo Domenicucci, 'Trusting Institutions' 3.

[164] Florentin Blanc, *From Chasing Violations to Managing Risks* 288–89: 'In this respect, inspections and enforcement create a "floor" of confidence, and a risk-mitigation mechanism. They are also an important driver of compliance, not primarily through deterrence, but by reassuring voluntary compliant actors that the rules of the game are enforced. Credible inspections and enforcement thus increase trust among businesses (towards suppliers and buyers), workers (towards employers), consumers (towards sellers) etc. In an optimal situation, it reduces the reliance on litigation, reduces uncertainty, thus decreases costs and ends up having a positive economic and social impact'. See also Christopher Hodges and Ruth Steinholz, *Ethical Business Practice and Regulation. A Behavioural and Values-Based Approach to Compliance and Enforcement*, esp 'Trust Within and in Organisations'.

[165] Diego Gambetta 'Can We Trust Trust?', in D Gambetta (ed), *Trust and Power* 214: 'a priori, we cannot always say whether greater trust and cooperation are in fact desirable'.

[166] Bernard Williams, 'Formal Structures and Social Reality', in Diego Gambetta (ed) *Trust: Making and Breaking Cooperative Relations* 3. See Diego Gambetta, 'Can We Trust Trust?', in Diego Gambetta (ed) *Trust: Making and Breaking Cooperative Relations* 213.

[167] Wayne D Collins 'Trusts and the Origins of Antitrust Legislation' (2013) 81 *Fordham Law Review* 2279.

[168] Augustin of Hippo, *The City of God*, IV-4: 'Justice being taken away, then, what are kingdoms but great robberies? For what are robberies themselves, but little kingdoms? The band itself is made up of men; it is ruled by the authority of a prince, it is knit together by the pact of the confederacy; the booty is divided by the law agreed on'. See also Adam Smith *The theory of moral sentiments* (1759) section II, ch 3: 'if there is any society among robbers and murderers, they must at least, according to the trite observation, abstain from robbing and murdering one another'.

against trust as private fact by prosecuting and sanctioning partnership in crime and any possible illicit and infringement. However, in so doing they intend to provide protection for trust as general and public value.[169] When corruption flourishes, these institutional functions (producing, protecting, scrutinising trust) are weakened in their credibility.

Strictly related to the first, there is a second aspect, 'the importance of *trust for institutions*':[170] 'institutions (e.g. democratic institutions, healthcare systems, banks) need public trust to function properly' and mere compliance ensured through coercion is not always enough. For this reason, trust is currently a major institutional goal in order to improve institutions' legitimacy, to increase compliance with and effectiveness of rules and to reduce costs associated to legislation and regulation, whatever their nature (for implementing and enforcing as well as for litigation). Trust makes single rules as well as legal systems more effective and, for this reason, it is regularly measured by barometers and indexes, such as the Eurobarometer (Trust in National and International Institutions),[171] the Edelman Trust Barometer[172] and the US Gallup Confidence in Institutions Index.[173]

A third aspect should be considered: the *alternativity between trust and controls is only limited*. Legal systems cannot be based only on trust, nor exclusively on controls.[174] Institutions work through a combination of methods. In fact, on the one hand, there is large agreement on the idea that overly strong systems of control will inhibit trust and that in the long run they will produce a greater number of infringements. On the other hand, there is also large agreement on the idea that trust without controls will inevitably lead to infringements and non-compliance. Moreover, not all possible combinations of trust and controls will produce optimal results: institutions, in fact, should accurately choose cases where it is preferable to establish controls, and cases where it is better to promote trust.[175]

---

[169] For a related but different perspective, see Annette Baier, 'Trust and Antitrust' (1986) 96(2) *Ethics* 231.

[170] Jacopo Domenicucci, 'Trusting Institutions' 3.

[171] The Eurobarometer standard was established in 1974. Each survey consists of approximately 1,000 face-to-face interviews per country. See Eurobarometer 92, *Autumn 2019. Public opinion in the European Union* (November 2019), esp 5, where there is the analysis of European and political Institutions, with reference to 'trust in national governments and parliaments and in the European Union: trend' and 6, with reference to 'trust in the European Union: national results and evolutions'.

[172] In the mid-1990s Francis Fukuyama's influential book *Trust: The Social Virtues and the Creation of Prosperity* (Simon & Schuster, 1996) laid the foundation for studies of societal trust and informed the creation of the Edelman Trust Barometer: 'Throughout 20 years of studying how trust is won, violated and lost, we have learned that the two essential elements of trust are *effectiveness* and *ethical conduct*. ... The initial study polled opinion shapers in the U.S., U.K., France, Germany, and Australia on their trust in NGOs relative to media, government and business. We were stunned to learn that NGOs were the most trusted institution in the world (now no longer the case), a clear sign of discontent with the effectiveness of traditional leadership.' (www.edelman.com/20yearsoftrust/.)

[173] https://news.gallup.com/poll/1597/confidence-institutions.aspx.

[174] On 'limits to the use of inspections to create trust' see Florentin Blanc, *From Chasing Violations to Managing Risks* 289.

[175] On this point see F David Schoorman, Roger C Mayer and James H Davis, 'An Integrative Model of Organizational Trust: Past, Present and Future' (2007) 32(2) *The Academy of Management Review* 346: 'when the risk in a situation is greater than the trust (and thus the willingness to take risk), a control

32 *Rules, Corruption and Controls: Setting the Scene*

Starting from these premises, when both trust is poor and controls are not wholly effective, this contributes to make corruption more frequent, even systemic. From this perspective, regulatory effectiveness and anticorruption policies necessarily include the restoration of confidence in institutions (or trust repairing, as some scholars say).[176] Trust, in other words, is an intangible but highly relevant factor for compliance, regulatory effectiveness and – conversely – an indispensable asset of anticorruption.

1.5. Corruption

1.5.1. Definition

Despite being 'as old as government itself',[177] corruption is, at the same time, difficult to define[178] and difficult to measure.[179]

Corruption is difficult to define, because albeit being a 'ubiquitous aspect of political society'[180] which crosses legal systems, history and cultures, it simultaneously expresses historical contingency and geographic localism: in other words, a behaviour can be considered corrupt in one country or at a certain time and not be considered corrupt elsewhere or at different times.

Corruption is difficult to measure, because corrupt behaviour – as with any kind of infringements – presupposes secrecy;[181] collecting strong evidence on corruption cases is quite impossible; and, as a consequence, each Index related to the corruption in a country is inevitably focused on perception

---

system can bridge the difference by lowering the perceived risk to a level that can be managed by trust'. See also, Florentin Blanc, *From Chasing Violations to Managing Risks* 155 (quoting Erich Kirchler, *The Economic Psychology of Tax Behaviour* (Cambridge University Press, 2007)): 'In a climate of distrust, the primary driver will be deterrence, in a climate of trust, social representations, norms and fairness perceptions will be the main drivers'.

[176] On trust repair, see F David Schoorman, Roger C Mayer and James H Davis, 'An Integrative Model of Organizational Trust: Past, Present and Future' 349.

[177] Robert Klitgaard, *Controlling Corruption* 7.

[178] On the academic debate about this point, see Maria De Benedetto, entry 'Administrative Corruption', in Jürgen Georg Backhaus, *Encyclopedia of Law and Economics* (Springer online, 2014) 1–2.

[179] See John A Gardiner, *Controlling official corruption and fraud: Bureaucratic incentives and disincentives* 40 and Frank Anechiarico and James B Jacobs, *The Pursuit of Absolute Integrity. How Corruption Control Makes Government Ineffective*, 14. See, also, Fabio Mendez and Facundo Sepúlveda, 'What Do We Talk About When We Talk About Corruption?' (2010) 26(3) *The Journal of Law, Economics and Organization* 493. On this point, see Danila Serra, 'Empirical determinants of corruption: A sensitive analysis' (2006) *Public Choice* 225 and Tudorel Andrei, Bogdan Oancea and Florin Dananau, 'The analysis of corruption in public administration. A quantitative method' (2010) 1(XVII) *Lex et Scientia International Journal (LESIJ)* 435.

[180] John A Gardiner, *The Politics of Corruption* 93.

[181] On this point, see Carlos Mariano Mosquera, 'Negotiation Games in the Fight against Corruption' (2014), *Edmond J Safra Working Papers*, No 46, 19 June 2014, esp 6.

rather than on reality.[182] In other words, any knowledge of corruption is mostly knowledge about people's perceptions of corruption.[183]

1.5.2. A Basic Definition for a Complex Issue: (Simple) Corruption

Literature on corruption has become huge and ever more multidisciplinary during recent decades. It can be briefly grouped into three major veins.

The first looks at corruption mainly as a moral issue,[184] by tending to consider it as evil,[185] which requires changes in 'values and norms of honesty in public life': the central idea of this current is that without 'active moral reform campaigns no big dent in the corrosive effects of corruption is likely to be achieved'.[186]

The second considers corruption as an economic issue. Important (but also debated) contributions have recognised not only that economics is a powerful and illuminating tool for the analysis of corruption[187] but that corruption might produce even positive effects by 'greasing the wheels' of an economy[188] or by influencing firm market entry[189] or, finally, by ensuring economic development.[190]

A third current emphasised corruption as an institutional issue, because it represents an 'extra-legal institution used by individuals or groups to gain influence over the action of the bureaucracy', a sort of participation in the decision-making.[191] Corruption could be considered functional to the agency's mission, when 'the agency cannot accomplish its mission through legally sanctioned techniques, and "cuts corners" to get *something done*';[192] sometimes corruption has

---

[182] The Transparency International Annual Report is based on a Corruption Perception Index. On this point, see Benjamin A Olken, 'Corruption perceptions vs. corruption reality' (2009) 93(7–8) *Journal of Public Economics* 950.

[183] See James B Jacobs, *Dilemmas of Corruption Controls*, in Cyrille Fijnaut and Leo Huberts (eds) *Corruption, Integrity and Law Enforcement* (Kluwer Law International, 2002) 287.

[184] Edward C Banfield, *The Moral Basis of Backward Society* (Free Press, 1958).

[185] Joseph S Nye, 'Corruption and political development: a cost-benefit analysis' (1967) 61(2) *American Political Science Review* 417 and in particular 419, where Nye provides one of the most important definitions of corruption: 'behaviour which deviates from the formal duties of a public role because of private-regarding (personal, close family, private clique) pecuniary or status gains; or violates rules against the exercise of certain types of private-regarding influence'.

[186] Pranab Bardhan, 'Corruption and development: a review of issues' 1335.

[187] See Susan Rose-Ackerman, *Corruption and government: causes, consequences and reform* xi; see also Robert Klitgaard, *Controlling Corruption*. and Anthony Ogus, *Corruption and Regulatory Structures*.

[188] Pierre-Guillame Méon, and Khalid Sekkat, 'Does corruption grease or sand the wheels of growth?', (2005) 122(1) *Public Choice* 69.

[189] Axel Dreher and Martin Gassebner, 'Greasing the wheels? The impact of regulations and corruption on firm entry' (2013) 155 *Public Choice*, 413.

[190] See Nathaniel H Leff, 'Economic Development Through Bureaucratic Corruption'. On this point, see also Paolo Mauro, 'Corruption and Growth' 681.

[191] Ibid 8: 'the existence of corruption *per se* indicates only that these groups participate in the decision-making process'.

[192] John A Gardiner, *Controlling official corruption and fraud: Bureaucratic incentives and disincentives* 35.

34 *Rules, Corruption and Controls: Setting the Scene*

been considered to be a tool to correct inefficient regulation, for instance when corruption reduces the administrative costs of regulatory processes.[193]

Moreover, scholars and academics have proposed a certain number of distinctions and typologies in the field of corruption. For instance, 'petty' administrative corruption has been distinguished from 'grand' political corruption which 'occurs at the highest level of government and involves major government projects and programs'.[194] There is also systemic corruption 'brought about, encouraged, or promoted by the system itself ... where bribery on a large scale is routine'.[195]

These classifications have made it evident that a definition of corruption should take into account so many elements and perspectives (history, geography, repression, prevention, criminal and administrative, politics and administration, ethics, economics, behaviour and so on) that the best – in the sense of more flexible to be used in different contexts – is unavoidably the simplest. In fact, the most famous and commonly used definition has been provided by the World Bank, and refers to a concept of corruption so vague as to fit into every national context and to include all typologies of corruption: 'the abuse of public power for private benefit'.[196]

1.5.3. A Slightly Complex Definition: Corruption as a Regulatory Issue

Alongside these major currents, further elements have contributed to complicating the search for a definition. For centuries, corruption has been considered a pathology,[197] to be approached from a criminal point of view, ie by ex-post reactions (prosecuting bribery or other kinds of corruption infringements). Historically the idea of the abuse of public power was defined between the seventeenth and eighteenth centuries, during the process of abolition of venal offices,[198] and developed in the context of the rule of law[199] which prohibits any private agreements or sale

---

[193] Anthony Ogus, *Corruption and regulatory structures* 333.

[194] On this point, see Susan Rose-Ackerman, *Corruption and Government: Causes, Consequences and Reform* 27, where 'petty' administrative corruption has been distinguished from political (or 'grand') corruption, which 'occurs at the highest level of government and involves major government projects and programs'.

[195] Colin Nicholls, Tim Daniel, Martin Polaine and John Hatchard, *Corruption and Misuse of Public Office* 4. See also Adam Graycar, 'Corruption and public value' (2016) 18 *Public Integrity* 339 where he describes corruption in poor countries as different from that in rich ones.

[196] World Bank, *Writing an Effective Anticorruption Law* (2001) 1; World Bank, *Helping countries combat corruption: progress at the World Bank since 1997* (2000).

[197] See John A Gardiner, *The Politics of Corruption* 93.

[198] On this point see William Doyle, *Venality. The sale of offices in eighteenth-century France* (Clarendon Press, 2006) and Roland Mousnier, *La vénalité des offices sous Henri IV et Louis XIII* (Kaugard, 1946).

[199] On this point see United Nations Secretary-General, *Report of the Secretary-General on the rule of law and transitional justice in conflict and post-conflict societies* (S/2004/616), para 6: 'It refers to a principle of governance in which all persons, institutions and entities, public and private, including the State itself, are accountable to laws that are publicly promulgated, equally enforced and independently adjudicated, and which are consistent with international human rights norms and standards. It requires, as well, measures to ensure adherence to the principles of supremacy of law, equality before the law,

regarding public activities. Starting from the end of the last century anticorruption policies have been introduced,[200] making it necessary to evaluate corruption even from an administrative point of view, carrying out procedures and mechanisms in order to prevent corruption cases by establishing ex-ante duties of disclosure, regulation of conflicts of interest, whistleblowers, anticorruption controls, ethical codes, staff rotation and so on. Administrative anticorruption looks at the risk of corruption as related to administrative activities.

How can these different approaches be taken together? Many academics have referred to the Principal-Agent-(Client) model[201] as a way to take a comprehensive look at infringements and corruption, at administrative prevention and criminal repression. The model involves three actors: the Principal (the state and its citizens), the Agent (civil servants in charge of administrative tasks) and the Client

Figure 1.3 Principal-Agent-Client Model: Infringements

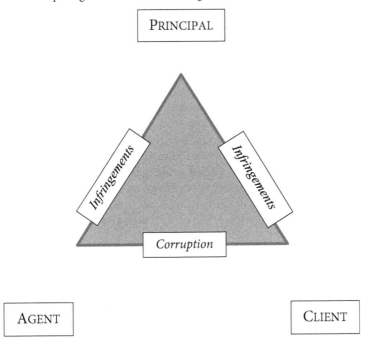

accountability to the law, fairness in the application of the law, separation of powers, participation in decision-making, legal certainty, avoidance of arbitrariness and procedural and legal transparency'.

[200] On this point, see Maria De Benedetto, entry 'Administrative Corruption', in J Backhaus (ed) *Encyclopedia of Law and Economics* (Springer online, 2014) 1–2.

[201] Edward C Banfield, 'Corruption as a Feature of Government Organization' (1975) XVIII *The Journal of Law and Economics* 587; Susan Rose-Ackerman, *Corruption. A Study in Political Economy*; Robert Klitgaard, *Controlling Corruption*; Donatella Della Porta and Alberto Vannucci, *The hidden order of corruption. An institutional approach*. See, finally, Staffan Andersson and Torbjörn Bergman, 'Controlling Corruption in the Public Sector' (2009) 32(1) *Scandinavian Political Studies* 45.

(enterprises or citizens, eg as taxpayer). Strict corruption occurs only in the Agent-Client relationship while simple infringements characterise the Principal-Agent (eg internal frauds) or the Principal-Client (eg tax evasion) relationship: in fact, a simple infringement is not necessarily 'considered to be corruption since it does not include the active (or passive) collusion of an agent of the state'.[202]

However, corruption is a regulatory issue because it is always (in one way or another) connected with rules.

In political corruption, raw illicit behaviour may be carried out, but not infrequently they are related to rent-creation via legislation, as when interested groups use bribery to obtain favourable rules.

In administrative corruption, a rule establishes administrative powers impacting on private activities; to be carried out, such corruption always needs an agreement between citizens/firms and a public agent; and finally, it always consists in a regulatory failure or in a regulatory side-effect. Regulatory anticorruption (as we will see later) looks at the risk of corruption as related to rules.

Two preliminary remarks should be taken into consideration in this regard.

Firstly, from the regulatory perspective the specific criminal connotation of corruption is not so relevant: in fact, the distinction between active or passive corruption or extortion and bribery 'means little because both parties must agree before corruption can occur'.[203] Secondly, simple infringements (breaking the law[204]) and corruption reveal the same rent-seeking activity – an effort to achieve an extra income via rules[205] – and share the character of secrecy, because 'operating in the dark' is needed in both cases in order to avoid detection and sanction: and this is the reason why infringements and corruption should be studied together.

For this slightly more complex rationale, when focusing on administrative corruption, the regulatory definition of corruption – based on that of the World Bank – could be *abuse of public power for private benefits, made it possible by bad quality or bad functioning of rules which establishes and regulates such public power.*

1.6. Corruption and Conflict of Interest

Corruption has often been associated with conflicts of interests, in the sense that they have been considered ever more frequently as being strongly and deeply related, in literature,[206] legislation[207] and institutional documents.[208]

---

[202] Mark Robinson (ed), *Corruption and development* 110.
[203] Susan Rose-Ackerman, *Corruption and Government: Causes, Consequences and Reform* 53.
[204] Robert Baldwin, Martin Cave and Martin Lodge, *Understanding Regulation* 232.
[205] Jacob Van Klaveren, 'The Concept of Corruption', in Arnold J Heidenheimer, Michael Johnston and Victor T Levine (eds), *Political Corruption. A Handbook* 25.
[206] On this point see, Jean-Bernard Auby, Emmanuel Breen and Thomas Perroud (eds), *Corruption and Conflicts of interest. A comparative Law Approach.*
[207] As in the case of the Georgian Law no 982/1997 on 'Conflict of Interest and Corruption in Public Service'.
[208] See OECD, *Managing Conflict of Interest in the Public Sector. A toolkit* (OECD, 2005) esp 19 et seq.

On the other hand, there are significant differences between the notion of corruption and that of conflicts of interest and it is important to establish clear boundaries between them.

1.6.1. Corruption as 'Actuality', Conflicts of Interest as 'Possibility'

Corruption is a fact at the end of a (more or less extended) process in which a public agent plays an active or passive (in any case, indispensible) role.

Conflicts of interest are independent from (and antecedent to) any possible fact or even process. Rather, a fact could in theory never occur, because a conflict of interest consists in the mere condition of an agent (public or private).[209] Conflicts of interest arise when people are in a position of dilemma 'between self-interest and their legal duty to other persons',[210] for instance when government employees have the opportunity to participate in official matters in which they have also a financial interest.

Conflicts of interest have been regulated by imposing ex-ante duties of disclosure or abstention, while for corruption both detection and criminal, ex-post punishment has been considered indispensible.

As a consequence of the emerging administrative anticorruption policies at different level of government, corruption and conflicts of interest have today become much closer than in the past: alongside traditional ex-post criminal regulation, in fact, anticorruption is currently moving ex ante. From a preventive perspective, corruption is considered a risk that a fact will occur and that it should be avoided, as far as possible.

Differences remain because regulation of conflicts of interest looks at certain sensitive charges and offices, while administrative anticorruption looks at the probability that certain facts occur. Despite their peculiarities, including (or at least, taking into consideration) conflicts of interest in a discourse on corruption prevention could be very useful, for a series of reasons.

In both corruption and in conflicts of interest, deviation from a *standard* of administrative activities and established procedures indicates procedures themselves as being at the centre; in both regulation of corruption and conflicts of interest the focus is on the problematic relationship between ethics (on one side) and law (on the other side); in both regulation of corruption and conflicts of interest the goal is how to steer human behaviour effectively.

---

[209] See Thomas L Carson, 'Conflicts of Interest' (1994) 13(5) *Journal of Business Ethics* 387, 396.
[210] Alison Grey Anderson, 'Conflicts of interest: efficiency, fairness and corporate structure' (1977–78) 25 *UCLA Law Review* 738. On this topic see also Jonathan R Macey and Geoffrey Parsons Miller, 'An economic analysis of conflicts of interest regulation' (1997) 82(4) *Iowa Law Review* 965, and Andrew Stark, *Conflict of Interest in American Public Life* (Harvard University Press, 2000). See, in general, Sabino Cassese, 'I conflitti di interesse e i modi per regolarli' (2005) 2 *Bancaria* 36.

In particular, the regulation of conflicts of interest tends to eliminate (or at least to reduce) any suspicion of impartiality[211] which is considered a menace for the clarity and fairness of public decisions[212] and for trust in institutions. For this reason, it constitutes a real challenge for administrative law.[213]

1.6.2. Criticisms and Paradoxes in Overregulating Conflicts of Interest

One of the most frequent way to regulate conflicts of interest is the increasing recourse to ethical codes, codes of conduct and other kind of ethical soft regulation adopted by institutions and companies in order to strengthen the moral engagement of their public/private agents. Following this path, conflicts of interest regulation has become pervasive.[214]

Upon closer inspection, conflicts of interest are an unavoidable human condition. People have many conflicts regarding competing interests:[215] each person, in fact, every day plays multiple roles, for instance, being a public officer but at the same time being a friend of a businessman; a citizen with political preferences and opinions but at the same time a consumer who would like to save money; a teacher in a school while also a parent; and so on. This makes conflicts of interest a markedly common situation in daily life.[216]

Moreover, the question of conflicts of interest has become nowadays more complex due to the exponential growth of specialised transactions which at the same time increases the possibility of 'competition for resources by illegitimate means'[217] by decreasing the likelihood of detection.

The same notion of conflict of interest tends to widen by becoming a broad umbrella[218] for a 'family' of related legal issues[219] and by also involving non-tangible interests.[220] It seems to be a tendency to make the conflict of interest a sort of paradigm.

---

[211] Jean-Bernard Auby, 'Conflits d'intérêts et droit administratif' (2010) 12 *Droit Administratif* 14.
[212] Ibid: 'la clarté de la décision publique'.
[213] Ibid: 'vrai défi pour le droit administratif'.
[214] Thomas L Carson, 'Conflicts of Interest' 393.
[215] On this point, see Robert B Reich, *Supercapitalism. The transformation of Business, Democracy and Everyday Life* (Alfred A Knopf, 2007), in the chapter dedicated to 'The two minds': 'the awkward truth is that most of us are of two minds: as consumers and investors we want the great deals. As citizens we don't like many of the consequences that flow from them'.
[216] See Joel S Demski, 'Corporate Conflicts of Interest' (2003) 17(2) *Journal of Economic Perspectives* 51, 69: 'multiple players'. See also Susan Rose-Ackerman, 'Corruption and conflicts of interest', in Jean-Bernard Auby, Emmanuel Breen and Thomas Perroud (eds), *Corruption and Conflicts of interest. A comparative Law Approach* 3. See, finally, Thomas L Carson, 'Conflicts of Interest' 391.
[217] Alison Grey Anderson, 'Conflicts of interest: efficiency, fairness and corporate structure' 742.
[218] Susan Rose-Ackerman, 'Corruption and conflicts of interest' 6. On this point, see also Thomas L Carson, 'Conflicts of Interest' 395.
[219] Sabino Cassese, 'I conflitti di interesse e i modi per regolarli' 36.
[220] See Thomas L Carson, 'Conflicts of Interest' 395.

Unfortunately, this faces a limited capacity regulation in matter of conflict of interest to effectively impact in practice[221] with the consequence that the crucial question is not 'how to regulate more effectively conflicts of interest' but 'if regulation is the best way to manage them'.

In this regard, there are a couple of relevant remarks.

Firstly, both conflicts of interest and anticorruption present regulatory criticisms because 'law operates more comfortably in retrospect, when a risk has been realised, when it can react to the certitudes of things past rather than seek to anticipate what might happen in future'.[222] If the problem is operating ex ante via rules (both in preventing corruption and in regulating conflicts of interest), the tendency towards an obsessive regulation of conflicts of interest, instead of being the solution could in the long run exacerbate the problem. Moreover, regulators do not always have clear ideas on the public interest which should be pursued,[223] while saying 'ought not' would imply a clear communication about what one 'should do otherwise'.[224]

Secondly, when talking about conflicts of interest we move at the boundary between ethics and law: albeit the moral status[225] of the question, regulators at every level of government have made recourse ever more frequently to legal mechanisms or legal sanctions.[226] Without prejudice for the most relevant disciplines (for instance, senior government positions), the obsessive regulation of minor conflicts of interest in administration[227] could lead to *the paradox of regulation ethics*. According to this paradox, overregulation will always be escapable by opportunists and people oriented towards voluntary circumvention or infringement; however, people who are motivated to behave honestly and with integrity, in the presence of prescriptive codes of conduct, are no longer free to choose an ethical behaviour which is (by its very nature) free. In other words, if I *must* do (to observe a legal obligation) what I *would do freely* (by my own willingness, to respond to my ethical values) my moral commitment to behaving will decrease and be impeded by the presence of rules. Behaviour, when regulated, stops being free (and moral) to become coerced (and legal).

---

[221] Ibid.
[222] Keith Hawkins, *Law as last resort. Prosecution Decision-Making in a Regulatory Agency* 438.
[223] Susan Rose-Ackerman, *Corruption and conflicts of interest* 7.
[224] Thomas L Carson, 'Conflicts of Interest' 396.
[225] Ibid, 395.
[226] See Susan Rose-Ackerman, *Corruption and conflicts of interest* 4.
[227] The California Political Reform Act (Government Code s 81000 et seq) requires state and local government agencies to adopt and promulgate conflict of interest codes. On this basis, the Fair Political Practices Commission has adopted a regulation (2 Cal Code of Regulations s 18730) that contains the terms of a standard conflict of interest code: among other agencies, the California Department of Education proposed in 2020 a Conflict of Interest Code. The State Ethic Commission of Massachusetts published *Public School Teacher FAQs on the Conflict of Interest Law. How the conflict of interest law generally applies to public school teachers*, www.mass.gov/service-details/public-school-teacher-faqs-on-the-conflict-of-interest-law.

Alongside these remarks, conflicts of interest regulation should consider also its own psychological impact,[228] in order to provide adequate incentives for 'good managerial performance',[229] according to the enforcement agency's mandate and performance indicators, consistently with its 'primary goal'.[230] But instead, overly pervasive regulation in this matter has been considered a disincentive for honest and competent persons to accept public offices.[231]

In summary, regulation of conflicts of interest tends to obsessively avoid risks, in a way very similar to anticorruption regulation; unfortunately, in so doing it reduces also the space for trust between people and institutions. There are good reasons to suspect that it would be better to accept and manage part of these risks by limiting regulation of conflicts of interest to indispensable cases, in so doing preserving the possibility for moral behaviour and trust, by saving huge administrative resources committed to conflicts of interest administration. In fact, perfect neutrality in performing public charges is not only impossible, but probably also undesirable.[232]

1.7. Corruption and Corruptibility

When corruption occurs it is an instance when 'you can't unscramble scrambled eggs' and there is little to do, apart from detecting and sanctioning. Hopefully, regulators may exploit such a situation at least by understanding the way in which corrupt infringements have been carried out and by learning lessons for the future from what happened. Despite its criminal character, in fact, the stock of corruption – corruption which has already occurred – presents a great interest from a regulatory point of view, because it constitutes a valuable and available knowledge, indispensible for improving regulatory capability and effective prevention.

1.7.1. Corruption as 'Actuality', Corruptibility as 'Probability'

However, as we have already seen, corruption is not only an instance (to be managed from a criminal point of view) but also a risk that an instance might

---

[228] Jean-Bernard Auby, *Conflits d'intérêts et droit administratif*: 'le probleme du conflit d'intérêt est en vérité plus une question de psychologie qu'une question d'éthique'.
[229] Alison Grey Anderson, 'Conflicts of interest: efficiency, fairness and corporate structure' 795.
[230] Florentin Blanc and Giuseppa Ottimofiore, 'The interplay of mandates and accountability in enforcement within the EU', in Miroslava Scholten and Michiel Luchtman (eds), *Law Enforcement by EU Authorities* (Edward Elgar Publishing, 2017) 285.
[231] Susan Rose-Ackerman, *Corruption and Government: Causes, Consequences and Reform* 68 and Susan Rose-Ackerman, 'Corruption and conflicts of interest' 5 and 7. See also Richard E Messick, 'Policy consideration when drafting conflict of interest legislation', in Jean-Bernard Auby, Emmanuel Breen and Thomas Perroud (eds), *Corruption and Conflicts of interest. A Comparative Law Approach* 123.
[232] Susan Rose-Ackerman, 'Corruption and conflicts of interest' 7.

occur in which regard, before the damage is done, there would be much to do from a regulatory and administrative point of view. Corruptibility is corruption which has not already occurred, for which there is a measurable risk that it could occur; corruption that effective regulation and administration may still in some way prevent. Upon closer inspection, there are two kinds of corruption and two related types of corruptibility.

Corruption can refer to persons whose behaviour[233] is reprehensible, corresponding to *corruptibility in a subjective sense* ('the quality of being corruptible'[234]) which focuses on individuals, mainly from an ethical or criminal point of view. As we will see later, subjective corruption (and subjective corruptibility) can also be of great interest from a regulatory perspective, because its understanding may represent relevant evidence to be introduced into the regulatory process as a proxy of corruption.

Corruption can also refer to 'objective factors' such as the institutional system, its organisation and its rules[235] and corresponds to *corruptibility in an objective sense*, which looks at aggregate behaviours, mainly from a regulatory and administrative point of view, by expressing the idea that corruption is more likely to occur in certain situations, in the presence of a given regulatory framework, during specific administrative procedures or when people come into contact with certain types of public administrations.

Both subjective and objective corruption should be taken into account when fighting corruption, because they both help to explain reasons why a certain incident has occurred. Both subjective and objective corruptibility are relevant for an integrated anticorruption policy because they both prepare the ground for future administrative corruption.

1.7.2. Objective Corruption and Corruptibility: Type AP (Administrative Powers) and Type C (Controls)

A further sub-distinction could help in developing the reasoning and to focus on specific administrative law issues relevant in a discourse about corruption, such as administrative organisation, administrative procedures and controls. It concerns *objective corruptibility* which does not always present the same structure: it is possible to distinguish OC type Administrative Powers and OC type Controls.

OC type AP was born together with administrative powers, exactly at the moment when administrative competences are established. To some extent, OC type AP could be considered the other side of the coin of administration.

---

[233] See Marco D'Alberti, *Combattere la corruzione. Analisi e proposte* (Rubbettino, 2016) 12.
[234] Webster's Dictionary, 1913.
[235] Marco D'Alberti, *Combattere la corruzione. Analisi e proposte* 12 where he mentions Jeremy Bentham speaking of corruption as 'inherent in the system of governance', distinguishing it from personal corruption.

When a client (citizen or firm) needs permits, asks for subsidies or other administrative performance (acts or services) which are necessary to operate in the market, which constitute incentives or which are simply required to live (to travel, to sell an apartment, to be treated in a public hospital, to be enrolled in oversupplied schools, to drive, to do renovation works in their own apartment, and so on), a public agent becomes the cornerstone of a potential illicit exchange. In fact, the power to issue licences, permits, passports, visas or any other kind of discretionary administrative permission makes it possible for government officials to take bribes from private agents.[236]

Starting from the idea that public powers regulate private activities and that they can be evaluated from economic (very often even monetary) point of view, some scholars have argued that in order to reduce corruption permanently, the government's role in the economy should be drastically cut back.[237] However, the mere act of cutting does not ensure efficient cutting. In fact, regulators should take into account that ad hoc evaluations are needed and that certain discretionary powers are indispensible[238] and should be well calibrated.

For this reason, attention is required when establishing regulation which presents more risk than others,[239] especially by creating or reinforcing monopolies and authorising powers (independently from their discretion), allowing bureaucratic agents to manage incentives and disincentives for other officials, citizens or enterprises[240] and providing public services.

It should be clear that corrupt infringements between the agent and the client (citizens or firms) may regard more than one aspect of administrative performance (administrative acts or public services), ie the *an* (if), the *quando* (when) and the *quomodo* (how, in the sense of to what extent).

This makes clear that corruption also means buying not only illegitimate results but also legitimate results, simply in order to attain them or to attain them fully and sooner: under the broad umbrella of corruption there are often disappointed expectations regarding good administration.

Let us consider the case of an administrative act, such as a building permit. The citizen's interest is not only to have the permit (if) but also to have it in a reasonable time (when) and to have a permit covering the whole elements of the original request and possibly without too much effort or cost (how and with what extent).

Let us consider an administrative service, such as major surgery in a public hospital. The citizen's interest is not only to be operated on in a good hospital

---

[236] Andrei Shleifer and Robert W Vishny, 'Corruption' (1993) 108(3) *Quarterly Journal of Economics* 492 : 'insofar as government officials have discretion over the provision of these goods (licenses, permits, passports and visas), they can collect bribes from private agents'.

[237] Gary S Becker, 'Want to Squelch Corruption? Try Passing Out Raises' 26: 'the only way to reduce corruption permanently is to drastically cut back government's role in the economy'.

[238] Kenneth Culp Davis, *Discretionary Justice. A Preliminary Inquiry* (Greenwood Press, 1980) 217: 'to eliminate unnecessary discretionary power in government, not to eliminate all discretionary power'.

[239] Robert Baldwin, Martin Cave and Martin Lodge, *Understanding Regulation. Theory, Strategy and Practice* 236, in particular 'predicting compliance'.

[240] Susan Rose Ackerman, *Corruption and Government: Causes, Consequences and Reform* 39.

(if), but also to be operated as soon as possible with respect to real but also to perceived urgency (when) and possibly by the most brilliant surgeon in the hospital (how and with what extent).

All these elements (if, when and how) have relevance for citizens and may be translated into money or other valuables becoming the price of a permit (for which there would be no right), maybe in a shorter time, via limited effort or with full authorisation to do what I would like do; or the price of having the operation done in a good hospital, quickly and by the best surgeon. Let us imagine how true and complex this analysis can be for firms in countless cases of licensing, subsidies, certifications, registers, authorisations regarding factories, and so on.

OC type C is generated together with controls, any possible kinds of control which follow directly from rules consisting of commands, prohibitions and permissions,[241] or which follow indirectly as control of possible infringements and transgressions connected to objective corruption type AP, for instance a control regarding a licence already issued.

Controls may consist in various kinds of audits, checks and inspections over private activities, and controls over administrative activities. What happens when an inspection or another kind of control comes along?

It could be possible that clients (citizens or firms) have committed no substantive infringements at all: no fiscal evasion, no frauds (agriculture, food, etc), no competition infringements, no false declarations (to achieve, for example, social benefits), no money laundering, and so on. Nonetheless, law enforcement officials and inspectors when controlling could abuse their powers, seeking to obtain an illicit extra income, in the presence of minor, formal or even imaginary infringements.

It could also be possible for clients (citizens or firms) to have committed some infringements, or even significant fiscal evasion. They have an interest in holding on to the extra income which comes from illicit activities (fiscal evasion), which is jeopardised by the inspection. The concrete contact between the agent and the client during inspections creates the opportunity for corrupt arrangements, independently of who takes the initiative.

These arrangements can present themselves as extortion or strict corruption and normally can be quantified in proportion to the illicit extra income.[242]

The relevance to approaching corruption also as corruptibility comes from the evidence that the transactions between agents and clients are at the very end of the process. When corruption occurs it is too late for prevention; only repression

---

[241] On the relationship between commands, prohibitions and permissions see Jeremy Bentham, *Collected Works*, Vol 2, *Principles of Legislation* (ed Herberth Lionel Adolphus Hart) (Athlone Press, 1945) esp 111.
[242] See Jessica Schultz and Tina Søreide, 'Corruption in emergency procurement' (2008) 32(4) *Disasters* 516, 521: 'bribes are often calculated as percentages of the total contract amount. The bigger the potential contract, the more important it is for a firm to acquire it, and the more willing they might be to take risks in the form of corruption'. See also Sadika Hameed, *The Costs of Corruption* (CSIS, 2014) 34–35.

44 Rules, Corruption and Controls: Setting the Scene

Table 1.2 Objective Corruption/Corruptibility

	Objective corruption/corruptibility	
Types	Role of Public Agents	Illicit agreements (actual/probable)
OC/C type AP Administrative powers	A public agent has *power over provision of goods* (licences, permits, authorisations, subsidies, and so on)	If
		When
		How
OC/C type C Controls	A public agent has the *power to control commands, prohibitions, permissions* as well as the *if, when, how* related to provision of goods (type AP)	Public agent *extortion* (even for minor transgressions)
		Client *corruption*

is needed, while a preventive approach necessitates the already mentioned 'very early detection'.[243] In order to understand corruption, it is important to take a comprehensive look at various transactions and related controls by attracting corruption-free infringements and non-criminal activities to the broad analysis of complex corruption processes: because corruption is a long time in preparation and must be stopped at its beginning.

1.8. Controls

1.8.1. Definition

Even though controls should be considered a crucial topic in a discourse on corruption, there are only a few titles in the literature which address the relationship between corruption and controls[244] focusing on the way in which controls should be regulated, planned, implemented and communicated in order to maximise compliance, and (in this way) reduce opportunities for infringements and corruption.

Arguments in favour of the relevance of controls for corruption can be grouped into three main fields of research: studies on human behaviour, legal theory and economic theory.

---

[243] Tom Vander Beken, 'A Multidisciplinary Approach for detection and Investigation of Corruption' in Cyrille Fijnaut and Leo Huberts (eds), *Corruption, Integrity and Law Enforcement* 275.

[244] On this point see Frank Anechiarico and James B Jacobs, *The Pursuit of Absolute Integrity. How Corruption Control Makes Government Ineffective*; Theodore R Lyman, 'The logic of corruption control'; Adam Graycar and Aiden Sidebottom, 'Corruption and control: a corruption reduction approach'; Robert Klitgaard, *Controlling Corruption*. See, more recently, Florentin Blanc, *From Chasing Violations to Managing Risks* 125 et seq: 'Regulations, inspections and corruption'.

According to innumerable contributions on the topic, human behaviour is always fallible and corruptible. It is fallible because human knowledge[245] is limited, affected by several biases,[246] unable to retain all possible elements which can interact each other and incapable of taking into adequate consideration innovation and development of scientific knowledge. It is corruptible (ie fallible from an ethical point of view) because people are free and they can choose everyday good or evil, they can decide to comply or not to comply with rules. Controlling is necessary to the purpose of influencing behaviour.

According to legal theory, controls alongside with sanctions constitute the traditional tool-box of enforcement: they operate as drivers of the effectiveness of law and contribute to transposing rules (words) into facts. In real life, compliance with rules (such as commands and prohibitions) does not come automatically, rules say 'what we have to do', never 'what we will do'[247] and they can only seek to persuade people to behave in a certain way. This is the reason why legislators establish sanctions as incentives for behaviour and controls to detect possible infringements.

According to economic theory, enforcement aims to achieve compliance with rules, in other words with the prescribed (or proscribed) behaviour.[248] From this perspective, economic literature has considered individual decisions about compliance as being central to the reasoning,[249] starting from the traditional (and later developed, criticised, revised and integrated) idea that the result of an economic evaluation connects the cost of compliance, the size of the penalty but also the risk of incurring the penalty, which is strictly connected with controls.

1.8.2. The Notion of Control from an Anticorruption Perspective

Starting from these premises, which notion of control best fits the purpose of preventing illicit and administrative corrupt behaviour? The concept of control

---

[245] Friedrich Von Hayek, 'The use of knowledge in society' (1945) 35(4) *American Economic Review* 519. See also Friedrich Von Hayek, *The Counter-revolution of Science. Studies on the Abuse of Reason* (The Free Press, 1952).

[246] On this point see Christine Jolls, Cass R Sunstein, Richard Thaler, 'A Behavioural Approach to Law and Economics'. See also George A Akerlof, Robert J Shiller, *Animal Spirits: How Human Psychology Drives the Economy, and Why It Matters for Global Capitalism*; Christopher Hodges and Ruth Steinholtz, *Ethical Business Practice and Regulation. A Behavioural and Values-Based Approach to Compliance and Enforcement*. See, among others, Richard H Thaler and Cass R Sunstein, *Nudge: Improving Decisions about Health, Wealth, and Happiness*.

[247] Georges Vedel, 'Le hasard et la nécessité' (1989) 50 *Pouvoirs* 27: 'si le droit dit "ce qu'il faut faire" il ne peut pas dire "ce qu'on en fera"'.

[248] George J Stigler, 'The Optimum enforcement of Law' 56: 'the goal of enforcement … is to achieve that degree of compliance with the rule of prescribed (or proscribed) behaviour that the society believes it can afford'.

[249] See Gary S Becker, 'Crime and Punishment: An Economic Approach' 169. For further aspects see Anthony Ogus, 'Corruption and regulatory structures' 329; see also Johann Graf Lambsdorff, 'Corruption and rent-seeking'. See finally Keith Hawkins, John M Thomas (eds), *Enforcing Regulation*.

(namely, the power of control conferred on various kinds of administrative bodies for a great variety of reasons, in all kinds of legal systems) is not completely uniform across different jurisdictions.[250] In some legal systems, control has been featured as a separate administrative function, operating almost in parallel with the regulation whose compliance should have been checked: for instance, controls of public procurements in Italy[251] are pervasive, very expensive but not always capable of detecting infringements.[252] Elsewhere controlling has been more strictly considered as regulatory enforcement,[253] a tool to make regulation effective. In this regard, the UK's Hampton Report[254] has strongly influenced reports and documents of international organisations in matter of inspections (such as the World Bank or the OECD[255]) right towards the instrumentality of controls with respect to public policies and regulation.[256]

The traditional divergence in the 'culture of control'[257] has today been mitigated due to EU regulations and to international treaties which over time have provided a common normative basis for national regulation and systems of control in many regulated sectors, such as food safety, competition law, anti-fraud, anti-money laundering, public procurements, environmental protection and so on. Even though this has contributed to a convergence towards a single notion of controls as a means of regulatory enforcement, a cross-border and functional definition can currently only be minimal: at this stage of the reasoning controlling would mean 'looking at something or someone in order to ensure that (public or private) activities conform to established standards and laid-down procedures'.[258]

---

[250] See Massimo Severo Giannini, 'Controllo: nozione e problemi' (1974) in *Rivista trimestrale di diritto pubblico* 1263, where he mentioned an 'English' concept of control alongside a 'French and Italian' one.

[251] See European Commission, *Annex Italy to the EU Anticorruption Report*, COM(2014)38 final, 3 February 2014, 12: 'The Court of Audit concluded on several occasions that the public procurement process is proper, procedures are respected, and winning bids indeed seem to be the most advantageous, but in contrast, the quality of deliverables is intentionally compromised in the execution phase. While not necessarily indicating corrupt practices, such irregularities, and the Eurobarometer indicators above, illustrate the vulnerabilities of the current control mechanisms, notably as regards the implementation phase of public contracts'.

[252] See Florentin Blanc, *Inspection Reforms: Why, How and with what Results* 41. See also OECD, *Regulatory Enforcement and Inspections* (OECD, 2014) 11.

[253] On this point, see Eugene Bardach and Robert A Kagan, *Going by the Book: The Problem of Regulatory Unreasonableness* 123.

[254] HM Treasury, Hampton Report, *Reducing administrative burdens: effective inspection and enforcement* 5.

[255] See, on this point, OECD, *Regulatory enforcement and inspections* (2014) and OECD, *Regulatory enforcement and inspections toolkit* (2018).

[256] HM Treasury, Hampton Report, *Reducing administrative burdens: effective inspection and enforcement* 28: 'Risk assessment needs to be comprehensive, and inform all aspects of the regulatory lifecycle from the selection and development of appropriate regulatory and policy instruments through to the regulators work including data collection, inspection and prosecution'.

[257] David Garland, *The Culture of Control: Crime and Social Order in Contemporary Society* (The University of Chicago Press, 2001).

[258] Maria De Benedetto, 'Corruption and controls' (2015) 4 *European Journal of Law Reform* 47.

However, very often when establishing controls, legislators also provide consequences which are crucial for their effectiveness (as we will see later) but which are not strictly part of their definition. In fact, controlling refers to achieving knowledge in view of adopting decisions, such as granting a licence, imposing a fine, making a tax assessment, suspending the activity of a firm, ordering a seizure, authorising construction works and so on.

Indeed, the comprehensive framework which seems to be more useful for the purposes of our reasoning about controls, is once again the Principal-Agent-(Client) model:[259] it allows an overview of the various fields in which different controls operate, by considering all kinds of infringements as part of the broad analysis of corruption processes and, conversely, as elements of preventive measures.

As already mentioned, corrupt transactions in a strict sense are performed downstream, in the Agent-Client relationship, at the very end of any institutional process, where only criminal ex-post controls focusing on repression are possible. How to ensure the desirable and already mentioned 'very early detection'[260] of corruption? Both relationships between Principal and Agent and those between Principal and Client are upstream of corruption and are subject respectively to controls of administrative activities and to controls of private activities with the purpose of making public officers, citizens and businesses compliant with rules, as far as possible. In this sense, they are incredibly relevant even from an anticorruption perspective because they give elements with which to identify corruptibility (see section 1.7), and for this reason they should be considered part of the anticorruption tool-kit.

Controls of administrative activities can be external or internal and include budgetary controls, controls performed by national courts of audit, internal inspections, anticorruption controls, whenever the object of controls is an administrative activity.

Controls of private activities include, among other things, desk-based or field-based controls (such as inspections[261]), whenever the object of controls is a regulated (economic or non-economic) private activity.

1.8.3. Criticism, Paradoxes and Dilemmas of Controlling

A number of criticisms seems to affect controls as a way to combat infringements and as tools for anticorruption, especially if looking at their concrete effectiveness.

---

[259] Edward C Banfield, 'Corruption as a Feature of Government Organization' 587; Susan Rose-Ackerman, *Corruption. A Study in Political Economy*; Robert Klitgaard, *Controlling Corruption*; Donatella Della Porta and Alberto Vannucci, *The hidden order of corruption. An institutional approach*. See, finally, Staffan Andersson and Torbjörn Bergman, 'Controlling Corruption in the Public Sector' 45.

[260] Tom Vander Beken, 'A Multidisciplinary Approach for detection and Investigation of Corruption' 275.

[261] OECD, *Regulatory Enforcement and Inspections* 11 defines inspections as 'any type of visit or check conducted by authorised officials on products or business premises, activities, documents, etc.'

Figure 1.4 Principal-Agent-Client Model: Controls

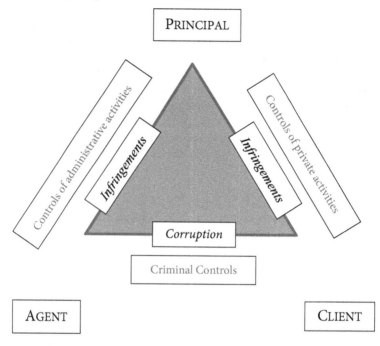

Adopting the *behavioural perspective*, if it is true that controls influence behaviour, people under observation do not always behave in a more cooperative way.[262] Literature on the topic has, in fact, observed that excessively intrusive controls may produce resistance and evasion[263] and that compliance also depends on the way in which controls are carried out,[264] and on perceived procedural justice.[265]

From the *legal theory perspective*, establishing controls does not once and forever solve the problem of infringements nor the risks that controls might produce side-effects (even corruption, as we have already seen in section 1.7.2). Their effectiveness is controversial and traditional controls have long been considered

---

[262] On this point, see Max Ernest-Jones, Daniel Nettle and Melissa Bateson, 'Effects of eye images on everyday cooperative behaviour: a field experiment' (2011) 32 *Evolution and Human Behaviour* 172, 173: 'there have been many demonstrations that the physical presence of other people in the room, or other non-verbal cues of proximity or visibility, produces more cooperative behaviour'.

[263] On this point see Erich Hoelzl, 'Modelling Taxpayers Behaviour as a Function of Interaction between Tax Authorities and Taxpayers' 1 onwards and Florentin Blanc and Giuliana Cola, 'The Impact of Inspections. Measuring Ourcomes from Occupational Safety and Health Inspections', in Graham Russell and Christopher Hodges (eds), *Regulatory Delivery* (Hart/Beck, 2019).

[264] See HM Treasury, Hampton Report, *Reducing administrative burdens: effective inspection and enforcement*.

[265] See John Braithwaite, *Improving Compliance: Strategies and Practical Applications in OECD Countries* 9. See also Tom R Tyler, 'Procedural Justice, Legitimacy, and the Effective Rule of Law' 283.

inadequate – 'outdated and counterproductive',[266] as in the case of anticorruption controls. A great number of public and private bodies are involved in performing different kinds of controls, at every level of government: courts of auditors, antifraud offices, several bodies of inspectors, police officers, independent authorities and so on. However, even in presence of so many controls and controllers, the efforts of controls too often fail.

From the *economic theory perspective*, controls raise the problem of information costs. They consist in valuable activities of collecting information, which are indispensable to the adoption of many other administrative decisions, to the attainment of administrative objectives and to adequate responses to public interests.[267] Moreover, albeit administrative knowledge via controls is a great cost, it must be paid in order to legitimate administrative decisions.[268]

Whatever perspective one adopts, controls are and remain a conundrum which often produces paradoxes and creates dilemmas. Although pervasive, controls can never eradicate the possibility of transgression, which is 'inscribed into the law as hidden possibility'.[269] Furthermore, the need for controls does not eliminate paradoxes such as 'who guards the guardians?' (*quis custodiet ipsos custodes?*[270]). Finally, there is no solution to the question of suboptimality in controlling, considering that a further level of control would be always necessary and this produces a regression without end.[271]

1.9. Controlling Administrative Activities

Comparative administration is a challenging and very complex field of research.[272] The same could be affirmed of the specific issue of 'controls of administrative activities'. In any case, although differently structured, in all jurisdictions public bodies tend to be in charge of tasks of revising and controlling their own administrative activities or administrative activities carried out by other administrative bodies.

---

[266] Frank Anechiarico and James B Jacobs, *The Pursuit of Absolute Integrity. How Corruption Control Makes Government Ineffective* 193.
[267] See, in general, on this topic, Georges J Stigler, 'The Economics of Information' (1961) 69(3) *Journal of Political Economy* 213.
[268] See Niklas Luhmann, *Legitimation durch Verfahren* (Suhrkamp, 1969; Italian edn Giuffré, 1995).
[269] Monique Nuijten and Gehrard Anders (eds), *Corruption and the Secret of law. A Legal Anthropological Perspective* 12.
[270] On this point see Juvenal, VI *Satyr*, 347–48 and Plato, *The Republic*, Book II, 421. See also, Martin M Shapiro, *Who guards the guardians? Judicial control of Administration* (The University of Georgia Press, 1988).
[271] Niklas Luhmann, *Legitimation durch Verfahren*, Italian translation 217.
[272] B Guy Peters, 'The Necessity and Difficulty of Comparison in Public Administration' (2014) 12 *Asian Journal of Public Administration* 3; see also Susan Rose-Ackerman, Peter L Lindseth and Blake Emerson (eds), *Comparative Administrative Law* and Jonathan Bendor, 'A Theoretical Problem in Comparative Administration' (1976) 36(6) *Public Administration Review* 626. See finally Francesco Merloni,

50 *Rules, Corruption and Controls: Setting the Scene*

Thus, in general it is possible to say that controls of administrative activities are established everywhere because all legal systems need to ensure legitimate and/or effective administration,[273] working both from the inside (internal controls) and from the outside of government agencies (external controls).

In past academic debates, external (political and institutional) controls have been considered as a competing model to that of internal ones;[274] however, currently this dichotomous approach has been largely overcome and controls of administrative activities are ever more frequently considered as being an integrated system which aims to bring the administrative performance (both from the perspective of its legitimacy and from that of its efficiency/effectiveness) 'under control'.[275]

1.9.1. External Controls

External controls of administrative actions play an important role in parliamentary democracies which are based on the separation of powers. Public administrations, in fact, operate as legitimate authorities within executive power, and are 'controlled' from the outside primarily by the legislative and judiciary branches, with the purpose of making it accountable.[276] *Parliamentary controls*[277] and *judicial review*[278] represent the political and legal external controls over

---

Corruption and Public Administration. The Italian Case in a Comparative Perspective (Routledge, 2018) 142.

[273] On this point see Florentin Blanc and Giuseppa Ottimofiore, 'The interplay of mandates and accountability in enforcement within the EU' 272 onwards.

[274] During the 1930s Carl Friedrich and Herman Finer (the Friedrich-Finer 'classic' debate) discussed the question of professionalism *vs* democratic accountability in public decision-making, with consequences on the system of controls (internal *vs* external). See Herman Finer, 'Better Government Personnel' (1936) 51(4) *Political Science Quarterly* 569; Carl Friedrich, 'Public Policy and the Nature of Administrative Responsibility' (1940) *Public Policy*, 3; Herman Finer, 'Administrative Responsibility in Democratic Government' (1941) 1(4) *Public Administration Review* 335. On this point see also Terry L Cooper, *The Responsible Administrator: An Approach to Ethics for the Administrative Role* (Wiley, 2012), and Kenneth Kernaghan, 'Responsible public bureaucracy: a rationale and a framework for analysis' (1973) 16(4) *Canadian Public Administration* 572.

[275] Giandomenico Majone, *Regulating Europe* 40: 'when such a system works properly no one controls an independent agency, yet the agency is "under control"'.

[276] See, again, Florentin Blanc and Giuseppa Ottimofiore, 'The interplay of mandates and accountability in enforcement within the EU'; see also Herman Finer, 'Better Government Personnel' 580: 'Responsibility necessarily requires the existence of a relationship of obedience on the part of the person acting to an external controlling authority. It is in this externality of reference that the essential nature of responsibility consists, and it is obvious what significance this has for the public service in a democratic state'.

[277] B Guy Peters and Jon Pierre (eds), *Handbook of Public Administration* (Sage, 2007) 288.

[278] Leonard Dupee White, *The Civil Service in the Modern State* (The University of Chicago Press, 1930): 'At one extreme, the vigour of judicial control may paralyse effective administration, at the other the result may be an offensive bureaucratic tyranny.'

administrative activities,[279] in the sense that they operate from outside the administrative sphere.[280] However, the idea of external control also expresses a stricter meaning[281] where it can also refer to controls performed by dedicated agencies, sometimes independent but – when characterised by administrative nature – in any case controls that are different and not dependent on those whom they control.

These external controls combine managerial, financial as well as legal standards. Supreme audit institutions (SAIs) exist in nearly all legal systems, even though they can have different structures because they 'vary reflecting different legal, financial and political traditions'.[282] In fact, SAIs control administrations[283] and adopt different possible models, which may be inspired by the French Court des Comptes (independent of the executive, sometimes provided with judicial powers) or by the UK Audit Office (never judicial, sometimes placed in the executive, sometimes in the legislative branch).[284] Controls operated by SAIs aim

---

[279] Jerry L Mashaw, 'Judicial review of administrative action: reflections on balancing political, managerial and legal accountability' (2005) 1 *Revista Direito GV* 154: 'Judicial review of administrative action simultaneously supports other accountability mechanisms that bolster democratic governance and undermines them. The institution of judicial review of administrative action is rife with paradox. It supports democratic governance by making officials accountable to unelected judges. It protects individual rights while simultaneously ensuring state control. It legitimizes expert administrative judgment by subjecting that judgment to review by bodies who often have limited knowledge of either the technical data upon which administrative action is premised or the concrete situations within which administration must function.'

[280] Susan Rose-Ackerman, 'Regulation and Public Law in Comparative Perspective' (2010) 60 *University of Toronto Law Journal* 534: 'Accountable administrative processes are costly and time consuming. Major rule makings in the United States can take years to complete, followed by court review. These practical difficulties, however, do not undermine the basic principle that administrative law needs to be concerned with effective democratic control of the administration.'

[281] Richard Allen, *Management Control in Modern Government Administration: Some Comparative Practices* (OECD, 1996), 12: 'Citing further examples of differences in definition and approach, the report of the EUROSAI Experts Meeting notes that, in France and Italy, "internal audit is seen to embrace aspects of internal control, such as public accountants and inspectors in France who perform key functions in the control of expenditure" while in countries such as Poland "internal audit is seen to embrace certain [state] regulatory and supervisory bodies; in addition to controls over public expenditure these bodies are responsible for controls over technical standards and safety issues"'; see also 93: 'In Germany, the internal audit is part of the external audit. Although the internal audit forms an integral part of the activities of the administrative agencies, the internal auditors are only subject to the professional and technical guidance of the FCA (the German supreme audit institution). They only report to the FCA and may not take any other professional orders. Therefore, the internal audit in Germany is called a "pre-audit", not in the sense of an a priori audit, but because they carry out their audits before the FCA.'

[282] OECD, *Good Practices in Supporting Supreme Audit Institutions* (OECD, 2011) 16. See also International Organisation of Supreme Audit Institutions-INTOSAI, *The Auditing Function of Supreme Audit Institutions: A Systematic Mapping of the Auditing Assignment of 31 Selected Supreme Audit Institutions Across the Regions of INTOSAI* (2010). See finally DFID, *Characteristics of Different External Audit Systems*, (2004).

[283] International Organisation of Supreme Audit Institutions-INTOSAI 'operates as an umbrella organisation for the external government audit community' (OECD, *Good Practices in Supporting Supreme Audit Institutions* 15). See also Elizabeth L Normanton, *The Accountability and Audit of Governments: A Comparative Study* (Manchester University Press, 1966).

[284] Ibid, 17: '*Westminster model*, also known as the Anglo-Saxon or Parliamentary model found in the United Kingdom and most Commonwealth countries including many in sub-Saharan Africa, a few European countries such as Ireland and Denmark, and Latin American countries such as Peru and

to combine legitimacy and regularity (in a financial audit, *audit financier*) with evaluation of the administrative performance (management audit) raising the very important question of 'what performance?'.[285] This is the reason why control by SAIs is increasingly considered crucial in combating corruption.[286]

Among these external controls, there are also controls performed by anticorruption bodies, even more frequently introduced in national legal systems as a consequence of anticorruption global policies[287] (as we will see later, chapter two, section 2.2). Specialised anticorruption agencies (ACAs) are in charge of curbing corruption via preventive measures according to established specific criteria: among them, independence, specialisation, adequate expertise and resources. These agencies have achieved an increasing influence over daily administrative activities,[288] even though 'there is no strong evidence that the existence of anticorruption bodies always helps to reduce corruption'[289] and despite the fact that they have encountered several difficulties[290] because 'preventive functions are so

---

Chile – often referred to as national audit offices; *Judicial or Napoleonic model*, found in the Latin countries in Europe, Turkey, Francophone countries in Africa and Asia, and several Latin American countries including Brazil and Colombia; – often referred to as courts of audit or courts of accounts. In Francophone Africa, this model may co-exist with general state inspectorates, some of whom may be nominated as the country's SAI. They are usually part of the executive but independent of specific ministries and departments; and *Board or Collegiate model*, found in some European countries including Germany and the Netherlands, Argentina, and Asian countries including Indonesia, Japan and the Republic of Korea'. See also World Bank, 'Features and Functions of Supreme Audit Institutions' (2001), in PREMnotes, October 2001, fn 59.

[285] Even controls of legality presents need principles and goals. On this point, see in general, Andrew Hopkins, 'Compliance with what? The Fundamental Regulatory Question' (1994) 34(4) *British Journal of Criminology* 431.

[286] See International Organisation of Supreme Audit Institutions-INTOSAI, *Lima Declaration of Guidelines on Auditing Precepts* (Ninth Congress of INTOSAI, Lima, Peru, 1977). See also Kenneth M Dye, Rick Stapenhurst, *Pillars of Integrity: Importance of Supreme Audit Institutions in Curbing Corruption* (World Bank Institute, 1998), Kenneth M Dye, *Corruption and Fraud Detection by Supreme Audit Institutions* (World Bank, 2008), Jorge Alejandro Ortiz Ramírez and José Adrián Cruz Pérez, 'Impact of Supreme Audit Institutions on the Phenomenon of Corruption; An International Empirical Analysis' (2016) 1(3) *Journal of Public Governance and Policy: Latin American Review* 34, and finally Ebrahim A Assakaf, Rose Shamsiah Samsudin, Zeleha Othman, 'Public Sector Auditing and Corruption: A Literature Review' (2018) 10(1) *Asian Journal of Finance & Accounting* 226.

[287] UN Convention against Corruption, adopted by the UN General Assembly Resolution 58/4 of 31 October 2003. See also OECD, *Specialised Anticorruption Institutions. Review of Models* (OECD, 2008) 5.

[288] Karen Hussmann, Hannes Hechler and Miguel Peñailillo, *Institutional arrangements for corruption prevention: Considerations for the implementation of the United Nations Convention against Corruption Article 6* (U4 Anticorruption Resource Centre, Issue 2009/4).

[289] OECD, *Specialised Anticorruption Institutions. Review of Models* 6. See also Claes Sandgren, 'Combating Corruption: The Misunderstood Role of Law' (2005) 39(3) *International Lawyer* 717, 729–30 and Kayla Crider and Jeffrey Milyo, 'Do State Ethics Commissions Reduce Political Corruption? An Exploratory Investigation' (2013) 3 *UC Irvine Law Review* 717.

[290] Luis De Sousa, 'Anticorruption Agencies: Between Empowerment and Irrelevance' (2010) 53 *Crime, Law and Social Change* 5: 'One distinctive feature of the anticorruption activity of the 1990s is the rise of new players, such as specialized anticorruption bodies. Anticorruption agencies (ACAs) are public bodies of a durable nature, with a specific mission to fight corruption and reducing the opportunity structures propitious for its occurrence in society through preventive and/or repressive measures. Independently of their format and powers, ACAs encounter various constraints to their mandate, which explains the meagre results obtained by some of them: difficulties (technical, statutory

numerous and diverse, covering all aspects of good governance, that they cannot be performed by a single institution'.[291]

1.9.2. Internal Controls

Internal controls as a research issue have been primarily developed in the field of business management,[292] even though there is historical evidence that forms of internal audit in government have been present since ancient times.[293] Internal accounting controls are intended to prevent fraud or unintentional errors, in order to check the accuracy and reliability of the accounting data and to promote operational efficiency.[294] They consist in 'internal audit (the management function which is intended to verify many of the aspects of the defined internal control system) and internal check (the procedures designed to safeguard assets against defalcations, etc.)'.[295]

Internal control, therefore, is potentially capable of bringing to light infringements and corruption, not only when firms are concerned (private-to-private corruption[296]) but also when there is corruption in a strict sense, involving administrative functions and public officers alongside private ones. For this reason, public internal controls (indicated by international organisations[297] and in EU documents with the acronym PIC[298]) have been systematically introduced by governments and by EU member states during the 1980s, in the general framework of the New Public Management Reforms:[299] their purposes are combining

---

or cultural) in unveiling corruption via complaints; difficulties in obtaining information about corruption and its opportunity structures from other state bodies/agencies; and difficulties in establishing a good working relationship with the political sphere.'

[291] OECD, *Specialised Anticorruption Institutions* 15.

[292] See Lawrence Robert Dicksee, *Auditing: A Practical Manual for Auditors* (Ronald Press, 1905) 54.

[293] Tom A Lee, 'The Historical Development of Internal Control from the Earliest Times to the End of the Seventeenth Century' (1971) 9(1) *Journal of Accounting Research* 150.

[294] Paul Grady, 'The Broader Concept of Internal Control' (1957) 103(5) *Journal of Accountancy* 36: 'Internal administrative control comprises the plan of organization and all of the co-ordinate methods and measures adopted within the business to promote operational efficiency and encourage adherence to prescribed managerial policies'.

[295] Tom A Lee, 'The Historical Development of Internal Control from the Earliest Times to the End of the Seventeenth Century' 151.

[296] Antonio Argandoña, 'Private-to-Private Corruption' (2003) 47(3) *Journal of Business Ethics* 253.

[297] See International Organisation of Supreme Audit Institutions-INTOSAI, *Guidelines for Internal Control Standards for the Public Sector* (2004), which has based its definition on the definition in the COSO Framework (Committee of Sponsoring Organisations of the Treadway Commission-COSO, *Internal Control – Integrated Framework*, 1992).

[298] European Commission, Directorate-General for Budget, *Compendium of the public internal control systems in the EU Member States* 2nd edn (2014) 2: 'This Compendium provides a structured overview of the various Public Internal Control (PIC) systems currently being applied by the public sector in each of the 28 EU Member States. These are systems primarily used to manage national funds, both revenues and expenditure rather than European funds'.

[299] Christopher Hood, 'A Public Management for All Seasons' (1991) 69(1) *Public Administration* 3.

better administrative performance with administrative accountability, as well as preventing non compliance of public officers (such as in the case of internal fraud) and incidents of corruption.[300]

However, the concept of internal control is differently nuanced across jurisdictions.[301] In any case, a comparison of internal controls systems (such as the PIC systems in the EU member states) contributes to the notion of internal control becoming ever more convergent with more effective and accountable public administration.[302]

1.9.3. Criticisms and Paradoxes in Controlling Administrative Activities

Despite the fact that controls of administrative activities present important specificities in different jurisdictions, some general remarks may be formulated.

First of all, controls of administrative activities indirectly exert a major influence over administration. In a certain sense they shape it, because controls sometimes consist in 'duplicating administration'. In the same way, as all kinds of oversight (regulatory, judicial, administrative), controls impact on what administration has done (or is going to do, when controls are preventive), in terms of legitimacy, regularity, opportunity, proportionality, and so on. These controls in turn establish the outline of administrative activities which will pass muster of future oversight or review:[303] in this sense controllers can be considered as co-administrators.

---

[300] OECD, *Internal Control and Risk Management for Public Integrity in the Middle East and North Africa* (OECD, 2017) 11: 'public internal control is increasingly recognised as an integral part of modern governance systems and an essential tool for preventing, detecting and responding to corruption'.

[301] European Commission, Directorate-General for Budget, *Compendium of the public internal control systems in the EU Member States* 7 and 9: 'PIC systems differ from country to country as they have to fit into the respective overall governance arrangements with each of the constitutional stakeholders – government, parliament and the supreme audit institution – as well as the accountability arrangements that exist between these stakeholders. Within the government, internal accountability arrangements are also a determining factor, as is the content of accountability of those responsible for carrying out public tasks. A distinction can be drawn here between legal accountability for compliance with rules and regulations and managerial accountability for the use of public resources to achieve goals. Budgeting and accounting arrangements also have to be taken into account.'

[302] Jerry Mashaw, 'Accountability and Institutional Design; Some Thoughts on the Grammar of Governance' in Michael W Dowdle (ed), *Public Accountability: Designs, Dilemmas and Experiences* (Cambridge University Press, 2006) 115. See also Mark Bovens, 'Public Accountability', in Ewan Ferlie, Laurence E Lynn and Christopher Pollitt (eds), *Oxford Handbook of Public Management* (Oxford University Press, 2005) 182. The term 'accountability' is used in other senses as well and is often difficult to translate appropriately.

[303] On this topic see Herbert A. Simon, *Administrative behaviour: a study of decision-making processes in administrative organization* (Macmillan Company, 1947). See also Hans Albert, *Treatise on critical reason* (Princeton University Press, 1985; 1st German edn 1968) 16 onwards. See finally Mathew D McCubbins, Roger G Noll, Barry R Weingast, 'Administrative procedures as instruments of political control' (1987) 3(2) *Journal of Law, Economics and Organization* 243.

Secondly, public officers are currently facing 'a mixed set of accountability regimes: … managerial accountability through processes of audit and systems design; and legal accountability through judicial review'.[304] There is probably an overload of regimes which should be analysed from the perspective of the administrative behaviour with the purpose of fine-tuning, in order to allow them to 'work together to produce accountable governance'.[305]

Thirdly, the systems of controls of administrative activities – each one according to their objectives – face the challenge of combining proportionality and effectiveness (in the light of administrative activities principles and goals), calibrating the right degree (sufficient to prevent and protect involved interests) without oppressing public officers. This is true for any kind of administrative control, but especially so in the case of anticorruption controls, which have in the last decade largely contributed to defensive decision-making and administration in some legal systems,[306] in this way confirming the idea that anticorruption controls might not produce less corruption, rather more bureaucracy.[307]

1.10. Controlling Private Activities

Public controls of private activities are directed towards a boundless and heterogeneous universe of addressees – sometime citizens, in other cases firms – with the goal of checking an enormous amount of prescriptions which establish obligations (commands or prohibitions) or which regulate private activities: let us consider fiscal rules, antitrust law, traffic regulations, public procurements, building regulations, smoking bans, regulated sectors in which licences and permits are required, and many other possible examples.

Compliance with rules is not automatic, and similarly, the effects of prevention or protection (which justifies rules) are not automatically achieved. This is the reason why controls are needed: decisions about compliance are intrinsically economic even though they do not always imply a rational evaluation, and are the result of strategies.[308] However, such decisions are based on cognitive biases,[309]

---

[304] Jerry L Mashaw, 'Judicial review of administrative action: reflections on balancing political, managerial and legal accountability' 157.
[305] Ibid.
[306] On 'defensive administration', see Florian Artinger, Sabrina Artinger and Gerd Gigerenzer, 'C. Y. A.: frequency and causes of defensive decisions in public administration' (2018) *Business Research* 10. With special regard to Italy, see Stefano Battini and Francesco Decarolis, 'L'amministrazione si difende' (2019) 1 *Rivista Trimestrale di Diritto Pubblico* 293.
[307] Frank Anechiarico, 'Law Enforcement or a Community-Oriented Strategy Toward Corruption Control', in Cyrille Fijnaut and Leo Huberts (ed), *Corruption, Integrity and Law Enforcement* 300. On this point see Florentin Blanc, 'Regulation, Regulatory Delivery, Trust and Distrust: Avoiding Vicious Circles', in Maria De Benedetto, Nicola Lupo, Nicoletta Rangone (eds), *The Crisis of Confidence in Legislation* (Nomos/Hart, 2020) 318–19.
[308] Gary S Becker, 'Crime and Punishment: An Economic Approach' 169.
[309] On this point, see Richard H Thaler and Cass R Sunstein, *Nudge: Improving Decisions about Health, Wealth, and Happiness.*

and (overall) they are unpredictable, especially in legal systems characterised by overregulation and creative compliance.

Controls over private activities have not frequently been studied as a single issue, while different typologies of controls have been, such as those concerned with taxation, antitrust, environmental protection, building regulations and so on. What has been more frequently studied is *inspection*, as the prototypical form of control. The reason for this lack of comprehensive research is probably due to the great quantity and variety of controls, covering the entire administrative area, which makes their study part of the study of individual sectors of regulation.[310]

Conceptually, there are three types of controls: *conformity controls*, concerning compliance with rules which establish obligations (commands or prohibitions) for citizens or firms; *controls related to administrative approvals*, whenever administrations have powers to confer something (such as subsidies or public procurement) and to issue permits or licences (which is already in itself a control); finally *controls by economic regulators*, when controls have to be framed in the context of some executive or independent authority's powers and, for this reason, should be considered as expressions of a wider and stable relationship between authority and firms.[311]

However, controls are no longer exclusively established at national, but also at European (eg by antitrust or anti-fraud regulations) and at global level (for instance, by anti-money laundering regulation). Moreover, controls are regulated not only by formal regulation (for instance, adopted by parliaments and governments) but by soft regulation, such as guidelines and manuals of inspection.[312] The 'verification function'[313] consists in controls or audits of private activities established to collect indispensible information[314] and (in this way) to make administrative

---

[310] On this point see Florentin Blanc, *From Chasing Violations to Managing Risks* 5–6; see also, Pierre Clèment, *Lettres, instructions et mémoires de Colbert* (Paris, 1869) t. VI, 29–30, quoted in Paolo Napoli, '"Police": la conceptualisation d'un modèle juridico-politique sous l'ancien régime' (II) (1995) 21 *Droits* 151: 'la difficulté en ces matières n'est pas de faire des règlements, mais de trouver des moyens pour le faire executer'.

[311] On this aspect, see Alfredo Moliterni, 'Controlli pubblici sui soggetti privati e prevenzione della corruzione' (2016) 1 *Diritto Pubblico* 204 et seq.

[312] In English-speaking countries recourse is frequently made to the *Inspection Guidelines* (or *Guides*) or to the *Inspection Handbook*: for instance, see the *School Inspection Handbook* (Handbook for inspecting schools in England under s 5 of the Education Act 2005, December 2017) or the US Food & Drug Administration *Inspection Guides* adopted in different fields (biotechnology, devices, drugs and so on).

[313] OECD, *Tax Administration 2019. Comparative Information on OECD and other Advanced and Emerging Economies* (OECD, 2019) 88: 'The verification function in tax administration has various names, but used here it encompasses those function that assess accuracy and completeness of taxpayer reported information. This function employs on average 30% of tax administration staff and verifies that tax obligations have been met, mainly still through the conducting desk or field based "tax audit".'

[314] OECD, *Tax administration 2013* (OECD, 2013) 212: 'Administrative controlling is the most important tool to reduce this information gap, both when controls are implemented in back office (*desk based*) and when are carried out on-site, via inspections (*field based*). No doubt that the sector in which the issue has been most developed and effective is the fiscal one'.

powers effective, capable of attaining administrative objectives, and adequately responding to the public interest.[315]

What do such greatly different controls have in common? They constitute a single issue because (all) controls affect the freedoms of individuals, and (all) enforcement agencies in charge of controls are required to follow established procedures in order to prevent any possible arbitrary use of their power, according to the constitutional protection of fundamental rights. Furthermore, (all) controls constitute a risky administrative activity in terms of probability of infringements, ie, illicit and corrupt transactions[316] (as we will see later in chapter four).

1.10.1. 'Desk-Based' Controls

Administrative knowledge of private activities can be the result, first of all, of a desk-based gathering of evidence carried out by public administrations.

Desk-based controls[317] take different forms. The simplest criterion to distinguish them is related to their character, meaning that resulting knowledge can be self-generated by public administrations or should be, in a certain way, out-sourced.

In the case of self-generated knowledge, there is increasing recourse to data and algorithms, especially the 'data matching' techniques,[318] which exploit the use of data banks in order to carry out controls by document matching programmes. These techniques can also be used to plan inspections. A special kind of control, increasingly relevant due to the 2020 Coronavirus pandemic, is remote surveillance, a smart tracking control of people via smart technologies to carry out preventive administration[319] generating relevant problems of data and fundamental protection of rights.

In the case of out-sourced knowledge, public administrations in charge of controls need to collect information[320] which is out of their reach. Public officers

---

[315] See, in general, on this topic, Georges J Stigler, 'The Economics of Information' 213.

[316] On this point see Maria De Benedetto, *Corruption and Controls* 479.

[317] On the relevance of back-office see Mervyn J King, *Back Office and Beyond: A Guide to Procedures, Settlements and Risk in Financial Markets* (Harriman House, 2003) 1.

[318] See Daniel J Steinbock, 'Data matching, data mining and due process' (2005) 40(1) *Georgia Law Review* 3–4: '"Data matching" – linking individuals with data about them – or "data mining" – identifying people who fit a designated computer-generated profile'.

[319] Jennifer Valentino-De Vries, 'Translating a Surveillance Tool into a Virus Tracker for Democracies', *The New York Times*, 19 March 2020: 'Health officials in Britain are building an app that would alert the people who have come in contact with someone known to have the coronavirus. The project aims to adapt China's tracking efforts for countries wary of government surveillance'.

[320] See Jean-Bernard Auby, 'Le pouvoirs d'inspections de l'Union européenne' (2006) *Revue Trimestrielle de Droit Européen* 132. See art 18, Council Regulation no 1/2003 on the implementation of the rules of competition, 'Request for information'.

may ask firms, citizens or third parties for any kind of data, information or documents. Their requests for information and documents are formally compulsory and must be observed within established deadlines; compliance with them is often ensured by establishing monetary fines or other penalties.

1.10.2. 'Field-Based' Controls

Field-based controls consist in investigating even via coercive means.[321] Inspections are potentially the most intrusive power[322] or the most evident aspect of public power.[323] They could affect fundamental rights and require specific guarantees to ensure that there will be no arbitrary exercise of their power, in this way 'preserving a reasonable balance between agency powers and target rights'.[324] Inspections (especially when unannounced) are a typical activity of 'fact-finding' administration.[325]

Even though inspection procedures have no common regulation in different jurisdictions,[326] in constitutional democracies they tend to refer to a common set of principles with regard to fundamental rights protection (such as the right to a fair trial, to liberty, to property, etc).[327]

From a strict procedural point of view, a decision (at least an internal decision) is normally required to conduct inspections.[328] Moreover, non-compliance during

---

[321] Ibid, 132–33. On this point, see arts 20–21, Council Regulation no 1/2003, 'Inspections'. See also Leonard E Martin, 'Investigatory Powers of Congress and Administrative Agencies' (1941) 26(4) *Washington University Law Review* 531.

[322] Mark Furse, *Competition Law of the EC and UK* 6th edn (Oxford University Press, 2008) 94.

[323] Jean-Bernard Auby, 'Le pouvoirs d'inspections de l'Union européenne' 133: 'façon plus marquée des attribution d'autorité'.

[324] John W. Bagby, 'Administrative Investigations: Preserving a Reasonable Balance between Agency Powers and Target Rights' (1985) 23(3) *American Business Law Journal* 319.

[325] The earliest and most famous example in this regard is the US Federal Trade Commission, strongly provided with investigative powers. In particular, with reference to the Federal Trade Commission, see Carl McFarland, *Judicial Control of the Federal Trade Commission and the Interstate Commerce Commission, 1920–1930* (Harvard University Press, 1933) 98. See also, Stephen G Breyer and Richard B Stewart, *Administrative Law and Regulatory Policy* 19, and Stephanie T Kanwit, *Federal Trade Commission*, (Shepard's McGraw-Hill, 1979). See, finally, Paul Rand Dixon, 'The Federal Trade Commission: Its Fact Finding Responsibilities and Powers' (1962) 46(1) *Marquette Law Review* 20, where the right of visitation is mentioned, s 9 of the Federal Trade Commission Act.

[326] Jean-Bernard Auby, 'Le pouvoirs d'inspections de l'Union européenne' 136: 'il n'existe pas de régime général de procédures d'inspections'.

[327] On this point, see Court of Justice, Case 136/79 *National Panasonic (UK) Limited v Commission of the European Communities*, 26 June 1980. Substantive and procedural requirements are needed everywhere for conducting competition inspections. From a substantive point of view, the presence of 'reasonable grounds for suspecting an infringement' is necessary.

[328] ECN Working Group Cooperation Issue and Due Process, *Investigative Powers Report*, 31 October 2012, 8 and ICN Agency Effectiveness Project on Investigative Process, *Investigative Tools Report*, 15 April 2013, 9. A specific discipline is established by EU Competition law in which inspections are possible on the basis of a mandate (directly adopted by the Commission, which need spontaneous cooperation of undertakings) or on the basis of a formal decision (which implies a binding nature).

investigations 'is sanctioned in almost all jurisdictions':[329] in other words, there is an obligation for citizens and undertakings to cooperate during inspections[330] and non-cooperation can be punishable in itself or can be considered an aggravating factor in the enforcement decision.

1.10.3. Criticisms and Paradoxes in Controlling Private Activities

Enforcement agencies operate between asymmetric information and protection of fundamental rights for citizens and firms. They should choose 'what to focus on' as well as the 'right depth' for each inspection: the object of the inspection should be well defined and inspection should be neither too great (because proportionality should be ensured when inspecting), nor too little (because controls should be effective).

A first problem regards just this narrow scope of decision. A definition of the 'what' and the 'how' of controls needs a minimum of information that it is not always available by determining a decisional short circuit, the consequence of which is that enforcement agencies are sometimes disproportionate[331] or ineffective. Alternatively, scarce information may be managed thanks to appropriate skills, methods and use of data.

A second problem concerns the organisational sustainability of the controls system, intended as a whole. Universal control of private activities presupposes such a large number of controls and controllers that it is impossible to ensure (and may be undesirable).[332] There is the need to make a complex series of choices: why, who, what, when and how should inspections be carried out, in order to maximise information and the deterrent effects of controls, ie planning controls (as we will see in chapter four section 4.3.4). This is not a way to improve controls but a structural feature of contemporary controlling.

---

[329] ECN, *Investigative Powers Report* 21, and ICN, *Investigative Tools Report*, 16.

[330] See European Commission, Decision of 20 December 1979, *Fabbrica Pisana*, 80/334/EEC, OJ L75/30, n 10, in which the undertaking had made its files available but had not assisted the Commission's officials in finding the relevant documents: 'The argument that Fabbrica Pisana had satisfactorily fulfilled its obligations by generally putting all its files at the investigators' disposal must be rejected, since the obligation on undertakings to supply all documents required by Commission inspectors must be understood to mean not merely giving access to all files but actually producing the specific documents required'.

[331] Furthermore, the problem of the target rights has also generated the most important litigation in the matter of inspections, focusing the conflict on the legitimate exercise of the inspection power and (especially) on proportionality in inspections. The problem has been analysed in Maciej Bernatt, 'Power of Inspection of the Polish Competition Authority. Question of Proportionality' (2011) 4(5) *Yearbook of Antitrust and Regulatory Studies* 47. See also Ingrid Vandenborre and Thorsten Goetz, 'EU Competition Law Procedural Issue' (2013) 4(6) *Journal of European Competition Law & Practice* 506.

[332] On the limits of 'total control' see Florentin Blanc, *From Chasing Violations to Managing Risks* 259 et seq.

60 *Rules, Corruption and Controls: Setting the Scene*

Finally, infringements can be detected during controls and, as a consequence, they may be sanctioned in so doing ensuring effective controls and disincentives to infringements. On the other hand, the disincentive effect of 'being caught' seems to be far higher than the effect of 'being punished'[333] and this suggests not to forget while controlling that compliance is strongly dependent upon cooperation and trust.[334]

---

[333] See Erich Kirchler and Erik Hoelzl, 'Modelling Taxpayers Behaviour as a Function of Interaction between Tax Authorities and Taxpayers'. On this point see also Florentin Blanc, *From Chasing Violations to Managing Risks* 146: 'it seems clear that the probability and severity of punishment are *not* the primary drivers of tax compliance – but rather, that the moral values of taxpayers, and their views on the legitimacy of the tax system and its rules, are the fundamental drivers, to which inspections and enforcement only come as an addition'.

[334] See Erich Kirchler, *The Economic Psychology of Tax Behaviour* (Cambridge University Press, 2007) xvi, where he describes the 'Slippery slope model': 'trust in the authorities and voluntary compliance integrate favourable social representations, that is, basic comprehension of tax law, favourable tax mentality, favourable personal, social and societal norms and a perceived fairness with regard to distribution of tax burden, benefits and procedures. Trust depends on cooperation and favours cooperation. A cooperative climate is based on and favours compliance, which is derived from commitment as a motivational posture and from high tax morale in the society. Rather than guaranteeing compliance, audits and fines may have opposite effects in a trustful climate and thus corrupt voluntary compliance'. See, finally, OECD, *Forum on Tax Administration's Compliance Sub-group, Strengthening Tax Audit Capabilities: General Principles and Approaches* 10: 'Given that audits can vary in terms of their scope and intensity revenue bodies should have a clear policy on the types (and numbers) of audits to be conducted, and the circumstances in which specific types of audits are to be carried out, so that audit officials (including managers) understand what is expected of them'.

2

Anticorruption: Strategies and Risks

2.1. Preventing Corruption: A Contemporary Issue

Despite the fact that there is little literature on its history, corruption has long been considered a regrettable yet unavoidable phenomenon.[1] In a sense, it represents the norm, while the ex post criminal prosecution of corrupt infringements has been exceptional.[2] This is probably due to several concurrent factors: on one side, the social tolerance for bribery, nepotism, conflicts of interests and any possible form of corrupt transactions, even though highly differentiated among countries and historical periods; on the other side, the concrete genuine difficulty in detecting, proving, and sanctioning corrupt transactions, as a largely shared criticism of legal systems, all over the world.

There is even less literature on the history of anticorruption.[3] Historically, anticorruption campaigns were mainly reactive, often following (or being connected with) political scandals. Criminal responses have been prominent, sometimes being accompanied by administrative adjustments and reforms. To give an example, at the end of the nineteenth century, scandals characterised central banking in Italy (eg, the Banca Romana scandal); while the core of the historical fact in 1893 consisted in political resignations and in penal trial for embezzlement and other fraudulent practices,[4] in the same year the Bank of Italy was founded as a response to the serious administrative dysfunctionalities at the heart of the scandal.[5]

---

[1] On this point, see Jacob van Klaveren, 'Corruption as a Historical Phenomenon', in Arnold J Heidenheimer and Michael Johnston (eds) *Political Corruption: Concepts and Contexts* 83: 'Corruption as a historical phenomenon is ... a problem that has never been dealt with systematically'. See also Pranab Bardhan 'Corruption and Development: A Review of Issues' 1320; Florian Ramseger, 'Historical perspectives on corruption in Europe' (2007) *Transparency International, U4ExpertAnswer*, 26 February 2007; Bruce Buchan and Lisa Hill, *An Intellectual History of Political Corruption* (Palgrave MacMillan, 2014) and Carlo Alberto Brioschi, *Corruption: A Short History* (Brookings Institution Press, 2017).

[2] Gerald. Caiden, OP Dwivedi and Joseph G Jabbra (eds), *Where Corruption Lives* (Kumarian Press, 2001) 23: 'corruption should be seen as the norm, not the exception'.

[3] See, on this topic, Ronald Kroeze, André Vitória and Guy Geltner, *Anticorruption in History: From Antiquity to the Modern Era* (Oxford University Press, 2018).

[4] Manfred Pohl and Sabine Freitag (eds), *Handbook on the History of European Banks* (Edwar Elgar 1994), 593.

[5] Mark Gilbert and Robert K Nilsson, *Historical Dictionary of Modern Italy*, 2nd edn (Scarecrow Press, 1961) 48.

However, administrative anticorruption intended as proactive and autonomous ex ante activity, different from mere criminal prosecution and designed to prevent corrupt infringements at an early stage, is definitely a contemporary issue, in the sense that it emerged and developed in the last part of the twentieth century. Why has corruption started to be perceived as an increased problem? Is this contemporary attention due to a higher level of corruption, or to reduced tolerance regarding it?

As we will see later, corruption became a central topic of public discussion in the early 1990s, when international organisations, non-governmental actors, the press, scholars and academics commenced to report on dysfunctions connected to huge corruption at global level, with special regard to inefficiencies in public services, widespread inequalities, waste of financial resources (for instance, in public procurement), negative effects on macroeconomic aspects, and so on. It is difficult to say whether this increased attention has been due to actual higher levels of corruption, given the fact that its measurement is still characterised by the prevalence of perception surveys. In any case, it stands to reason that both greater opportunities for corruption (due to the increased role of states, to the rise in global transactions, and to economic growth) and stronger awareness about its hidden costs have contributed to this greater attention and to better understanding of the problem.

Contemporary anticorruption presents two structural novelties in comparison with the previous approach to fighting corruption.

On the one hand, *economic reasoning* has become much more relevant, while the specific criminal qualification of corrupt infringements has proven to be less crucial to the purpose of administrative prevention. However, if there is wide agreement on the idea that economics is indispensable for the analysis (and the prevention) of corruption[6] (because it contributes to explaining its causes and to arranging possible solutions), then ethics too maintains a central role: not only because economics has its roots in moral philosophy,[7] but because ethics and intangible factors (such as trust) strongly impact on the effectiveness of anticorruption policies.[8]

On the other hand, contemporary anticorruption embodies a genuine *administrative connotation* by operating ex ante and by resorting to an administrative toolkit constituted by risk-based controls (directed towards sensitive activities and sectors characterised by higher risk of corruption, such as public procurements); internal audits; ethical codes; whistleblower regulation; a duty of abstention in case of conflicts of interest; staff rotation in inspections; duty of disclosure; anticorruption plans and so on.

---

[6] See Susan Rose-Ackerman, *Corruption and government: causes, consequences and reform*, xi; see also Robert Klitgaard, *Controlling Corruption* and Anthony Ogus, 'Corruption and regulatory structures'.
[7] See Lisa Hill, 'Adam Smith and the Theme of Corruption' (2006) 68 *Review of Politics* 636.
[8] On this point, see among others Peter Koslowski, *Principles of Ethical Economy* (Springer, 2001) and Christopher Hodges and Ruth Steinholtz, *Ethical Business Practice and Regulation. A Behavioural and Values-Based Approach to Compliance and Enforcement* (Hart, 2017).

In any case, contemporary anticorruption is characterised by a number of administrative activities focused on the way in which public administering is carried out, living together with the criminal prosecution of corruption.

2.1.1. The Great Temptation: Justifying

Separation from its moral roots is at the basis of modern value-neutral economics[9] and has produced a quantitative discipline which has at least a great merit in coldly considering many previously underestimated aspects of corruption.

However, the value-neutral perspective has sometimes led to overestimation of the positive effects of corruption and even to justification of corruption as a necessary evil. According to this perspective, corruption consists in 'greasing the wheels'[10] of the economy, making possible what would otherwise be hindered by the rigidities of legitimate regulation and administration: corruption may express positive effects when it secures economic development,[11] when functional to an agency's mission[12] or when it corrects bad (inefficient) regulation[13] by introducing 'an element of competition into what is otherwise a comfortably monopolistic industry'.[14]

The limited vision of value-neutral economics[15] has been widely discussed. From a theoretical point of view, criticism has been formulated, by behavioural economics and by ethical economy,[16] among others. From a practical perspective,

---

[9] On this topic see Hilary Putnam and Vivian Walsh (eds), *The End of Value-Free Economics* (Routledge, 2012).

[10] See Nathaniel Leff, 'Economic Development Through Bureaucratic Corruption' 11: 'If the government has erred in its decision, the course made possible by corruption may well be the better one'. See also Samuel P Huntington, *Political order in changing societies* (Yale University Press, 1968) 69: 'In terms of economic growth, the only thing worse than a society with a rigid, over-centralised, dishonest bureaucracy is one with a rigid, over-centralised, honest bureaucracy.'

[11] Ibid.

[12] John A Gardiner, 'Controlling official corruption and fraud: Bureaucratic incentives and disincentives' 35.

[13] Anthony Ogus, 'Corruption and regulatory structures' 330–31.

[14] Nathaniel Leff, 'Economic Development Through Bureaucratic Corruption' 10.

[15] On this point see Lionel Robbins, *An Essay on the Nature and Significance of Economic Science* (Macmillan, 1932): 'Economics, we have seen, is concerned with that aspect of behaviour which arises from the scarcity of means to achieve given ends. It follows that Economics is entirely neutral between ends; that, in so far as the achievement of *any* end is dependent on scarce means, it is germane to the preoccupations of the Economist. Economics is not concerned with ends as such'. See also Gary Becker, *The Economic Approach to Human Behavior* (University of Chicago Press, 1976) 5: 'The combined assumptions of maximizing behavior, market equilibrium, and stable preferences ... form the heart of the economic approach as I see it'.

[16] On this point, see Amartya Sen, 'Rational fools: A critique of the behavioral foundations of economic theory' (1977) 6(4) *Philosophy and Public Affairs*, 317 and Amartya Sen, *On Ethics and Economics* (Blackwell Publishing, 1987) 2–3, where 'economics has had two rather different origins ... concerned respectively with "ethics", on the one hand, and with what may be called "engineering", on the other' and 6: 'Given the nature of economics, it is not surprising that both the ethics-related origin and the engineering-based origin of economics have some cogency of their own'. On this issue see also John Neville Keynes, *The Scope and Method of Political Economy* (Macmillan and Co, 1917) and Hilary Putnam and Vivian Walsh (eds), *The End of Value-Free Economics*.

research and studies argue that the positive economic effects of administrative corruption would be controversial as the effects of corruption on administrative performance are themselves controversial.[17]

For these reasons, even though the temptation to justify corruption is not completely outdated, there is large agreement on the idea that the results of corruption may be considered positively only by adopting a very limited perspective in the short run, while the long run view (including a wider, integrated evaluation) would make evident that corruption could be sanding the wheels, rather than greasing them.[18]

2.1.2. The Right Choice: Combating

Contemporary administrative anticorruption is based on a set of motivations which combine and integrate moral, social, economic, regulatory and administrative arguments.

From a *moral perspective*, when people behave corruptly, they operate in a parallel reality by managing a dual truth: the 'true truth' regarding what has happened in corrupt transactions, which is secret in nature; and the 'apparent truth' which regards the public dimension.[19] This duplicity requires lies and hypocrisy, and impedes integrity (indispensable especially for public officers).

From a *social perspective*, corruption presupposes an agreement between a public agent and at least a citizen or a firm. Such an agreement is based on a private trust, indispensable to carrying out cooperative illegal behaviours. This private, intra-group trust undermines public and general trust, ie the trust of citizens and firms in institutions, trust of institutions in citizens and firms, trust among institutions, trust among firms and among citizens. This negatively affects social relationships[20]

---

[17] David J Gould and Jose A Amaro-Reyes, *The Effects of Corruption on Administrative Performance. Illustrations from Developing Countries* (1983) World Bank Staff Working Papers, no 580, Management and Development Series, number 7; see also Joseph S Nye, 'Corruption and political development: a cost-benefit analysis'.

[18] On this point see Paolo Mauro, 'Corruption and Growth' and Susan Rose Ackerman, *Corruption and Government: Causes, Consequences and Reform*.

[19] Mark E Warren, 'Political Corruption as Duplicitous Exclusion' (2006) 39(4) *Political Science and Politics* 803, 806 where – regarding political corruption – he wrote: 'The distinctive marks of corruption in the legislative domain are those that contravene inclusive public deliberation, namely, secrecy in decision-making, and duplicity in speech. Secrecy can have many motives – some quite proper – but in legislative matters it is often a sign that influences are improper and voices are excluded for reasons that could not be justified in public. Duplicity in speech, what many people call a "lack of sincerity" in politicians, is a sign that the deliberative process has been corrupted: the arguments made and displayed are not those motivating the decisions. The harms to democracy are direct and extensive: corruption of this sort severs representative linkages, breaks the relationship between deliberation and decision-making, and undermines the creative elements of democratic conflict resolution'.

[20] Ibid, 804: 'Political corruption attacks democracy by excluding people from decisions that affect them. The very logic of corruption involves exclusion: the corrupt use their control over resources to achieve gains at the expense of those excluded from collective decision-making, or organization of collective actions'.

because corruption has a 'destructive effect ... on the fabric of society ... where agents and public officers break the confidence entrusted to them'.[21]

From an *economic perspective*, corruption operates in the economic process, artificially separating economic activity and its result into two abstract concepts:[22] the result benefits someone else (even though it belongs to others).[23] In so doing, corruption changes the value (ie, the result of the economic activity, which simultaneously represents a moral and an economic value) into mere advantage, with the consequence that the economic process in itself is corrupted. Moreover, even though the economic effects of corruption are controversial, there is large agreement about the fact that corruption impedes innovation and that – in the presence of corruption – 'economic and political development are crippled'.[24]

From a *regulatory perspective*, corruption has an impact on regulation and on the system of incentives arranged in order to achieve regulatory purposes. Corruption, for instance, has been regarded as a 'sister activity' of taxation, but at the same time it has been considered as more costly due to the fact that corruption presupposes secrecy, which 'makes bribes more distortionary than taxes'.[25] Moreover, corruption has been considered a way to determine who benefits and who bears the costs of government action,[26] characterised by secrecy: this 'distorts incentives, undermines institutions, and redistributes wealth and power to the undeserving'.[27]

From an *administrative perspective*, corruption distorts public officers from the public interest and from proper administrative behaviour (which has to be legitimate, fair and impartial, according to rules[28]). Corruption creates an illegitimate and secret market for public functions and services, and this represents a threat to the integrity of public officials and to trust in them, in so

---

[21] Colin Nicholls, Tim Daniel, Martin Polaine and John Hatchard, *Corruption and misuse of public office* (Oxford University Press, 2006), 1; see also Oliver E Williamson, 'Transaction-Cost Economics: The Governance of Contractual Relations' (1979) 22(2) *Journal of Law and Economics* 233, 242: 'Governance structures which attenuate opportunism and otherwise infuse confidence are evidently needed'.

[22] Maria De Benedetto, entry 'Administrative Corruption', in Juergen G Backhaus (ed), *Encyclopedia of Law and Economics* (Springer on line, 2014) 3–4, quoting the Italian legal philosopher Giuseppe Capograssi.

[23] See Alison Grey Anderson, 'Conflicts of Interest: Efficiency, Fairness and Corporate Structure' (1978) 25 *UCLA Law Review* 794.

[24] Robert Klitgaard, *Controlling Corruption* 2 and Paolo Mauro, 'Corruption and Growth'. See also Anthony Ogus, 'Corruption and regulatory structures' 229: 'the connection between corruption and the lack of growth is more often assumed than demonstrated'.

[25] Andrei Shleifer and Robert W Vishny, 'Corruption' (1993) 108(3) *Quarterly Journal of Economics* 599, 600. See also, in general, Giacomo Di Gennaro and Antonio La Spina, 'The costs of illegality: a research programme' (2016) 17(1) *Global Crime* 1.

[26] Susan Rose Ackerman, *Corruption and Government: Causes, Consequences and Reform* 9.

[27] Robert Klitgaard, *Controlling Corruption* 2.

[28] Mark E Warren, 'Political Corruption as Duplicitous Exclusion' 803, 804: 'Administrative officials fulfill their offices by holding a public trust and acting impartially in the public interest, ideally insulated from political pressure'.

doing weakening an intangible but incredibly relevant factor of institutional life (see chapter one section 1.4.3).[29]

All these moral, social, economic, regulatory and administrative reasons contribute to the conclusion that combating corruption is important: even though some economic and bureaucratic benefits of corruption can sometimes be recognised or even justified by the bad functioning of regulation, in the large majority of cases they will be significantly outweighed by the costs.[30]

2.2. Anticorruption between Global Stance and Domestic Strategies

An important aspect of contemporary anticorruption policies is their dual nature: on one side, they present a global design, in the sense that there are ever stronger directives and constraints from international organisations regarding corruption prevention for national governments; on the other side, they present local implementation, because domestic regulations establish at countries' level administrative bodies, burdens and procedures specifically oriented to achieving anticorruption purposes.[31]

However, anticorruption global policies and domestic strategies are not always consistent with each other. Rather, they very often coexist by expressing different visions and cultures. Anticorruption systems are affected by apparent contradictions, often leading to serious inconsistencies: sometimes they are in the form of procedures and institutions which tend to work formally; at other times they produce side-effects; in any case, anticorruption has proved to be a very costly system and problematic in terms of effectiveness.[32]

2.2.1. Global Anticorruption Policies

Since the last decade of the last century, there has been a wide and increasing interest in anticorruption policies by international actors and, consequently, a deeper involvement of national governments. By operating at every

---

[29] Colin Nicholls, Tim Daniel, Martin Polaine and John Hatchard, *Corruption and Misuse of Public Office* 1: corruption has a 'destructive effect ... on the fabric of society ... where agents and public officers break the confidence entrusted to them'.
[30] Anthony Ogus, 'Corruption and regulatory structures' 333.
[31] On this point see Ina Kubbe and Annika Engelbert (eds), *Corruption and Norms. Why Informal Rules Matter* (Palgrave Macmillan, 2018).
[32] See Gilles Badet, Luc Damiba, Stéphane B Enguéléguélé, Emmanuel Gaima, Chijioke K Iwuamadi, Semou Ndiaye and Shine Williams, *Effectiveness of Anticorruption Agencies in West Africa – OSIWA* (Open Society Foundation, 2016).

Anticorruption between Global Stance and Domestic Strategies 67

level of government, international anticorruption policies have produced a complex framework of states' 'soft law' obligations to repress and to prevent corruption.[33]

Throughout the 1990s, a global movement aiming at transparency and integrity in government has started a number of institutional activities, reporting and regulation: alongside the Transparency International Corruption Perceptions Index (CPI) introduced in 1995, the OECD has adopted recommendations[34] alongside Council of Europe resolutions[35] and conventions, and also establishing the GRECO group of states against corruption, in order 'to improve the capacity of its members to fight corruption';[36] among other initiatives, at the European Union level, communications have been adopted[37] and the OLAF was introduced.[38]

In the first decade of the new century, there was an acceleration of the process, due to the OECD recommendations,[39] to a further European Commission Communication[40] but overall to some international conventions: alongside the already adopted Inter-American Convention[41] and the conventions of the Council of Europe, in 2003 the African Union Convention[42] and, most notably, the United Nations Convention against Corruption (UNCAC) were approved.

---

[33] Cecily Rose, *International Anticorruption Norms: Their Creation and Influence on domestic legal systems* (Oxford University Press, 2015) 15 et seq; see Julio Bacio Terracino, *The International Legal Framework Against Corruption. State's Obligation to prevent and Repress Corruption* (Intersentia, 2012). For a first analysis see OECD, *Public Sector Corruption. An International Survey of Prevention Measures* (OECD, 1999).

[34] OECD, *Recommendation of the Council for Further Combating Bribery of Foreign Public Officials in International Business Transactions*, 26 November 2009.

[35] Council of Europe, Resolution (97)24 *On Twenty Guiding Principles for the Fight Against Corruption*, 1997. In 1999 the Criminal Law Convention on Corruption (27 January 1999) was adopted and opened to signature followed by the Civil Law Convention on Corruption (4 November 1999).

[36] Statute of the GRECO, Appendix to Resolution (99)5, art 1. On this point see GRECO, *Compliance Report on Italy*, adopted at its 51st Plenary Meeting, Strasbourg, 23–27 May 2011, Greco RC-I/II (2011) 1E.

[37] European Commission, Communication, *A Union policy against corruption*, COM (97) 192 final, 21 May 1997.

[38] EC, ECSC, Euratom, Commission Decision of 28 April 1999/352, *Establishing the European Anti-fraud Office* (OLAF).

[39] *Recommendation on integrity in public procurement* (C(2008)105); *Recommendation on Guidelines for managing conflict of interest in the public service* (C(2003)107); *Recommendation on improving ethical conduct in the public service including principles for managing ethics in the public service* (C(98)70/FINAL); *Recommendation for Enhanced Access and More Effective Use of Public Sector Information* (C(2008)36), *Recommendation on Improving the Quality of Government Regulation* (C(95)21/FINAL); *Recommendation of the Council for Further Combating Bribery of Foreign Public Officials in International Business Transactions* 26 November 2009 – C(2009)159/REV1/FINAL, Amended on 18 February 2010 – C(2010)19); *Recommendation of the Council on Principles for Transparency and Integrity in Lobbying*, 18 February 2010 – C(2010)16.

[40] European Commission, *Communication on a comprehensive EU policy against corruption* (COM/2003/0317).

[41] Inter-American Convention against Corruption (B-58), 29 March 1996.

[42] African Union Convention on Preventing and Combating Corruption, 1 July 2003, date of last signature 10 February 2020.

UNCAC – considered the 'standard-bearer of anticorruption efforts in the world'[43] – represented the launch of a complex global process of 'nationalising' anticorruption. Alongside criminal provisions and provisions about international cooperation, UNCAC established the need for preventive measures: article 5 (preventive anticorruption policies and practices) disposed that states 'develop and implement or maintain effective, coordinated anticorruption policies that promote the participation of society and reflect the principles of the rule of law, proper management of public affairs and public property, integrity, transparency and accountability'.[44] More specifically, art 6 requires states to establish preventive anticorruption bodies in charge of implementing anticorruption policies as well as increasing and disseminating knowledge about the prevention of corruption: such bodies should be provided with the necessary independence, material resources and specialised staff.[45]

Regarding the specific administrative system of preventive measures, UNCAC requires states to operate at several administrative levels. Looking at the question from an administrative law point of view, many chapters in this field of research are interested in and contaminated by anticorruption regulation. First of all, it addresses civil service legal regimes, both with regard to systems for the 'recruitment, hiring, retention, promotion and retirement of civil servants'[46] and to those for promoting integrity, honesty and responsibility among public officials,[47] including codes of conduct and conflicts of interest regulation. Secondly, public procurement, for which the UNCAC requires appropriate systems, based on transparency, competition and objective criteria in decision-making, that are effective, inter alia, in preventing corruption.[48] Management of public finances is involved in order to promote transparency and accountability.[49] It also concerns public reporting, in order to enhance transparency in organisation, functioning and decision-making

---

[43] Alina Mungiu-Pippidi and Niklas Kossow, 'Rethinking the way we do anticorruption' (2016) *NatoReview*, www.nato.int/docu/review/articles/2016/12/08/rethinking-the-way-we-do-anticorruption/index.html.

[44] Art 5.3 of UNCAC establishes also the need 'to periodically evaluate relevant legal instruments and administrative measures with a view to determining their adequacy to prevent and fight corruption'.

[45] United Nations, Conference of the States Parties to the United Nations Convention against Corruption, CAC/COSP/WG.4/2014/2, 25 June 2014, Open-ended Intergovernmental Working Group on the Prevention of Corruption, 'Mandates of anticorruption body or bodies in respect of prevention' (art 6 of the United Nations Convention against Corruption) – Note by the Secretariat, 11, 'Measures to grant the necessary independence, resources and staff to enable corruption prevention authorities to carry out their functions effectively'.

[46] Art 7, 'Public sector'.

[47] Art 8 'Codes of conduct for public officials', also establishing measures and systems requiring public officials to make declarations regarding their outside activities, employment, investments, assets and substantial gifts or benefits from which a conflict of interest may result with respect to their functions as public officials.

[48] Art 9.1.

[49] Art 9.2.

processes, with consequences for administrative procedures or regulations processes, on the protection of privacy and personal data as well as on simplification of administrative procedures and on publishing information.[50] Participation of society is relevant, by promoting the contribution of the public to decision-making processes and by ensuring that the public has effective access to information.[51] And finally, measures to prevent money-laundering are also addressed.[52]

Since 2003, states have subscribed to the Convention and have progressively introduced anticorruption systems into their national legal systems, including bodies and regulation.

For the sake of completeness, international and European actors have influenced national governments in matters of anticorruption not only directly – by requiring an extremely high number of administrative burdens – but also following other, more indirect tenets such as *conditionality*.[53] The World Bank, for example, gives loans to developing countries requiring (among other things) the putting in place of regulatory and institutional mechanisms to fight corruption.[54] The EU pursues conditionality in order to improve governance and control corruption in aspiring member states.[55] Anticorruption prerequisites express real conditions for obtaining some kind of benefit, whether it is a loan or admission to the EU.[56] In all likelihood, if they were analysed as real incentives, it would be clear that they can work not only by reversing distortions derived from corruption but that they also may produce further distortionary results.[57]

---

[50] Art 10.
[51] Art 13.
[52] Art 14.
[53] Celine Tan, 'The new disciplinary framework: conditionality, new aid architecture and global economic governance', in Julio Faundez and Celine Tan (eds), *International Economic Law, Globalization and Developing Countries* (Edwar Elgar, 2010) 112.
[54] See Anthony Ogus, 'Corruption and regulatory structures' 329; World Bank, *Guidelines on Preventing and Combating Fraud and Corruption in Projects Financed by IBRD Loans and IDA Credits and Grants* (World Bank, 2006; revised 2011).
[55] Patrycja Szarek-Mason, *The European Union's Fight Against Corruption: The Evolving Policy Towards Member States and Candidate Countries* (Cambridge University Press, 2010) esp 135 et seq ('Conditionality in the EU accession process'). On this aspect, see also Alina Mungiu-Pippidi and Jana Warkotsch, 'For a More Effective Link Between EU Funds and Good Governance', in Alina Mungiu-Pippidi and Jana Warkotsch, *Beyond the Panama Papers. The Performance of EU Good Governance Promotion*, The Anticorruption Report 4 (Barbara Budrich Publishers, 2017) 7 and Digdem Soyaltin, 'Turkey: The Paradoxical Effects of EU Accession', ibid, 79: 'the strategy of reinforcement by reward, [has] enabled the EU to induce governments to comply with its conditions and adopt certain policies to fight against corruption'; see also Agnes Batory, 'Post-accession malaise? EU conditionality, domestic politics and anticorruption policy in Hungary' (2010) 11(2) *Global Crime*: Anticorruption for Eastern Europe, 164.
[56] See World Bank, *Guidelines on Preventing and Combating Fraud and Corruption in Projects Financed by IBRD Loans and IDA Credits and Grants*; see also Anthony Ogus, *Corruption and regulatory structures* 329.
[57] Johann Lambsdorff, *The Organization of Anticorruption – Getting Incentives Right*, Passau University Discussion Paper 57-08, October 2008.

2.2.2. Domestic Administrative Strategies

National governments which pledged to respect international anticorruption agreements and treaties (or even conditionalities) have experienced restricted space for completely independent strategies. The goals of global anticorruption policies to be implemented at national level and to influence national institutional cultures are very difficult to pursue and (even more so) to achieve. Governments may not choose *whether to* combat corruption (because they are obliged to by agreements and treaties, by loan agreements or by other conditions). They also have limited scope in *how* to combat corruption (because national anticorruption systems look necessarily at the consolidated anticorruption toolkit, developed at an international level, including the regulation of conflicts of interest, whistleblower regulation, codes of conduct for public officers, and so on).[58]

At the end of the day, the autonomy national Governments' mainly regards the design of anticorruption institutions (*who* has to combat corruption) which should aim 'to adapt the model and form of specialised anticorruption preventive and repressive functions to the local context'.[59] Upon closer inspections, in this respect too, there are recommendations, international standards and practices: national anticorruption bodies, in fact, should in any case feature 'mandate and functions; forms of specialisation; independence, autonomy and accountability; adequate material resources, specialised and trained staff; adequate powers; co-operation with the civil society and the private sector; inter-agency co-operation'.[60]

However, the *institutional design* also has much to say regarding countries' anticorruption preventive strategies.[61] To this purpose international organisations have provided broad classifications by indicating three main typologies of anticorruption bodies (ACBs).

Firstly, there are ACBs in charge both of prevention and investigation, alternatively defined as 'specialised anticorruption bodies with a dual prevention

---

[58] See Eastern Partnership-Council of Europe Facility Project on 'Good Governance and Fight against Corruption'. *Designing and Implementing Anticorruption Policies Handbook* (March 2013).

[59] OECD, *Specialised Anticorruption Institutions. Review of Models* 2nd edn (OECD, 2013) 43; Lala Camerer, *Prerequisites for effective anticorruption ombudsman's offices and anticorruption agencies*, 10th International Anticorruption Conference, Prague, IACC (Transparency International 2001), www.10iacc.org/download/workshops/cs06.pdf.

[60] Ibid, 23.

[61] See UNDP, *Report of the Regional Forum on Anticorruption Institutions* (Vienna International Centre, 2005), http://europeandcis.undp.org/files/uploads/Lotta/AC%20Forum%20Report.pdf; Patrick Meagher, *Anticorruption Services. A Review of Experience*, IRIS (Center for Institutional Reform and the Informal Sector at the University of Maryland 2004); Alan Doig, 'A Good Idea Gone Wrong? Anticorruption Commissions in the Twenty First Century', EGPA 2004 Annual Conference, Ljubljana; Jeremy Pope, *The Need and Role of an Independent Anticorruption Agency* (Working Paper for Transparency International 1999); Council of Europe *Anticorruption Services – Good Practices in Europe* (Council of Europe Publishing, 2004); see also Alina Mungiu-Pippidi and R Dadasov, 'When do laws matter? The evidence on national integrity enabling contexts' (2017) *Crime, Law and Social Change*, 387 and Alina Mungiu-Pippidi, *The Quest for Good Governance: How Societies Develop Control of Corruption* (Cambridge University Press, 2015).

and investigation mandate' by the UN[62] or as 'multi-purpose agencies with law enforcement powers' by the OECD.[63]

Secondly, there are law enforcement-type institutions, which can take on different kinds of specialisation implemented in detection, investigation and prosecution bodies, sometimes including elements of prevention, coordination and research functions.[64]

Thirdly, there are genuine preventive institutions – according to the OECD definition – defined as 'Specialised anticorruption bodies with a primarily prevention-related mandate' by the UN.[65] They are considered 'the broadest model' but can have different features. Some are devoted to coordination between government agencies in the field of corruption prevention,[66] as non-permanent institutions which operate through regular meetings; some are dedicated corruption prevention bodies, permanent, with a broader mandate including the coordination of anticorruption strategies and other functions 'such as assessment of corruption risk and integrity plans for public institutions and sectors, anticorruption awareness-raising and education, conflict of interest prevention, asset declarations, political party financing and lobbying and anticorruption assessment of legal acts'.[67]

However, the effectiveness of anticorruption systems varies among countries. First of all, not all countries share the same 'philosophy' of anticorruption (the already mentioned *if, how* and *who* of anticorruption), while anticorruption(ism) has been perceived as an ideology, 'a set of postulates about what corruption is, how it emerges, why it needs to be controlled, and how to control it'.[68] Moreover, countries' governments may present 'differences between the willingness and capacity … to create, design and administer an effective anticorruption strategy'.[69] Finally the recommendation to create agencies specifically devoted to corruption prevention as an important piece of the country's anticorruption strategy[70] meets doubts about their relevance,[71] being no strong evidence that the existence of

---

[62] United Nations, Conference of the States Parties to the United Nations Convention against Corruption, CAC/COSP/WG.4/2014/2, 25 June 2014, Open-ended Intergovernmental Working Group on the Prevention of Corruption, *Mandates of anticorruption body or bodies in respect of prevention* 6.

[63] OECD, *Specialised Anticorruption Institutions. Review of Models* 40.

[64] Ibid.

[65] United Nations, Conference of the States Parties to the United Nations Convention against Corruption, CAC/COSP/WG.4/2014/2, 25 June 2014, Open-ended Intergovernmental Working Group on the Prevention of Corruption, *Mandates of anticorruption body or bodies in respect of prevention* 4.

[66] Ibid, 7.

[67] OECD, *Specialised Anticorruption Institutions. Review of Models* 41. See also Oscar Capdeferro Villagrasa, 'The role of the Anti-Fraud Office of Catalonia in the fight against corruption in the Catalan public sector. Analysis and suggestions for reform to mark its 10th anniversary' (2020) 60 *Revista Catalana de Dret Públic* 35.

[68] Steven Sampson, 'The anticorruption industry: from movement to institution' (2010) 11(2) *Global Crime* 261, 262.

[69] Rob McCusker, *Review of anticorruption strategies* (Australian Institute of Criminology, Technical and Background Paper No 23, 2006) 10.

[70] Alina Mungiu-Pippidi, *The Quest for Good Governance: How Societies Develop Control of Corruption*.

[71] Luís Sousa, 'Anticorruption agencies: between empowerment and irrelevance' (2009) 53 (1) *Crime, Law and Social Change* 5.

ACBs always help to reduce corruption,[72] even though recent research projects are seeking to advance and investigate the question more accurately.[73]

2.3. Anticorruption: Conventional, Behavioural and Beyond

As long as corruption has been considered from a criminal perspective the institutional battle has been reactive, designed to punish ex post previously committed infringements and crimes. The struggle has become ever more stringent even by becoming proactive and by orienting institutions to prevent, ex ante, any possible infringements or crimes before they have been committed. In the general framework of anticorruption regulation and practice it is possible to distinguish different approaches: far from being alternatives to each other, they represent incremental improvements in the institutional capacity to combat corruption.

They may be defined as conventional, behavioural and regulatory anticorruption.

2.3.1. Conventional Anticorruption

Conventional anticorruption (CAC) represents the war machine of anticorruption, born when regulation first established corruption prevention purposes by structuring dedicated administrative offices and by focusing on administrative activities (and on public agents). It is mainly informed by the traditional deterrence approach, of incentives and disincentives and the need for controls,[74] even though it aims also to promote ethical engagement of public officers and business. CAC has been based on Principal-Agent-(Client) theory, considering criminal behaviour the final result of an illicit agreement motivated by rent-seeking.[75] CAC has been articulated in a number of new administrative activities with the aim of taking all other administrative functions under its control, especially those characterised by a higher risk of corruption, such as in the field of public procurement,

---

[72] See OECD, *Specialised Anticorruption Institutions. Review of Models* 5. On the topic of special anticorruption bodies, see also Claes Sandgren, 'Combating Corruption: The Misunderstood Role of Law' (2005) 39(3) *International Lawyer* 729–30. On this point, see Kayla Crider and Jeffrey Milyo, 'Do State Ethics Commissions Reduce Political Corruption? An Exploratory Investigation' (2013) 3 *UC Irvine Law Review* 717.

[73] Daniel L Feldman, 'The Efficacy of Anticorruption Institutions in Italy' (2020) *Public Integrity*.

[74] Nicoletta Rangone, *A behavioural approach to administrative corruption prevention*, in Agustì Cerillo-I-Martinez and Juli Ponce (eds), *Preventing Corruption and Promoting good Government and Public Integrity* (Bruylant, 2017) 69.

[75] On this point see Luca Di Donato, *A behavioral Principal-Agent theory to study corruption and tax evasion*, Luiss School of Government, Working Paper Series, SOG-WP34/2016.

permissions, grants and so on. In this sense it is a figurative battle and requires an incredible number of footsoldiers to play their part because 'preventive functions are so numerous and diverse, covering all aspects of good governance, that they cannot be performed by a single institution'.[76]

The CAC regulatory framework consists of two levels of regulation: the international one, especially related to the already mentioned UN Convention against corruption, which establishes (among other things) the obligation for states to introduce anticorruption bodies; and the state level, related to national regulations transposing global anticorruption in the legal systems of individual countries.

Conventional anticorruption has been structured as an administrative function, in the most traditional sense, because three concurrent conditions are given. The first is that a national anticorruption regulation has been adopted by establishing administrative powers and procedures, according to the principle of legality of administration.[77] The second condition is that anticorruption offices (AC bodies) have been established at state level, both as central anticorruption bodies and/or as decentralised anticorruption offices. The third and last condition is the presence of anticorruption public officers, in charge of the anticorruption institutional mission, who can operate alternatively in central anticorruption bodies or locally, as anticorruption officers in a large variety of administrations.

Conventional anticorruption is the frame of a number of activities to be carried out before infringements and corruption occur. Among others, assessing the risk of corruption; monitoring and coordination of the implementation of national and local anticorruption strategies and action plans; reviewing and preparing relevant legislation; monitoring the conflict of interest rules and declaration of assets requirement for public officials; elaboration and implementation of codes of ethics; assisting in anticorruption training of officials; issuing guidance and providing advice on issues related to government ethics; facilitating international cooperation and cooperation with the civil society, and other matters.[78]

2.3.2. Behavioural Anticorruption

Behavioural anticorruption (BAC) represents the advancement of conventional anticorruption, both in the sense of its fine tuning and of its updating to include developments in theories of compliance and in cooperative enforcement practices. It focuses on human behaviour and exploits the great contributions which come from behavioural and cognitive insights in the field of corruption prevention by questioning the traditional deterrence approach based on the idea of

---

[76] OECD, *Specialised Anticorruption Institutions. Review of Models* (OECD, 2008) 21.

[77] Carol Harlow and Richard Rawlings, *Law and Administration*, 3rd edn (Cambridge University Press, 2009); Christopher L Atkinson, 'Legitimacy in Public Administration', in Ali Farazmand (ed) *Global Encyclopedia of Public Administration, Public Policy, and Governance* (Springer, 2018).

[78] OECD, *Specialised Anticorruption Institutions. Review of Models* 32.

rationality and by concentrating on real people, who are much more influenceable, characterised by bias and with limited capacity to assess risk and probability.[79] Behavioural and cognitive sciences, in fact, have over time investigated many significant aspects of infringements and corruption which may be incredibly useful for anticorruption, making it possible for preventive interventions to be better informed and targeted, and more effective. BAC also consists in reorienting Principal-Agent-(Client) theory by putting greater emphasis on the individual's motivations and values[80] and consists in a reframing of traditional anticorruption administrative tools[81] by considering their impact on individual behaviour.[82]

It works at two different levels: by strengthening the CAC consolidated toolkit, as in the case of whistle-blower protection[83] or staff-rotation;[84] and by changing the way in which some regulatory and administrative functions are carried out – as in the case of good quality behaviour-informed regulation or controls carried out according to procedural justice standards, in this way making them more effective and reducing opportunities for infringements and corruption.

The contribution coming from behavioural and cognitive insights to institutional performances is widely recognised, starting from the special relevance of laboratory experiments[85] on tax evasion in the area of fiscal studies. Many governments have introduced behavioural units or groups of experts in order to support the behavioural and cognitive orientation of regulation and in regulatory delivery:[86] in other words, a behavioural change approach to policymaking is today seriously considered capable of affecting how people behave and make decisions and, in so doing, of contributing to preventing corruption thanks to increased regulatory effectiveness. Furthermore, growing literature is currently focusing specifically on behaviour and anticorruption,[87] on people deciding to engage in

---

[79] Nicoletta Rangone, *A behavioural approach to administrative corruption prevention*, in Agustì Cerillo-I-Martinez and Juli Ponce (eds), *Preventing Corruption and Promoting good Government and Public Integrity* 69.
[80] Luca Di Donato, *A behavioral Principal-Agent theory to study corruption and tax evasion*.
[81] Nicoletta Rangone, *A behavioural approach to administrative corruption prevention* 69.
[82] Ibid, 92.
[83] Ibid, 76.
[84] Ibid. 79.
[85] Luigi Mittone, 'Dynamic behavior in tax evasion. An experimental approach' (2006) 35 *Journal of Socio-Economics* 813.
[86] In this regard, it suffices to remember the influential book of Richard H Thaler and Cass R Sunstein, *Nudge: Improving Decisions About Health, Wealth, and Happiness* (Yale University Press, 2008) and Pete Lunn, *Regulatory Policy and Behavioral Economics* (OECD, 2014). See also Nicoletta Rangone, 'Making Law Effective: Behavioural Insights into Compliance' (2018) 9(3) *European Journal of Risk Regulation* 483.
[87] On this point see Luca Di Donato, 'Behavioural research and corruption: A new promise for governments?,' (2017) *European Law Journal* 24; Johann Graf Lambsdorff, 'A Behavioral Science Approach to Preventing Corruption' (2016) *The Global Anticorruption Blog*; Richard Mulgan and John Wanna, 'Developing Cultures of Integrity in the Public and Private Sectors', in Adam Graycar and Russel G Smith (eds), *Handbook of Global Research and practice in Corruption* (Edward Elgar, 2011) 416; Levke Jessen-Thiessen and Laura McDonald, 'A nudge in the right direction: applying behavioural

corrupt transactions. In keeping with the purposes of BAC, specific behavioural and cognitive expertise is required in the regulatory process as well as to deliver regulation.

Two different veins of research have contributed to the development of BAC.

The first concerns the fields of psychology and neurology of corruption, involving the cost-benefit calculation of engaging in corruption, which is influenced by mental shortcuts, false intuitions, how individuals process and organise information, emotions, and is even based on people's physiology.[88] Starting from the idea of bounded rationality and from the need for a fairly drastic revision[89] of rationality of economic behaviour, people's preference function starts by including ethical considerations, intrinsic motivations as well as bias, inertia, heuristics, as demonstrated by laboratory experiments: 'this paradigmatic shift can be relevant for anticorruption'.[90]

A second vein of research concerns the social environment and, more generally, the culture in which people take decisions,[91] bringing the approach of ethnography and anthropology[92] as well as that of sociology in the evaluation of contextualised corruption and in the analysis of possible drivers for sustainable anticorruption. One promising approach in the field of behaviour comes from research into the area of social norms and corruption, and was especially developed to strengthen the effectiveness of anticorruption programming in fragile states[93] where corruption is the rule. Social norms consist in 'mutual expectations about the right way to behave'[94] and their consideration allows a contextually grounded analysis[95] by taking into account the relevance of collective action in this way integrating the principal-agent approach which has been revealed not to be always effective in

---

insights to public integrity', https://oecdonthelevel.com/2018/03/12/a-nudge-in-the-right-direction-applying-behavioural-insights-to-public-integrity/; Agata Slota, 'The Subtle Science of Nudging Anticorruption', *Palladium*, 9 December 2018; Ruta Mrazauskaite, 'Where Is the Behavioral Insights Revolution in Anticorruption?', in *The Global Anticorruption blog*, 25 January 2019.

[88] Adolf Tobeña, *Cerebro y poder: política, bandidaje y erótica del mando* (La Esfera de los libros, 2008).

[89] Herbert A Simon, 'A Behavioral Model of Rational Choice' (1955) 69(1) *Quarterly Journal of Economics* 99.

[90] Johann Graf Lambsdorff, 'Behavioral and Experimental Economics as a Guidance to Anticorruption', in Danila Serra and Leonard Wantchekon (eds), *New Advances in Experimental Research on Corruption* (2012) 15 *Research in Experimental Economics* 282.

[91] On this point see Alberto Vannucci, 'Three paradigms for the analysis of corruption' (2015) 1(2) *Labour & Law Issues* 10. See also Nieves Zúñiga, 'Behavioural changes against corruption', U4 Anticorruption Resource Centre, U4 Helpdesk Answer 2018/11, 29 July 2018.

[92] On this point see Susan Rose-Ackerman, 'Corruption: greed, culture and the State' (2010) 120 *Yale Law Journal Online* 125, Yale Law & Economics Research Paper No 409; see also Tim Ingold, 'Anthropology contra ethnography' (2017) 7(1) *Journal of Ethnographic Theory* 21.

[93] World Bank, Revised Classification of Fragility and Conflict Situations for World Bank Group Engagement. FCAS is the acronym for 'fragile and conflict-affected states', www.worldbank.org.

[94] Cheyanne Scharbatke-Church and Diana Chigas, *Understanding Social Norms: A Reference Guide for Policy and Practice* (Henry J Lier Institute, 2019) 25.

[95] Ibid, 11.

reducing corruption.[96] In any case, moving towards multi-faceted anticorruption strategies which include social norms is suggested, because ignoring them may undermine the effectiveness of the anticorruption efforts[97] and paradoxically may also exacerbate corruption,[98] depending on the context.

2.3.3. Towards Regulatory Anticorruption

Regulatory anticorruption (RAC) is intended to develop a diagnostic intelligence by limiting the use of troops in the war against corruption, in a certain sense by winning without fighting,[99] to the greatest extent possible. It focuses on rules, rather than on single administrative activities, being an approach which aims at preventing infringements and corruption not only before they occur but before they can be even conceived of, by looking at and working remotely on opportunities for infringements and corruption which are provided by rules, whether already adopted or in course of adoption. In other words, RAC exploits the regulatory perspective – which is comprehensive and realistic[100] – for the purpose of preventing corruption by considering it as regulatory ineffectiveness, as regulation which has failed in achieving its goals. According to RAC, considering corruption realistically via accurate and evidence-based diagnosis is much better than chasing single violations.[101] In fact, in order to implement adequate and effective remedial preventive actions, anticorruption requires a deep understanding of the reasons why some legal systems express more corruption than others or why, in the same legal system, some rules are more frequently occasions for corruption than others.

RAC accepts the CAC incentives/disincentives framework as well as the contribution which comes from behavioural and cognitive insights (BAC), by considering that despite corruption being mostly the result of 'cold' individuals' decisions, it is always important to focus on real people. In any case RAC places

---

[96] Ibid, 12.
[97] Ibid, 21.
[98] Ibid, 22.
[99] On this point is very important the approach expressed by François Jullien, *Traité de l'efficacité* (Editions Grasset & Fasquelle, 1996), English translation *A Treatise on Efficacy. Between Western and Chinese Thinking* (University of Hawaii Press, 2004), esp 16 when he describes the Chinese alternative way of behaving: 'Instead of constructing an ideal Form that we then project on to things, we could try to detect the factors whose configuration is favourable to the task at hand; instead of setting up a goal for our actions, we could allow ourselves to be carried along by the propensity of things'. On this point see also see also Peter N Grabosky, 'Using non-governmental resources to foster regulatory compliance' (1995) 8(4) *Governance: An International Journal of Policy and Administration* 527, 528, where he mentions Lao Tzu, *Tao te ching* (Penguin Books, 1963).
[100] Jean-Bernard Auby, 'Régulations et droit administratif' 232.
[101] Very relevant to this point is the book of Florentin Blanc, *From Chasing Violations to Managing Risks* (Edward Elgar, 2018).

its anticorruption assessment much earlier and works upstream, on the 'genetics' of corruption (by looking at rules as endogenous in the analysis of corruption[102]) instead of downstream, seeking to impede many thousands of specific possible acts of corruption (by looking at administrative procedures). As we will see below (chapter three), the effort to make anticorruption as effective as possible correctly suggests this focus on rules, especially those rules which establish administrative powers and powers of controls.

Regulatory Anticorruption requires specific intelligence expertise, and can be developed at two separate levels.

Firstly, when rules are produced and reformed, in law-making, in rule-making and in legislative/regulatory reforms and maintenance. At this stage, mechanisms to assess the impact of regulation on corruption have been introduced in some legal systems (as we will see below, in chapter three) while a corruptibility assessment would also improve the RAC toolkit (chapter five).

Secondly, when public officers are in charge of implementing and enforcing rules, in regulatory delivery. At this stage, planning controls as well as guidelines and manuals to ensure responsive enforcement, procedural justice and regulatory effectiveness have been ever more frequently adopted, including in order to keep corruption under control (chapter four).

Regulatory anticorruption is characterised by interdisciplinarity,[103] in social sciences and beyond. Law and economics must be integrated in the wider perspective of the social and human sciences, including statistics, psychology, anthropology, and sociology while other scientific and technological expertise may be occasionally involved.

In sum, CAC, BAC and RAC are not alternatives. Rather, RAC works as an integrated strategy, focusing especially on rules and on the whole regulatory framework which delimits the scope of individual and collective behaviour, whether rational or beyond rationality.

2.4. Risks of Anticorruption

Anticorruption is far from a magic wand. The widespread affirmation of anticorruption policies (in the different ways in which they have been introduced at national level) is not exempt from some risks and they have sometimes paradoxically produced adverse consequences.

---

[102] See Johann Graf Lambsdorff, *The Institutional Economics of Corruption and Reform. Theory, Evidence and Policy* (Cambridge University Press, 2007) 58: 'I claim that a sound assessment of the effects of corruption on public welfare remains inconclusive when regulations are considered exogenous to the analysis. This results because corruption and bad regulation are often two sides of the same coin'.

[103] Christel Koop and Martin Lodge, 'What is regulation? An interdisciplinary concept analysis' (2017) 11(1) *Regulation and Governance* 95.

78 *Anticorruption: Strategies and Risks*

Table 2.1 Types of Anticorruption Strategies

Anticorruption	Scope	Time and target
Conventional	Administrative activities	Before infringements and corruption (informed about and targeted on *administrative activities* characterised by risk of corruption)
Behavioural	Behaviour (*as a response to rules and to administrative activities*)	Before infringements and corruption (informed about and targeted on the *behaviour of citizens and firms*)
Regulatory	Rules	Long before infringements and corruption (informed about and targeted also on *rules which have produced more infringements and corruption than others*)

This is clear when talking about the role of anticorruption institutions. In this regard, it has been noted that '(i) a new institution can create yet another layer of ineffective bureaucracy; (ii) its can divert resources, attention and responsibilities from existing control institutions and donor resources from priority areas of reform; (iii) it can invoke jurisdictional conflicts and turf battles with other institutions; and (iv) it can be abused as a tool against political opponents'.[104]

Moreover, while the general purpose of anticorruption policies (preventing corruption) is largely agreed, the concrete design and implementation of anticorruption regulation may catalyse undesirable side-effects: these side-effects should be accurately considered both when regulating and in regulatory delivery using accurate preventive analysis concerning the cultural, social, economic and legal scenario in which anticorruption regulation will be applied.

Inaccurate analysis could prepare the ground for failures. There are indeed many risks which affect conventional anticorruption, such as backfire, anticorruption as a mere appearance of prevention, metastatic bureaucracy, defensive administration and difficulty recruiting honest and competent people in government. Regulatory anticorruption may provide some responses.

---

[104] OECD, *Specialised Anticorruption Institutions. Review of Models* (OECD, 2013) 42. See also Council of Europe, *Anticorruption Services – Good Practices in Europe*, Institutional Arrangements (Council of Europe Publishing, 2004); Patrick Meagher, *Anticorruption Services – A Review of Experience*, IRIS (Center for Institutional Reform and the Informal Sector at the University of Maryland, 2004); Jeremy Pope, *The Need and Role of an Independent Anticorruption Agency*, Working Paper for Transparency International, 1999; Alan Doig, *A Good Idea Gone Wrong? Anticorruption Commissions in the Twenty First Century*, EGPA 2004 Annual Conference, Ljubljana.

2.4.1. Backfire

Equilibrium in legal systems (in the same way as in the market) is 'concerned with present',[105] instantaneous. People, firms and administrations themselves tend to find arrangements continuously in order to protect their own interests, to maintain their advantages or possibly even to increase them: on one hand, this is possible because every law has its loophole; on the other, because opportunism and rent-seeking are unstoppable. While this informal adaptation occurs in real time, most institutional responses come too slowly, and are very often too late.

Let us now apply this reasoning to anticorruption purposes.

When there are political or administrative scandals which bring corruption into the light of day, in most cases politicians (at least in Italy) will propose ever more severe penalties for criminal infringements or administrative breaches. Their intention is to increase deterrence by strengthening the institutional response to illegality. In terms of political communication the strategy can work, the message is very simple and plausible: it can also be received positively by public opinion, alleviating citizens' anxiety in the face of such political or administrative scandals. Unfortunately, political communication is not reality. In fact, economic literature, based on evidence, has long made it clear that increasing the fine without a corresponding increase in the risk of incurring such penalties would produce not fewer infringements, but merely an increase in the size of the bribe necessary to corrupt.[106]

In other words, when regulation is used principally as a form of political communication, and adopted without accurate preventive analysis regarding its possible impact, individual interests may adapt to the new normative framework, and regulatory outcomes can drastically backfire, even exacerbating illegality and corruption.

2.4.2. Perception vs Reality

If secrecy is an aspect of corruption, as a consequence it is no simple matter to be adequately informed about it, nor to consolidate sufficient knowledge to achieve an adequate understanding of corruption processes. Scholars and academics have highlighted the lack of data in this area,[107] and have experienced difficulties in measuring it.[108]

---

[105] Gerald P O'Driscoll Jr and Mario J Rizzo, *The Economics of Time and Ignorance* (Routledge, 2015; 1st edn Basil Blackwell, 1985) 59.

[106] See Anthony Ogus, 'Corruption and regulatory structures' 336.

[107] John A Gardiner, 'Controlling official corruption and fraud: Bureaucratic incentives and disincentives' 40.

[108] Frank Anechiarico and James B Jacobs, *The Pursuit of Absolute Integrity. How Corruption Control Makes Government Ineffective* 14.

80 *Anticorruption: Strategies and Risks*

On the other hand, there is an international public debate which tends to compare countries and legal systems periodically, based on scores mainly of perceived corruption. For instance, the World Bank includes 'control of corruption' as one dimension of governance in the Worldwide Governance Indicators (WGI) project;[109] Transparency International produces a Corruption Perception Index every year, which ranks 180 countries and territories by their perceived levels of public sector corruption according to experts and businesspeople.[110]

Therefore, the already mentioned difficulty in collecting data about corruption goes hand in hand with the habit of referring to corruption perception as the trend indicator of real corruption, in this way contributing to a bias which affects the institutional debate: it risks focusing on corruption perception rather than on corruption reality.

Correspondingly, anticorruption which cannot be based on adequate knowledge about the phenomenon which intends to combat risks to be unavoidably reduced to an appearance of prevention rather than to real prevention.[111]

For this reason, despite the fact that corruption is very difficult to detect and even more difficult to measure in its real dimension,[112] efforts towards mixed methods[113] and operational guidelines[114] for quantitative, accurate and reliable representation of the effective levels of corruption are considered crucial[115] in order to 'fine-tune prevention and repression strategies' and to 'better assess policies that are implemented at national and international level'.[116]

---

[109] 'Control of corruption captures perceptions of the extent to which public power is exercised for private gain, including both petty and grand forms of corruption, as well as "capture" of the state by elites and private interests', https://datacatalog.worldbank.org/control-corruption-percentile-rank.

[110] www.transparency.it/corruption-perceptions-index/.

[111] See James B Jacobs, 'Dilemmas of Corruption Controls', in Cyrille Fijnaut and Leo Huberts (eds), *Corruption, Integrity and Law Enforcement* 287.

[112] On this point, see Danila Serra, 'Empirical determinants of corruption: A sensitive analysis', (2006) in *Public Choice*, 225 and Tudorel Andrei, Bogdan Oancea and Florin Dananau, 'The analysis of corruption in public administration. A quantitative method' (2010) 17(1) *Lex et Scientia* 435.

[113] On this point see Leslie Holmes, *Corruption. A very short introduction* (Oxford University Press, 2015) who indicates, among types of measurements: official statistics, perception surveys and experience-based surveys. Measurement may also consist in tracking surveys. See also Miriam A Golden and Lucio Picci, 'Proposal for a new measure of corruption, illustrated with Italian data (2005) 17 *Economics & Politics* 37.

[114] See United Nations Office on Drugs and Crime, *Manual on Corruption Surveys – Methodological guidelines on the measurement of bribery and other forms of corruption through sample surveys* (2018).

[115] On this point, see the Italian Institute of Statistics, www.istat.it/en/archive/204383: 'For the first time, Istat has introduced a series of questions in its 2015–2016 survey on the Safety of citizens, in order to examine the phenomenon of corruption. It is estimated that 7.9% of households have been directly involved in corrupt events during the course of their lives, such as, requests for money, favours, gifts or other in exchange for services or facilitations of transactions (7% in the past 3 years, 1.2% in the past 12 months)'. See also Alina Mungiu-Pippidi, 'For a New Generation of Objective Indicators in Governance and Corruption Studies' (2016) 22 *European Journal of Criminal Policy Research* 363. See also Daniel Kaufmann, Aart Kraay and Massimo Mastruzzi, *Measuring Corruption: Myths and Realities* (The World Bank, 2006), www1.worldbank.org/publicsector/anticorrupt/corecourse2007/Myths.pdf.

[116] G7 Chair Summary of the High-Level Workshop on Corruption Measurement, 27 October 2017.

2.4.3. Metastatic Bureaucracy

Current anticorruption consists mainly in bureaucratic activities intended to reduce the risk of corruption occurring in certain sensitive conditions, while managing certain procedures or when some public charges are interested: for instance, in public procurement, during inspections, when planning, when declaring a conflict of interests, when establishing a staff rotation and so on.

On the other hand, in the literature anticorruption has been considered to be a specific risk in terms of bureaucracy itself; anticorruption actually produces more bureaucracy ('corruption control and bureaucracy are mutually dependent'[117]), and if bureaucracy is one of the causes of corruption, there could be the paradox that anticorruption may contribute to creating more corruption, in a sort of vicious circle,[118] or even a pathological metastatic process.

This seems to be very clear in public procurement, one of the high-risk areas for corruption. Over the years, this regulation all over the world has increasingly established obligations and checks in order to strengthen transparency and competition as well as to prevent infringements and corruption (the 'bane' of public procurement[119]). In such a significant economic sector and in one of the government activities which is most vulnerable to corruption,[120] the OECD itself has stressed that 'corruption risks are exacerbated by the complexity of the process, the close interaction between public officials and businesses, and the multitude of stakeholders'.[121] However, from a regulatory perspective, such monumental legal framework – which is justified by the need to promote transparency and competition and to impede infringements and corruption – at the end of the day consists in a series of administrative burdens which operate fatally as further opportunities for infringement and corruption.[122]

In other words, there may be a deep contradiction (or at least a risk which should be specifically considered and managed) in the idea that to combat corruption – a consequence of bureaucracy – additional bureaucracy is needed.

---

[117] Frank Anechiarico, 'Law Enforcement or a Community-Oriented Strategy Toward Corruption Control', in Cyrille Fijnaut and Leo Huberts (eds), *Corruption, Integrity and Law Enforcement* 299.

[118] Frank Anechiarico and James B Jacobs, *The Pursuit of Absolute Integrity. How Corruption Control Makes Government Ineffective* 204.

[119] OECD, *Preventing Corruption in Public Procurement* (OECD, 2016) 6.

[120] On this topic see Gabriella Margherita Racca, Christopher Yukins (eds), *Integrity and Efficiency in Sustainable Public Contracts. Balancing Corruption Concerns in Public Procurement Internationally* (Bruylant, 2014) and Gabriella M Racca and Christopher R Yukins (eds), *Joint Public Procurement and Innovation Lessons Across Borders* (Bruylant, 2019).

[121] OECD, *Preventing Corruption in Public Procurement* (OECD, 2016) 6.

[122] See Tom Vander Beken and Annelies Balcaen, 'Crime Opportunities Provided by Legislation in Market Sectors: Mobile Phones, Waste Disposal, Banking, Pharmaceuticals' (2006) 12(3–4) *European Journal on Criminal Policy and Research* 299, 320: 'A last side effect relates to legislation that tries to regulate too much, which might cause the ineffectiveness of the law'.

2.4.4. Defensive Administration

Where adopted, anticorruption policies and regulation have introduced various kinds of increasingly stringent procedural constraints and obligations aiming at ensuring that public officers will behave honestly and that transactions between them and citizens/firms proceed according to the law.

On the other hand, too strict and detailed regulation does not always produce desirable results, rather it sometimes promotes and contributes to possible defensive bureaucratic responses.[123] Let us consider an anticorruption public official, operating anywhere in an Italian public administration as 'anticorruption officer' (*responsabile della prevenzione della corruzione*). He/she is compelled by a number of rules, among which is a rule establishing that in cases of corruption occurring in his/her administration, he/she will be considered triply responsible (as a manager, for liability related to damages to the Treasury, and to the reputation of the Italian administration) unless he/she gives proof of proper and full compliance with rules governing his/her tasks.[124]

At a first glance, this regulatory precision seems to make obligations stronger and more severe by expressly requiring what one has to do (for instance, developing coordination activities, promoting the adoption of codes of conduct, performing a certain number of checks, ensuring oversight and surveillance over anticorruption plans and so on).

In reality, even in the presence of strict regulatory provisions, it is always possible for public officers to behave in ways that benefit private interests, and for corruption to occur without being detected. Moreover, honest public officers may be disincentivised from taking good decisions according to the public interest, if it means deviating from extremely detailed normative schemes. They would definitely prefer to adopt decisions which were formally consistent with rules because this may preserve them from undesirable consequences, expressed in terms of different responsibility regimes.[125] In so doing, regulation is failing because it

---

[123] On defensive decision-making see Florian Artinger, Sabrina Artinger and Gerd Gigerenzer, 'C. Y. A.: frequency and causes of defensive decisions in public administration' (2018) *Business Research* 10: defensive decisions 'occur when professionals opt for the second-best option rather than (what they believe to be) the best option for their organization or client in order to protect themselves from potential negative consequences in the future'. See also Blake E Ashforth and Raymond T Lee, 'Defensive behavior in organizations. A preliminary model' (1990) 43(7) *Human Relations* 621.

[124] On this point see the Italian Anticorruption Law, Legge 6 novembre 2012, no 190, *Disposizioni per la prevenzione e la repressione della corruzione e dell'illegalità nella pubblica amministrazione*, art 1.12.

[125] Florian Artinger, Sabrina Artinger and Gerd Gigerenzer, 'C. Y. A.: frequency and causes of defensive decisions in public administration' 11: 'In organizations where failures are wrongly attributed to the decision maker, managers feel threatened and in need of protecting themselves'. For this reason public officers in some legal system, as in Italy, use to stipulate professional insurances. Italian Court of Auditors has estimated that in public works, the effects of defensive administration in a key sector for the economy are huge. See Stefano Battini and Francesco Decarolis, 'L'amministrazione si difende' (2019) 1 *Rivista Trimestrale di Diritto Pubblico* 293.

prescribes exactly what the public officer must do in order to avoid established penalties, independently from the substantial fact that this will be really useful to the purpose of reducing corruption. It is reasonable to believe that the prevalent work of anticorruption officers will be to pre-establish proof of their compliance, much more than working for effective anticorruption.

Rules as guided paths: making not the right thing but exactly what is established will ensure immunity for public officers against any possible complaint, in a way very similar to the case of compliance programmes for companies (chapter one). In some legal systems more than in others, public officers are incentivised to adopt such a defensive approach. Whether it is due to heavy responsibility regimes, to weak administrative cultures, to poor integrity or to all these things together is not so important; it is important to prevent the future of anticorruption from being 'not less corruption, but more bureaucracy'.[126]

2.4.5. Difficulty in Recruitment of Honest and Expert People

Studies and research on the topic of corruption have highlighted that where anticorruption is too strict, it is more difficult to recruit capable, honest and expert people in government.[127] This insight is especially important not only to progress in the understanding of the best way to prevent corruption but also to avoid the undesirable side-effect of a 'skills drain' from institutions as well as of poor integrity in government.

However, even though it should lead to a deep reconsideration of the logic of anticorruption, this insight has been largely underestimated. What is the real problem? In other words, what is the reason why honest and expert people would prefer to operate without overly strict anticorruption regulation if one rules out the possibility that they want to infringe and to make illicit profit?

A first possible response is that trust is indispensable to cooperation, both in personal life and in institutional relationships. Anticorruption regulation (as with any kind of strict regulation) means that in this field there is no (or there cannot be) any trust. In fact, rules are considered to be a surrogate for trust:[128] when rules are, trust shall not be.[129]

---

[126] Frank Anechiarico, 'Law Enforcement or a Community-Oriented Strategy Toward Corruption Control', in Cyrille Fijnaut and Leo Huberts (eds), *Corruption, Integrity and Law Enforcement* 300.

[127] James B Jacobs, 'Dilemmas of Corruption Controls', in Cyrille Fijnaut and Leo Huberts (eds), 'Corruption, Integrity and Law Enforcement' 285. On this point, see also Susan Rose-Ackerman, *Corruption and Government: Causes, Consequences and Reform* 68; Susan Rose-Ackerman, 'Corruption and conflicts of interest', in Jean-Bernard Auby, Emmanuel Breen and Thomas Perroud (eds), *Corruption and Conflicts of interest. A comparative Law Approach* 5. See, finally, Richard E Messick, 'Policy consideration when drafting conflict of interest legislation', in Jean-Bernard Auby, Emmanuel Breen and Thomas Perroud (eds), *Corruption and Conflicts of interest. A comparative Law Approach* 123.

[128] Mark E Warren, *Democracy and Trust* (Cambridge University Press, 1999) 266.

[129] Ibid, 265.

However, honest and expert people in the civil service or experts theoretically available for government, are strongly motivated by trust in their *expertise, benevolence* and *integrity*[130] and by social recognition of their reliability. In fact, the sentiment of trust is characterised by the presence 'of risk, uncertainty, vulnerability and the need for interdependency with another person'[131] while the structure of incentives for professional or appointed bureaucrats is not to please the voters but to focus on long-term goals and on professional prestige.[132]

Literature has highlighted that mechanisms for growing trust is counter-intuitive, because trust is not a material resource (subject to consumption): it *grows with use and is reduced by disuse.*[133] For this reason, the more that strict anticorruption regulation constitutes the context in which public officers must operate, the less trust there can be and the more difficult it is to recruit honest and competent people in government or to have conditions where they can work comfortably.

2.5. Feasible Objectives of Anticorruption

If corruption is an unavoidable phenomenon, and if anticorruption itself is not without risks, scholars and academics have therefore argued that governments should in any case accept a certain amount of corruption[134] rather than the institutional attempt to eradicate corruption, which is not only impossible to achieve[135] but also dangerous because 'anticorruption policy should never aim to achieve complete rectitude'.[136]

On the other hand, there is an optimal amount of corruption for each legal system directly connected with the capacity of their controls, both in terms of quantity and of quality:[137] a low capacity of control implies the need to accept a higher rate of corruption. If 'the optimal level of corruption is not zero'[138] and controls oriented to anticorruption are expensive,[139] so could it be necessary

---

[130] F David Schoorman, Roger C Mayer and James H Davis, 'An Integrative Model of Organizational Trust: Past, Present and Future' (2007) 32(2) *Academy of Management Review* 345.

[131] David Schoorman, Roger C Mayer and James H Davis, 'An Integrative Model of Organizational Trust' 709–34; Niklas Luhmann, *Trust and Power* (Polity Press, 2017; 1st German edn 1973) 50.

[132] On the different structure of incentives for bureaucrats and politicians, see Alberto Alesina and Guido Tabellini, 'Bureaucrats or Politicians? Part I: A Single Policy Task' (2007) 97 *American Economic Review* 169 and Alberto Alesina and Guido Tabellini, 'Bureaucrats or Politicians? Part II: Multiple Policy Tasks' (2008) 92 *Journal of Public Economics*, 426.

[133] On this point see, Albert O Hirschman, 'Against Parsimony: Three Easy Ways of Complicating Some Categories of Economic Discourse' (1984) 74(2) *American Economic Review*; Papers and Proceedings of the Ninety-Sixth Annual Meeting of the American Economic Association (May, 1984) 93.

[134] Robert Klitgaard, *Controlling Corruption* 27.

[135] Anthony Ogus, 'Corruption and regulatory structures' 342.

[136] Susan Rose Ackerman, *Corruption and Government: Causes, Consequences and Reform* 68.

[137] Robert Klitgaard, *Controlling Corruption* 27.

[138] Ibid, 24.

[139] Frank Anechiarico and James B Jacobs, *The Pursuit of Absolute Integrity. How Corruption Control Makes Government Ineffective*.

to decide the extent to which we should combat corruption by identifying 'the optimal amount of corruption' (see below, chapter four, section 4.2.4).

Eradicating corruption cannot be the objective of anticorruption. What then should be the set of feasible goals of institutional activities intended to prevent corruption?

There is no doubt that anticorruption regulation has a strong expressive function in the sense that it affirms combating corruption as a value. However, as with any kind of regulation, anticorruption regulation may also be counterproductive; it is therefore necessary to effectively achieve convincing anticorruption outcomes.

For this reason, anticorruption should aim to create specific, realistic and sustainable goals[140] which should involve all actors on the scene (citizens, firms, administrations), but – from the regulatory perspective – first and foremost, regulators at any level of government (European, national parliaments and governments, independent authorities, sub-national regulatory entities and so on).

The first goal is *reducing corruption* instead of eliminating it, by making anticorruption as effective and real as possible, aiming to keep corruption under control, as far as possible. This apparently less severe approach will imply more intelligent anticorruption by always considering that anticorruption itself can produce undesirable and counterproductive effects.

The second goal is *avoiding bureaucracy and restoring trust*, by regulating only if indispensable and controlling only when necessary. The increased widespread and enormous power of bureaucracy[141] developed during the last century is strictly related to regulatory inflation processes and to a deep crisis of public trust. In other words, the more that social and economic sectors have been regulated and the more that public officers have had occasions of managing bureaucratic incentives and disincentives, the more rapidly corruption has become systemic and reduced the possibility of public trust and cooperation.

The third goal is *reducing the number of rules* which stimulate illicit appetites; or, if you prefer, 'leaving the larder empty': in the same way as during a diet – when it is better for food not to be in the larder – each rule which has contributed to making public officers potential partners of illicit and corrupt economic transactions should

---

[140] Johann Graf Lambsdorff, 'Behavioral and Experimental Economics as a Guidance to Anticorruption' 293: 'Anticorruption has been a moral crusade, highly successful in initiating legal reform at the global level. But we are at risk of falling into some of the traps that can be identified in experimental ethics. These risk arise when reform assumes excessive levels of individual rationality that are in contrast to us morally fallible creatures'.

[141] In a historical perspective, see James Q Wilson, 'The rise of the bureaucratic State' (1975) 41 *Public Interest*; online (2020) 43 *National Affairs*. See Dwight Waldo, *The Administrative State. A Study of the Political Theory of American Public Administration* (The Ronald Press Company, 1948). See also Gary Lawson, 'The Rise and Rise of the Administrative State' (1994) 107(6) *Harvard Law Review* 1231–54. See finally Edward L Rubin, 'Bureaucratic Oppression: its Causes and Cures' (2012) 90(2) *Washington University Law Review* 291, 297: 'The increasing power and extent of the bureaucracy also created serious potential for the mistreatment of the individuals who were subject to, and dependent on, this new mode of governance'.

86 *Anticorruption: Strategies and Risks*

be reconsidered in terms of its Actuality, Necessity and Proportionality in protecting some kind of public interest or in preventing some kind of risk, according to consolidated simplification criteria (chapter three). If the 'ANP test' does not produce clear indications for maintaining them, rules, connected procedures and related administrative powers are eligible for cutting or reform.

In short, these feasible objectives require anticorruption to be looked at as if it were upside down: while current conventional anticorruption focuses mainly on infringements, regulatory anticorruption should also enhance compliance with rules and make it more simple and as convenient as possible; while current conventional anticorruption is informed by distrust in citizens, firms and public officers, regulatory anticorruption should indirectly promote trust and make it possible for a greater number of honest and competent people to be available for government; while current conventional anticorruption concentrates on a countless number of possible violations, regulatory anticorruption should start considering links between evidence of corruption and its 'genetics', by looking mainly at rules.

Table 2.2 Regulatory Anticorruption: Risks and Objectives

ANTICORRUPTION		INSTITUTIONAL RESPONSES (REGULATORY ANTICORRUPTION)
RISKS OF CONVENTIONAL ANTICORRUPTION	Backfire	Good quality regulation and effectiveness of rules
	Perception vs reality	Objective indicators for corruption
	Metastatic bureaucracy	Reducing administrative burdens and bureaucracy
	Defensive administration	Clear mandate and objectives
	Difficulty in recruitment of competent and honest people in government	Restoring trust policies
FEASIBLE OBJECTIVES OF REGULATORY ANTICORRUPTION	Reducing corruption	Realistic anti-corruption
	Reducing bureaucracy and promoting trust	Regulating only if indispensable, controlling only if necessary (and responsively)
	Reducing the number of rules	Maintenance of the regulatory stock based on the Actuality/Necessity/Proportionality (ANP) test

3

Anticorruption: Rules

(Can Good Rules Reduce Opportunities for Corruption?)

3.1. As with Corruption, Anticorruption Starts from Rules

Regulation used to be considered the first, and probably most powerful tool for preventing and combating corruption: in other words, adopting rules (especially rules which provide more severe sanctions) is perceived by governments and public opinion as the proper way to react when a corruption scandal occurs.

Many institutional reforms all over the world can be regarded as responses to serious corruption incidents. In particular, corruption has been defined 'as a justification for financial regulation',[1] when rules are counter-measures for 'defects in the governance of financial regulation [which] allowed regulators to deviate from the public interest'.[2] In the same way, corruption represents the background of all legislation in the field of public procurements.[3] Moreover, civil service regulation is also traditionally a response to the need to prevent corruption, even though there are bureaucracies which seem to be less corruptible than others,[4] from the

---

[1] See Imad A Moosa, 'Good Regulation, Bad Regulation: The Anatomy of Financial Regulation and Financial Regulation as a Response to Corruption and Fraud' (2016) *Contemporary Issues in the Post-Crisis Regulatory Landscape* 49. As already mentioned (ch 2.1), at the end of the nineteenth century, an 'enormous scandal' characterised central banking in Italy (the *Banca Romana* scandal) and a new Banking Law was adopted; on this point see Vera Zamagni, *The Economic History of Italy 1860–1990. Recovery After Decline* (Clarendon Press, 1993) 143.
[2] Ross Levine, 'The Governance of Financial Regulation: Reform Lessons from the Recent Crisis' (2012) 12(1) *International Review of Finance* 39.
[3] On this point, Tina Søreide, *Corruption in public procurement. Causes, consequences and cures*, Michelsen Institute Report, 2002. See also OECD, *Preventing Corruption in Public Procurement* (2016); Sope Williams-Elegbe, *Fighting Corruption in Public Procurement: A Comparative Analysis of Disqualification or Debarment measures* (Hart Publishing, 2012). More in general, on the topic, see Jean Tirole and Jean-Jacques Laffont, *A Theory of Incentives in Procurement and Regulation* (MIT Press, 1993).
[4] On this point, Susan Rose-Ackerman, 'Which Bureaucracies are Less Corruptible?', in Arnold J Heidenheimer, Michael Johnston, Victor T Levine (eds), *Political Corruption. A Handbook* (Transaction Publishers, third printing 1993, first printing 1989) 803; Robert Klitgaard, *Cleaning Up and Invigorating the Civil Service* (World Bank Operations Evaluation Department, November 1996).

points of view both of independence[5] and of incentive payments.[6] Finally, anticorruption legislation constitutes the relatively more recent institutional answer to the increasing sensitiveness of the public to corruption incidents, even though such legislation has been adopted by countries according to specific obligations established at international level, with special regard to the United Nations Convention against Corruption (see above, chapter two): in this framework there is legislation which establishes, for instance, whistleblower protection, transparency, staff rotation and other measures already mentioned (chapter two section 2.2).

3.1.1. No Rules, No Corruption?

On the other hand, paradoxically, regulation must take great responsibility in producing opportunities for corrupt transactions.

The idea is not new and affects law structurally.

It could suffice, in this regard, to remember the contribution of Saint Paul in his Letter to the Romans, where he expounded his doctrine on law and sin: the law, even though 'good' in itself,[7] in a certain way incites sin by giving the opportunity to infringe,[8] because 'where there is no law, there also is no violation'.[9] The connection between law and sin is so strict that Saint Paul wrote 'the Law came in so that the transgression would increase'.[10] Although indispensable, law is considered, at the same time, to be the logical premise of sin: 'in other words, the Law served as a guide to define sin, for if we did not know what sin was, how could we choose?'.[11]

In his *Annals*, Tacitus expressed another aspect of the same perspective when he wrote '*plurimae leges corruptissima republica*':[12] in this regard, it has been observed that 'the point is not that the laws themselves were bad in every case but that there was need for an increasingly large number of them …; and the number of laws proverbially reflected the extent of corruption in society's *mores*'.[13]

---

[5] See Frank Anechiarico and James B Jacobs, *The Pursuit of Absolute Integrity. How Corruption Control Makes Government Ineffective* (University of Chicago Press, 1996) 203.

[6] See Pranab Bardhan, 'Corruption and Development: A Review of Issues' (1997) XXXV (September) *Journal of Economic Literature* 1339.

[7] Saint Paul, Letter to the Romans, ch 7: '7. What shall we say then? Is the Law sin? May it never be! On the contrary, I would not have come to know sin except through the Law; for I would not have known about coveting if the Law had not said, "You shall not covet". 8. But sin, taking opportunity through the commandment, produced in me coveting of every kind; for apart from the Law sin is dead. 9. I was once alive apart from the Law; but when the commandment came, sin became alive and I died.'

[8] Ibid, 4, 15; see also 1 Letter to the Corinthians, ch 15, 56. On this point, see Orello Cone, *The Pauline Doctrine of Sin* (1898) 2(2) *American Journal of Theology* 241.

[9] Ibid.

[10] Ibid, 5, 20.

[11] Rebecca Denova, 'Paul the apostle', in *The Ancient History Encyclopedia*, December 2013.

[12] Tacitus, *Annales*, Book 3, 27. See also Shreyaa Bhatt, 'Useful Vices: Tacitus's Critique of Corruption' (2017) 50(3) *Arethusa* 311.

[13] *The Annals of Tacitus*, Book 3, edited with a commentary of AJ Woodman, RH Martin (Cambridge University Press, 2004) 255.

Even though the idea is far from a new one, however, it has recently been renewed by scholars who have focused on (and prepared the ground for) a real regulatory approach to corruption which, starting from the idea (and the evidence) that regulation has an important and causal effect on corruption:[14] as we will see, this may help in reshaping anticorruption policies and in developing a more effective prevention toolkit.

A first point is that policy makers and regulators contribute to corruption by creating rent opportunities, whether intentionally or not.[15] Rent-seeking (the attempt to profit from policies and rules) and rent-extraction (the activity necessary to realise rent) would be simply impossible without rent-creation.[16]

Intentional rent-creation may be the consequence of *political* or 'legislative' corruption,[17] when politicians in the legislative are lobbied and engage in corruption by taking bribes to favour a certain group of interests. This was the case of the *MoSE* (Italian for Moses) scandal, concerning the major public works project to protect the historical city of Venice from the threat of devastating high tides. The scandal has been adopted as a prototype of the so-called '*corruzione a norma di legge*'[18] (corruption going by the book), the method for achieving extra income by corrupting legislation rather than infringing it.[19]

Maybe unintentional (or, better, unpredictable) rent-creation[20] is the basis of the most part of administrative corruption, when legislators and regulators have not adequately considered in the legislative/regulatory process (or even, when they have accepted) that they are creating rent opportunities which will result in rent-seeking, rent-extraction and rent-sharing at the street-level government. This normally happens when regulation establishes strict and expensive obligations, as in matters of hazardous waste treatment,[21] subsidy programmes, controls, taxes

---

[14] George RG Clarke, 'Does over-regulation lead to corruption? Evidence from a multi-country survey' (2014) 14(1) *Southwestern Business Administration Journal* 28.

[15] Roger D Congleton, 'The nature of rent seeking', in Roger D Congleton and Arye L Hillman (eds), *Companion to the Political Economy of Rent Seeking* (Edward Elgar, 2015) 4: 'The existence of rent-seeking activities and losses are thus relevant for the study of policy making and public economics, and many other areas of social science'.

[16] Roger D Congleton, 'The Political Economy of Rent Creation and Rent Extraction', in Roger D Congleton, Bernard Grofman, and Stefan Voigt (eds) *The Oxford Handbook of Public Choice*, Vol 1.

[17] Mark Philp, 'Defining Political corruption' (1997) XLV *Political studies*, 436; see also Jeremy Pope, 'Parliament and Anticorruption legislation', in Rick Stapenhurst, Niall Johnston, Riccardo Pelizzo (eds), *The role of Parliament in curbing corruption* (WBI Development Studies; 2006) and Barry M Mitnick, 'Capturing "Capture": Definition and Mechanisms', in David Levi-Faur (ed), *Handbook on the Politics of Regulation* (Edward Elgar, 2011) 34.

[18] Giorgio Barbieri and Francesco Giavazzi, *Corruzione a norma di legge. La lobby delle grandi opere che affonda l'Italia* (Rizzoli, 2014).

[19] In this case, corruption was carried out by providing directly via legislation the choice of enterprise to be in charge of public procurement (*Consorzio Venezia Nuova*).

[20] Fred S McChesney, 'Rent Extraction and Rent Creation in the Economic Theory of Regulation' (1987) 16(1) *Journal of Legal Studies* 101: 'Finally, "government" itself has come to be treated, not as a unit, but as a complicated network of individuals, each with an incentive to maximize his own interest'.

[21] See, for this example, Tom Vander Beken and Annelies Balcaen, 'Crime Opportunities Provided by Legislation in Market Sectors: Mobile Phones, Waste Disposal, Banking, Pharmaceuticals' (2006) 12(3-4) *European Journal on Criminal Policy and Research* 299, 306.

or whenever regulation determines a way to obtain gains or to avoid losses at the administrative level.

In this regard, corruption can be considered a consequence of regulation, an always possible side-effect which should be taken into account by regulators especially when they establish and regulate sensitive administrative powers.

In fact, regulation can fail in the sense that it may be 'counterproductive' because 'regulatory initiatives may defeat themselves or may otherwise inflict collateral damage'.[22] Moreover, 'bad' or non-effective regulation may induce corruption as a necessary response.[23] Finally, regulation very often provides opportunities for direct contacts between the Agent (public officers in any kind of agencies and public bodies) and the Client (citizens or enterprises), opportunities which constitute, at the same time, the precondition and the concrete occasions for corruption, as we have already seen (chapter one section 1.3). Corruption, in fact, is strictly linked with 'regulatory structures', regulatory procedures[24] and bad regulatory enforcement: the more regulation, the more opportunities for contact (and transactions), the more possible violations and corruption.[25]

This is true for administrative (or petty) corruption but also for political (or grand) corruption, at parliamentary level as well as in regulation adopted by governments and regulatory agencies, where the danger of regulatory capture is always present.

3.1.2. Rules, their Market and their Profit

In other words, the idea that *corruption starts from rules* means that infringements, extortion, bribes and all kinds of illicit behaviour presuppose rules which impose obligations, establish incentives and regulate administrative activities.

Even though corruption is a consequence of legal systems, nobody would argue that legal systems should be eliminated in order to eradicate corruption. Rather, if illicit and corrupt transactions are oriented to achieve extra-income, it would be important to understand the way in which rules produce opportunities for rent-seeking and, in this sense, prepare and facilitate corruption,[26] in a given context and in certain conditions: academics underlined this point even by insisting that 'program elimination is sometimes better than more subtle reform strategies'.[27]

---

[22] See Peter Grabosky, 'Counterproductive regulation' (1995) 23 *International Journal of the Sociology of Law* 347.

[23] See Anthony Ogus, 'Corruption and regulatory structures' (2004) 26(July–October) *Law & Policy* 330–31.

[24] Ibid, 329.

[25] See Vito Tanzi, *Corruption Around the World: Causes, Consequences, Scope, and Cures* (1998) 45(4) *IMF Staff Papers*.

[26] See Donatella Della Porta and Alberto Vannucci, *The hidden order of corruption. An institutional approach* (Ashgate Publishing, 2012) 58.

[27] Susan Rose-Ackerman, *Corruption and Government: Causes, Consequences and Reform* (Cambridge University Press, 1999) 39.

A confirmation that corruption starts from rules comes indirectly from the existence of a real 'market'[28] of legislation so that while 'regulation might lead to corruption ... corruption might lead to more regulation':[29] interest groups, in fact, lobby legislators and regulators in order to obtain (sometimes 'buy') favourable rules just because rules represent tools for their own profit.

Extra-income can be achieved via rules in three different ways: breaching a duty in order to *avoid a cost* (as in the case for fiscal evasion); obtaining *a benefit which is not due* (eg a subsidy received without entitlement); *obtaining a regulation which favours a certain interest*. In all these cases, a rule, ie a specific regulatory provision, is at the core. Alongside these three ways, rent-seeking is also related to creative compliance (or creative adaptation), facilitated by the exponential growth of legislation.[30]

If rules could be used as a tool to make profit, regulators and public officers must be conscious of this possibility.[31] As a consequence, rules which impose duties and establish benefits should be adopted with special caution and monitored in their application at administrative level; regulation which favours specific interests should be traceable and transparent; creative compliance should be predicted, as far as possible, thanks to specific consultations and prognostic evaluation; finally, anticorruption measures should be regulated and monitored in order to check their concrete functioning and effectiveness.[32]

If regulation leads to corruption and corruption leads to more regulation, creating a vicious circle, the other side of the coin is that good quality regulation could express a strong potential as a tool to combat and prevent corruption. In this light, according to the principles of subsidiarity and proportionality,[33] good quality regulation can help in reversing the direction of the circle and, in so doing, can contribute to: limiting the number of rules (and taking under control

---

[28] On this point see Marcur Olson, *The logic of collective action. Public goods and the theory of groups* (Harvard University Press, 1965) 144: 'When a large firm is interested in legislation or administrative regulations of unique importance to itself, there is little doubt that it will act in its interest ...' and 44. See also George J Stigler, 'Economic Competition and Political Competition' (1972) 13 *Public Choice* 91. See finally Francesco Lagona and Fabio Padovano, 'The Political Legislation Cycle' (2008) 134 *Public Choice* 201 and Francesco Lagona, Fabio Padovano and Monica Auteri, 'Il ciclo politico-legislativo italiano dal 1948 ad oggi' (2018) 199/200 *Studi parlamentari e di politica costituzionale* 57.

[29] George RG Clarke, 'Does over-regulation lead to corruption? Evidence from a multi-country survey' 29.

[30] On this point, see Svein Eng, *Legislative inflation and the quality of law*, in Luc J Wintgens (ed), *Legisprudence* (Hart Publishing, 2002) 65–66 et seq.

[31] See Bernardo G Mattarella, *La trappola delle leggi* (Il Mulino, 2015) 67, where he talks about *disobbedienza incentivata* ('incentivised non-compliance').

[32] On this point, see Nicoletta Rangone, 'A behavioural approach to administrative corruption prevention', in Agustí Cerillo-I-Martinez and Juli Ponce (eds), *Preventing Corruption and Promoting good Government and Public Integrity* (Bruylant, 2017) 70: 'while such measures are widely recognised as crucial corruption prevention tools, their effectiveness is strictly related to the juridical regime adopted'.

[33] Art 5 of the Treaty on European Union.

legislative inflation), by minimising opportunities for corruption; reducing opportunistic use of regulation, creative compliance and non-compliance, by making full compliance definitely more convenient; establishing mechanisms in order to strengthen (where and when necessary) effectiveness of controls and sanctions as well as of any other traditional anticorruption tool. In other words, the 'vicious circle' between excessive regulation and corruption[34] needs to be managed.[35]

The regulatory perspective, indeed, enhances anticorruption policies, developing and widening their potential: alongside conventional anticorruption tools, prevention of infringements and corruption needs (in fact) also early diagnosis of dangerous connections between interests and rules. Regulatory anticorruption holds together different elements, combining all aspects of regulation and regulatory delivery, working as a single and integrated framework for anticorruption policies[36] because if we agree with the idea that corruption starts from (or at least is strictly related to) rules, as a consequence so should anticorruption.

3.2. Managing Rules, Combating Corruption

The current 'crisis of confidence'[37] in regulation is a general phenomenon, shared by different legal systems but more serious in those countries affected by widespread systemic corruption. However, academics agree that corruption is many times 'propitiated by the fact that the public regulation ... [is] too cumbersome to comply with or ... applied in opaque and discretional manners, and, therefore, this makes it convenient for some regulated actors and public officials to take advantage for themselves and avoid compliance'.[38]

---

[34] Johann Graf Lambsdorff, *The Institutional Economics of Corruption and Reform: Theory, Evidence, and Policy* (Cambridge University Press, 2008, 60: 'A vicious circle can exist whereby inefficient regulation leads to corruption, which in turn cultivates the further spread of troublesome regulation so as to enhance administrative power and the opportunity to exact further payoffs'; see also 61: 'Considering this vicious circle a welfare analysis of corruption must incorporate the investigation of institutions and regulation and must not consider them exogenous to the analysis'.

[35] On this point, Frank Anechiarico and James B Jacobs, *The Pursuit of Absolute Integrity. How Corruption Control Makes Government Ineffective*, 173: 'in many circumstances, red tape is a response to corruption and an attempt to control it. And yet the very complexities and time-consuming factors introduced by a red-tape control system invite enterprising people to find or bore shortcuts'.

[36] See Adam Graycar and Tim Prenzler, *Understanding and Preventing Corruption* (Palgrave Macmillan, 2013).

[37] See Maria De Benedetto, Nicoletta Rangone and Nicola Lupo (eds) *The Crisis of Confidence in Legislation* (Nomos/Hart Publishing, 2020); see also Cary Coglianese, *Regulatory Breakdown: The Crisis of Confidence in U.S. Regulation* (University of Pennsylvania Press, 2012).

[38] R Villareal, *Regulatory quality improvement for preventing corruption in public administration: a capacity building perspective*, Expert Group Meeting on Countering Corruption in the Public Sector, held on 25–28 June 2012 in New York, as part of the Public Service Forum 2012 organised by the Public Administration Capacity Branch (PACB), Division for Public Administration and Development Management (DPADM), United Nations Department of Economic and Social Affairs (UNDESA), 26.

In this context, anticorruption needs to be designed as a 'comprehensive strategy' which should include a number of built-in tools:[39] anyway, preventing corruption implies early detection of infringements, thanks to traditional anticorruption tools (such as for whistle blowers, transparency and so on), but also a still earlier detection of rent-seeking offered by regulation. To give an example, transparency over several concrete deliberations regarding subsidies is important from an anticorruption perspective but, inevitably, comes much later than the rule which has established subsidy criteria and procedures: because this rule creates opportunities for rent, early anticorruption evaluation is needed.

This is the reason why 'managing rules' could mean 'combating corruption', both when managing rules has to be intended as adequate evaluation in law-making and rule-making processes (before the adoption) or evaluation, revision, abrogation or reform (after the adoption). In other words, ex-ante as well as ex-post evaluation of legislation (and regulation) can determine not only the quality of regulation policies but also of anticorruption strategies themselves: by following the zero-option approach (the less regulation, the smaller the scope of corruption); by resorting to regulatory quality improvements, in order to prevent side-effects of regulation;[40] by designing appropriate and sustainable enforcement (avoiding 'too much law, too little enforcement'[41]); by monitoring the impacts of regulation in order to limit corruption; by cutting obsolete legislation or by consolidating scattered rules.

Therefore, if the regulatory approach to corruption requires effective rules (rules which achieve objectives, solve problems and avoid as far as possible regulatory failures) and if legislation (and regulation) should be strongly oriented towards being effective,[42] anticorruption policies presuppose *maintenance of rules*.[43] Alongside law-making, law-maintenance demands that governments implement specific activities not only to produce but also to manage the stock

---

[39] See Susan Rose-Ackerman, *Corruption and Government: Causes, Consequences and Reform* 6 and John A Gardiner and Theodore R Lyman, 'The logic of corruption control', in Arnold J Heidenheimer, Michael Johnston and Victor T Levine (eds), *Political Corruption. A Handbook* 827.

[40] R Villareal, *Regulatory quality improvement for preventing corruption in public administration: a capacity building perspective* 3: 'corruption is propitiated in many cases because the public regulation applicable on many subjects by the public administration (from regulations on civil and property registries, to regulations on public procurement and financing of political parties and campaigns, passing through regulations for construction, imports and exports, tax administration, business licenses, and many more) are too costly to comply with and, thus, this opens room for some regulated actors and public officials to engage in corruption as an alternative to the application of the corresponding penalties for non-compliance with these public regulations'.

[41] Michael Pinto-Duschinsky, 'Financing Policies: a Global View' (2002) 13(4) *Journal of Democracy* 80.

[42] Anthony Ogus, *Regulation. Legal Form and Economic Theory* (Hart Publishing, 2004) 90. See also, Jean-Bernard Auby and Thomas Perroud (eds), *Regulatory Impact Assessment/La evaluación de impacto regulatorio*, (Global Law Press/Inap, 2013).

[43] On this topic see Maria De Benedetto, 'Maintenance of Rules', in Ulrich Karpen and Helen Xantachi (eds), *Legislation and Legisprudence in Europe. A Comprehensive Guide for scholars and practitioners* (Hart Publishing, 2017) 215.

as well as the flow of regulation,[44] identifying unintended and unexpected consequences[45] of rules and, among them, opportunities for corruption.

In this sense, widespread maintenance activities can represent a driver for anticorruption, by contributing to making law 'capable of leading to efficacy of regulation'.[46]

Moreover, there are some compelling arguments in favour of the 'managing rules' perspective, which moves directly from the regulatory approach to anticorruption.

First of all, working on rules gets there first, allowing detection not of corruption incidents but of corruption opportunities, at a very early stage. This aims to impede, from the beginning, a number of infringements and corrupt transactions.

Second, the regulatory approach is cheaper because it implies a very focused, sustainable and expert work 'in the open' on a limited number of rules (schemes for behaviour) instead of chasing several concrete infringements (behaviours) performed 'in the dark' whose detection needs huge police forces and inspection bodies.[47]

Third, the regulatory approach aims to integrate into a system a number of anticorruption tools along the entire chain of regulation, from law-making and rule-making to regulatory delivery (for instance by strengthening effectiveness of controls).

As a consequence, the regulatory approach to corruption considers maintenance of rules as a very relevant aspect of a broad anticorruption strategy. Managing rules should be directed both to the regulatory stock and the regulatory flow.

From an anticorruption perspective, the *regulatory stock* can be managed through simplification (reducing the number of rules, their costs and time necessary to comply with) and by providing advocacy powers to national anticorruption bodies. The *regulatory flow* can be managed with quality of regulation tools (also oriented to evaluate ex ante the risk of infringements and corruption incidents connected to a specific rule in course of adoption) and through the tracing of interests in legislation (making transparent who pays for and who benefits from each rule).

---

[44] APEC_OECD, *Co-operative initiative on Regulatory Reform*, Symposium on Structural reform and Capacity Building, 2005, 29. See also, OECD, Report *From intervention to regulatory Governance* (OECD, 2002).

[45] European Commission, *Strengthening the foundations of Smart Regulation – improving evaluation*, COM (2013) 686 final, 3. On this point, see Claudio M Radaelli and Oliver Fritsch, *Evaluating Regulatory Management Tools and Programs* (2012) OECD Expert Paper No 2.

[46] Helen Xantaki, 'Quality of legislation: an achievable universal concept or an utopia pursuit?', in Luzius Mader and Marta Tavares de Almeida (eds), *Quality of Legislation. Principles and Instruments* (Nomos, 2011) 81.

[47] See Florentin Blanc, *From Chasing Violations to Managing Risks* (Edward Elgar, 2018).

3.3. Regulatory Stock

3.3.1. Simplification

Better regulation programmes require both administrative simplification and simplification of the regulatory stock; anticorruption policies too, in the sense that they can take great advantage from effective simplification programmes.

Simplification (on one side) and anticorruption (on the other side) are public policies.[48] Both policies are pursued by governments according to a common understanding and to a number of guidelines coming from international organisations (such as the OECD, the World Bank and the UN)[49] as well as from European institutions.[50] Sometimes they can come into conflict: simplification can lead to harmful consequences when reducing or even eliminating guarantees and standards concerning legality, and in so doing it can facilitate and allow more infringements and corruption; anticorruption tends to produce, inevitably, further complication by establishing additional bureaucracy and administrative burdens which are added to several institutional core-business activities.

---

[48] Regarding simplification as public policy, see OECD, *Overcoming Barriers to Administrative Simplification Strategies. Guidance for policy makers* (OECD, 2009); see also Edward Donelan, *Administrative Simplification. An Overarching Policy to Maintain a Balance between the Protection of the Public Interest and Interests of Businesses*, SIGMA-Support for Improvement in Governance and Management (OECD and the European Union), Seminar On Administrative Simplification, Ankara, 8-9 May 2008. Regarding anticorruption as public policy, see André Nijsen, John Hudson, Cristoph Müller, Kees van Paridon, R Thurik (eds), *Business Regulation and Public Policy: The Costs and Benefits of Compliance* (Springer, 2009); see also, UN Office for Drugs and Crime, *Guide for Anticorruption policies*, November 2003; see finally, Rema Hanna, Sarah Bishop, Sara Nadel, Gabe Scheffler and Katherine Durlacher, *The effectiveness of anticorruption policy: what has worked, what hasn't, and what we don't know – a systematic review. Technical report* (EPPI-Centre, Social Science Research Unit, Institute of Education, University of London, 2011).

[49] Regarding simplification see OECD, *From Red Tape to Smart Tape* (OECD, 2003); OECD, *Cutting Red Tape: National Strategies for Administrative Simplification* (OECD, 2006); World Bank Group – Small and Medium Enterprise Department, *Simplification of Business Regulations at the Sub-National Level: A Reform Implementation Toolkit for Project Teams*, 2006. Regarding corruption, see the United Nation Convention against Corruption, adopted by the UN General Assembly, 31 October 2003, Resolution 58/4 and also The World Bank, *Helping Countries Combat Corruption: The Role of the World Bank*, Washington, DC: World Bank Group, 1997. On this point, Heather Marquette, 'The World Bank's Fight Against Corruption' (2007) 13(2) *Brown Journal of World Affairs* 27; Paolo Mauro, 'World Bank Researchers and the Study of Corruption' (2007) 13(2) *Brown Journal of World Affairs* 67 and finally Susan Rose-Ackerman, 'Role of the World Bank in Controlling Corruption' (1997) 29 *Law & Policy in International Business* 93. On the OECD contribution, see several documents starting from the OECD *Principles for Managing Ethics in the Public Service* (OECD, 1998), to OECD *Trust in Government Ethics Measures in OECD Countries* (OECD, 2000), to OECD *Convention on combating bribery of foreign public officials in international business transactions*, 1997 and subsequent documents.

[50] On this point, about simplification see European Commission, *Communication EU Regulatory Fitness*, COM (2012) 746 final; about corruption see European Commission, *EU Anticorruption Report*, COM (2014) 38 final. See, in general on the topic, Nicholas Charron, Victor Lapuente and Bo Rothstein, *Quality of Government and Corruption from a European Perspective: A Comparative Study on Good Government in EU Regions* (Edward Elgar, 2013).

However, instead of working in parallel as competing (sometimes conflicting) policies, simplification and anticorruption should cooperate in the common framework provided by the regulatory approach to corruption and in a better regulation perspective: in fact, simplification may represent a powerful anticorruption tool and anticorruption constitutes an indispensable criterion to select priorities for simplification, to calibrate simplification interventions and to effectively steer simplification activities.

Unfortunately, even though it has been argued that '90 per cent of injustice in administration flow[s] from discretionary activity'[51] the question cannot be solved in an excessively simple way, adopting a 'rules versus discretion' approach of calling for more rules and exaggerating their virtues in order to minimise discretionary powers.[52] Simplification is difficult to achieve, because it implies complex and ad hoc evaluations 'to eliminate unnecessary discretionary power in government, not to eliminate all discretionary power'[53] avoiding the risk that discretionary power 'can be either too broad or too narrow'.[54]

Starting from this premise, no simplification change should be made without an anticorruption assessment, and no anticorruption results can be realistically achieved without properly simplifying the statute book and reducing the administrative burdens.

Let us now analyse the topics separately.

3.3.1.1. Simplification and Good Quality Regulation Per Se

From a regulatory perspective, simplification has become progressively more relevant as a tool for better regulation in OECD regulatory reform programmes and 'it seems highly likely that in many countries administrative simplification and burden reduction programmes will continue to become more embedded within the broader regulatory quality system'.[55] It is possible to argue that 'administrative simplification may simply become synonymous with regulatory quality'; in the same way, 'high quality regulation may increasingly be regarded as that which minimises burdens'.[56]

This idea is also the focus of the World Bank *Doing Business* report, which has highlighted that the regulatory environment influences business and competitiveness.[57]

---

[51] Robert Baldwin, *Rules and Government* (Clarendon Press, 1995) 20, quoting Davis (below).
[52] Ibid, 19.
[53] Kenneth C Davis, *Discretionary Justice. A Preliminary Inquiry* (Greenwood Press, 1980; 1st edn, Louisiana State University Press, 1969) 217.
[54] Ibid, 52.
[55] OECD, *Cutting Red Tape – National Strategies for Administrative Simplification* (OECD, 2006).
[56] Ibid.
[57] World Bank, *Doing Business 2010, Reforming through difficult times*: 'Doing Business functions as a kind of cholesterol test for the regulatory environment for domestic businesses. A cholesterol test does not tell us everything about the state of our health. But it does measure something important for our health'. See also Kenneth W Dam, *The Law-Growth Nexus. The Rule of Law and Economic Development*

Many countries are involved in simplification processes, both of rules and of administrative procedures. In particular, there is an increasing importance in 'reducing administrative burdens',[58] initially with the purpose of limiting costs for administrations and later with the aim of reducing costs for both businesses and citizens.[59]

Moreover, simplification has even been considered as a regulatory tool by the US Executive, because it has been viewed as 'the possibility of improving outcomes by easing and simplifying people's choices':[60] as a consequence, agencies should consider 'how best to eliminate unnecessary complexity'.[61]

Furthermore, the European Commission Regulatory Fitness and Performance Programme (REFIT)[62] has attached great importance to simplification. In other words, the programme is based on the idea that when 'there is a reduction in time and costs associated to regulatory compliance, efficiency gains in the economy will follow'.[63]

Even though simplification processes express a single tendency of legal systems towards 'less' (fewer rules, fewer costs, fewer administrative burdens), it is nevertheless important to distinguish between simplification of the statute book and simplification at administrative level, because different kinds of simplification imply different competencies and procedures as well as specific precautions.

From this perspective, countries have carried out activities of statute consolidation by adopting sectorial codes (such as in the field of the environment, etc, as in the case of Italy, but also of France)[64] or by establishing stable institutions, such as the UK Law Commission.[65] Regulatory simplification and codification of

---

(Brookings Institution Press, 2006) and Atur A Dar, Sal Amirkhalkhali, *On The Impact Of Regulation On Economic Growth In OECD Countries* (2011).

[58] On this point, HM Treasury, Hampton Report, *Reducing administrative burdens: effective inspection and enforcement*, March 2005.

[59] See David T Osborne and Ted Gaebler, *Reinventing Government: How the Entrepreneurial Spirit is Transforming the Public Sector* (Reading, 1992) and the US National Performance Review Report *From Red Tape to results: Creating a Government that Works Better and Costs Less. Report of the National Performance Review* (1993).

[60] OMB, Memorandum to the Heads of Executive Departments and Agencies, *Disclosure and Simplification as Regulatory Tools*, 2010, 9. On this point see the Paperwork Reduction Act 1980, US Code 44, ch 35.

[61] Ibid, 12.

[62] European Commission, Communication *EU Regulatory Fitness*, COM(2012) 746 final, and European Commission, Communication *Regulatory Fitness and Performance Programme (REFIT): State of Play and Outlook*, COM(2014) 368 final.

[63] OECD, *Overcoming Barriers to Administrative Simplification Strategies: Guidance for Policy Makers* (OECD, 2009).

[64] On this point, see Maria De Benedetto, *Maintenance of Rules*, in Ulrich Karpen and Helen Xantachi (eds), *Legislation and Legisprudence in Europe. A Comprehensive Guide*, 224.

[65] The Law Commission was established in 1965 to keep the law of England and Wales under review and to recommend reform where it is needed, in particular 'to ensure that the law is as fair, modern, simple and as cost-effective as possible; to conduct research and consultations in order to make systematic recommendations for consideration by Parliament; and to codify the law, eliminate anomalies, repeal obsolete and unnecessary enactments and reduce the number of separate statutes', see ww.lawcom.gov.uk.

existing laws and regulations aim to make simpler access and improve transparency in legislation.

At the same time, countries have started administrative simplification strategies also by resorting to administrative burden reduction programs while at EU level[66] institutions 'agree to cooperate in order to update and simplify legislation and to avoid overregulation and administrative burdens for citizens, administrations and businesses, including SMEs, while ensuring that the objectives of the legislation are met'.[67]

3.3.1.2. Simplification and Anticorruption

From an anticorruption perspective, simplification (both of the statute book and at administrative level) has been considered crucial to fighting corruption which is presupposed to be strictly connected to legislative inflation and bureaucratic power.

As already mentioned, regulation itself has been recognised as a direct factor that promotes corruption.[68] It could be useful to pay attention at two particularly important aspects.

First of all, over-regulation could increase bureaucratic and discretionary powers as well as monopolies[69] and in this way could create more favourable conditions for corruption: if government officials 'have discretion over the provision of ... goods [such as licences, permits, passports and visas], they can collect bribes from private agents'.[70] However, if discretionary powers are still necessary (as argued above), there is a need for counter-measures and adequate controls.

Secondly, over-regulation multiplies the number of legal schemes which are available for opportunistic use. In fact, regulatory inflation leads to increasing opportunities for creative compliance, the strategy of achieving extra-income through regulation by circumventing the scope of the rules. This contributes to nurturing a corruptible social environment and allows ever more corruption (see above, chapter one section 1.3.1).

The idea is that reducing the number of rules, their costs and the time connected to procedures will work as an effective anticorruption tool. In other words simplification can allow better accessibility to rules and can make them more understandable and enforceable, weakening bureaucratic power as well as intermediation and, in this way, can give a strong help in incentivising compliance and reducing opportunities for rent seeking, infringements and corruption.

---

[66] European Commission, *Communication better Regulation for Growth and Jobs in the European Union*, COM (2005) 97 fin.
[67] European Parliament, The Council of the European Union and the European Commission, *Interinstitutional agreement on Better law-making*, 13 April 2016, 48.
[68] See Vito Tanzi, *Corruption Around the World: Causes, Consequences, Scope, and Cures*, 10.
[69] See Anthony Ogus, *Corruption and regulatory structures*, 331.
[70] Andrei Shleifer and Robert W Vishny, 'Corruption' (1993) *Quarterly Journal of Economics* 599.

In anticorruption the tendency seems to be *less is better*. There should be less legislation which implies less enforcement, fewer compliance costs, fewer sanctions, less litigation. In other words, reduced constraints arising from regulation and diminished opportunities for rent seeking through legislation would mean less corruption.

If we adopt an integrated regulatory approach which includes an anticorruption perspective, not only fewer but also better rules are needed, simplification (both of the statute book and at administrative level) is indispensable to achieving both a good regulatory regime as well as effectively fighting corruption.

Even though simplification is complicated,[71] the conclusion of the OECD is that 'simplification of regulation is often a more effective way to address corruption than specific anticorruption strategies and measures'.[72]

This is also the approach expressed by the World Bank: 'the high correlation between the incidence of corruption and the extent of bureaucratic red tape as captured, for instance, by the Doing Business indicators suggests the desirability of eliminating as many needless regulations while safeguarding the essential regulatory functions of the state'.[73] Moreover, a connection has been made between bureaucracy and corruption even by Transparency International[74] when they mention 'evidence of linkages' between them.[75] Academics have long agreed on this point.

If it is true that 'sometimes more rules and regulations not only strangle efficiency but actually create opportunities for corruption',[76] the consequent idea is to simplify and to reduce the public sector in order to prevent corruption.

---

[71] OECD, *Cutting Red Tape: Why is Administrative Simplification so Complicated?* (OECD, 2010). On this point see Jeroen Nijland, *Making Simplification More Simple*, OECD Regulatory Reform Group, Ministry of Finance and Economic Affairs of the Netherlands, presentation of 18–19 June 2008; on the specific topic of tax simplification, see also S James, A Sawyer, T Budak (eds), *The Complexity of Tax Simplification: Experiences From Around the World* (Palgrave Macmillan, 2016).

[72] OECD Anticorruption Network for Eastern Europe and Central Asia, Istanbul, *Anticorruption Action Plan, Second Round of Monitoring, Armenia, Monitoring Report*, 29 September 2011, 55–56.

[73] On this point see World Bank, in particular *Strategies against corruption*, 'Cutting red tape', http://blogs.worldbank.org/futuredevelopment/six-strategies-fight-corruption: 'The sorts of regulations that are on the books of many countries – to open up a new business, to register property, to engage in international trade, and a plethora of other certifications and licenses – are sometimes not only extremely burdensome but governments have often not paused to examine whether the purpose for which they were introduced is at all relevant to the needs of the present'.

[74] Maira Martini, *Reducing bureaucracy and corruption affecting small and medium enterprises*, 'U4 Expert Answer', Transparency International, 8 April 2013.

[75] Ibid: 'As a result, red tape imposes a disproportionate bureaucratic burden on firms and citizens. It can manifest itself through excessive or overly rigid administrative procedures, requirements for unnecessary licenses, protracted decision-making processes involving multiple people or committees and a myriad of specific rules that slow down business operations. There is a broad consensus that unnecessary and excessive administrative requirements for complying with regulations create both incentives and opportunities for bribery and corruption.'

[76] Robert Klitgaard, Ronald MacLean-Abaroa and H Lindsey Parris, *Corrupt Cities. A Practical Guide to Cure and Prevention* (World Bank, 2000) 65; see also Alessia Damonte, Claire A Dunlop, Claudio M Radaelli, *Hindering Corruption* (Paper APSA 2015), 5: 'this is the world of byzantine regulations where cronyism becomes a way for even legitimate beneficiaries to jump queues or circumvent red tape'.

100   Anticorruption: Rules

The opinion that anticorruption objectives could be achieved thanks to reducing monopoly and discretion[77] is widely shared. Nonetheless, even though 'the only way to reduce corruption permanently is to drastically cut back government's role in the economy',[78] it is necessary to proceed with caution: the risk of 'throwing out the baby with the bathwater' is not entirely possible to avoid.

3.3.2. Advocacy Powers

Administrative advocacy has been defined as 'any attempt by interested parties, which may include individuals, organisations and governments, to shape or influence the policies or regulations of administrative agencies when they implement responsibilities given to them by the legislature by means of enacted legislation'.[79]

Therefore, advocacy is not an exclusive prerogative of groups of interests, charities or other kind of social actors. Advocacy, in fact, can take the form of a real public power when institutions are in charge of specific missions and formally provided by tasks 'beyond merely enforcing'.[80] Advocacy powers refer, in other words, to all mechanisms other than strict enforcement which are considered very important in many fields of administrative regulation[81] in order to establish 'a continuum, as a policy mix of "soft" and "harsh" actions', in terms of 'monitoring, promotion of … compliance, and recommendation to government at large'.[82] Among them, powers to advise government, to report annually to parliament or to propose regulatory reforms. However, in the advocacy area, success is considered 'more related to the power of persuasion than the power of decision'.[83]

The increasing importance of advocacy powers can be explained in terms of renewal of traditional policies[84] which move towards a cooperative[85] 'enforcement

---

[77] Susan Rose-Ackerman, *Corruption and Government: Causes, Consequences and Reform*.

[78] Gary S Becker, *Want to Squelch Corruption? Try Passing Out Raises* (1997) *Business Week*, 3 November, 26.

[79] See entry *Administrative Advocacy*, in Larry E. Sullivan (ed), *The Sage Glossary of the social and behavioural sciences* (Sage Publications, 2009). See also different definitions of advocacy, in Andrea Figari and Casey Kelso, *Developing an anticorruption advocacy plan. A step-by-step guide* (Transparency International, 2013) 5.

[80] John Clark, 'Competition Advocacy: challenges for developing countries' (2005) 6(4) *OECD Journal: Competition Law and Policy* 70.

[81] On this point, see P Norton, 'Advocacy powers in Canada', in *Encyclopedia of Canadian Laws*.

[82] Bruno Lasserre, 'The Future of the European Competition Network' (2013) *Rivista italiana di antitrust/Italian Antitrust Review* 13.

[83] OECD, Note by the OECD Secretariat, *Second Meeting of the Latin American Competition Forum*, 14–15 June 2004, 7.

[84] On this point, Richard A Posner, 'Antitrust in the New Economy' (2001) 68 *Antitrust Law Journal* 925.

[85] See James Alm, Erich Kirchler and Stephan Muehlbacher, 'Combining Psychology and Economics in the Analysis of Compliance: From Enforcement to Cooperation' (2012) 42(2) *Economic Analysis and Policy* 133. See also Scott A Anderson, 'The Enforcement Approach to Coercion' (2010) 5(1) *Journal of Ethics and Social Philosophy* 1. See finally, John T Scholz, *Voluntary compliance and Regulatory enforcement*, 385: 'enforcement strategy that potentially can reduce both enforcement and compliance costs by encouraging cooperation rather than confrontation between agencies and regulated firms'.

style',[86] focused on promoting compliance[87] and searching for a more complete and effective administrative toolkit which work as a component of successful public policies.[88]

3.3.2.1. In Competition Law

One important field in which agencies have been provided by structured advocacy powers is competition law, probably the sector of regulation characterised by one of the most intensive quests for effectiveness. The terms 'advocacy powers' in competition law started to be used in the US,[89] but had a dissemination early in the first decade of this century, on the occasion of the setting up of the International Competition Network between antitrust authorities all over the world;[90] advocacy 'rather refers to the non-enforcement activities of competition agencies that seek to prevent or redress distortions of competition created by state intervention'.[91]

The idea at the basis of this power is simple but strong and particularly relevant also in an anticorruption perspective: it is not only firms and businesses which engage in anti-competitive behaviour, but also institutions and regulators, so that is possible to meet 'public restrictions of competition: the state is often responsible for restrictions and distortions of competition, for example as a result of legislative measures, regulations, licensing rules or the provision of subsidies'.[92] This has led to the idea of strengthening competition policy by introducing advocacy powers alongside traditional competition enforcement in order 'to scrutinise "public" restrictions of competition and to play a

---

[86] Robert A Kagan, 'Understanding Regulatory Enforcement' (1989) 11 *Law and Policy* 91.
[87] On this point, see Jean Carbonnier, *Flexible droit. Pour un sociologie du droit sans rigueur* (LGDJ, 2001).
[88] Regarding competition, see Robert Pitofski, *Competition Policy in a Global Economy: Today and Tomorrow*, The European Institute's Eighth Annual Transatlantic Seminar on Trade and Investment, Washington DC, 4 November 1998.
[89] Arnold C Celnicker, 'The Federal Trade Commission's Competition and Consumer Advocacy Program' (1989) 33 *St Louis University Law Journal* 379 and James C Cooper, Paul A Pautler and Todd J Zywicki, 'Theory and Practice of Competition Advocacy at the FTC' (2005) 72 *Antitrust Law Journal* 1091.
[90] See Terry Murrisa, *Materials of the First International Competition Network*, Naples, September 2002; see also William Landes and Richard Posner, 'Market Power in Antitrust Cases' (1981) 94 *Harvard Law Review* 937.
[91] G Roebling, SA Ryan, D Sjöblom, 'The International Competition Network (ICN) two years on: concrete results of a virtual network' (2003) 3 *Competition Policy Newsletter* 40; see also Mario Todino, 'International Competition Network. The State of Play after Naples' (2003) 26(2) *World Competition* 283 and Eleanor Fox, *A Report on the First Annual Conference of The International Competition Network*, www.internationalcompetitionnetwork.org.
[92] Richard Whish and David Bailey, *Competition Law* 8th edn (Oxford University Press, 2015) 3 and 25. See also Nicoletta Rangone, 'New Frontiers for Competition Advocacy and the Potential Role of Competition Impact Assessment', in Josef Drexl and Fabiana Di Porto (eds), *Competition Law as Regulation* (Edwar Elgar, 2015) 118.

"competition advocacy" role by commenting on, and even recommending, the removal of such restrictions'.[93]

Advocacy powers in competition law have been defined in an extensive way, including all 'softer regulatory provision'.[94] Advocacy is a 'manifold notion',[95] a process which includes 'all activities of the competition authorities to promote and protect competition which does not fall under the legislation'.[96]

In the present context, the most important advocacy power is the already mentioned power to scrutinise legislation and regulation as possible drivers of inconsistencies, distortions and side-effects in the legal system,[97] also resorting to 'prior warning before the adoption of anti-competitive regulatory norms' or to 'joint activities in the field of law-making'.[98]

In order to promote a competitive environment, Competition Authorities all over the world have been provided with advocacy powers.[99]

3.3.2.2. In Anticorruption

If this idea works for competition, it could work for anticorruption.

A first suggestion, from this perspective, comes from a non-governmental context and has been given by the Transparency International anticorruption advocacy plan.[100]

---

[93] Ibid.

[94] Irina Knyazeva, 'Competition Advocacy: Soft Power in Competitive Policy' (2013) 6 *Procedia Economic and Finance* 281.

[95] Bruno Lasserre, 'The Future of the European Competition Network' 13.

[96] Irina Knyazeva, 'Competition Advocacy: Soft Power in Competitive Policy' 282 where there is a list of tools.

[97] Ibid: 'advocacy tries to convince the authorities not to take anti-competitive measures to protect the interests of certain groups which at the same time may harm the public interest'.

[98] Ibid; on this point, see also Anna Argentati and Rita Coco, 'Success Rates of Competition Advocacy by Italian Competition Authority: Analysis and Perspectives' (2016) 3(1) *Rivista italiana di antitrust/Italian Antitrust Review*.

[99] See ICN Advocacy Working Group, *Framework of Competition Assessment Regimes*, presented at the ICN 14th Annual Conference Sydney, April 2015. See Richard Whish and David Bailey, *Competition Law*, 25: 'some competition authorities are specifically mandated to scrutinize legislation that will distort competition', especially where they mentioned the South Africa Competition Act 1998, s 21(1)K (which requires the Competition Commission to 'review legislation and public regulations and report to the Minister concerning any provision that permits uncompetitive behaviour') and the Indian Competition Act 2002, s 49(1) (which provides that the Competition Commission of India can review legislation but only if a reference is made to it by either the central or the state governments). See also, Michele Ainis, 'The Italian Competition Authority's maieutic role' (2016) 3(2) *Rivista italiana di antitrust/Italian Antitrust Review*. On this point see International Competition Network, Advocacy Working Group, Report *Advocacy and Competition Policy*, prepared by the Advocacy Working Group for the ICN's Conference, Naples, Italy, 2002, 25. On this point see again Richard Whish and David Bailey, *Competition Law*, 25: 'In the UK, the OFT, acting under section 7 of the Enterprise Act 2002, can bring to the attention of Ministers laws or proposed laws that could be harmful to competition'.

[100] Andrea Figari and Casey Kelso, *Developing an anticorruption advocacy plan. A step-by-step guide* (Transparency International, 2013).

However, especially in cases in which legislation and regulation have produced more frequently opportunities to infringe and corrupt, there should be a stronger response on the institutional (governmental) side. In fact, as already mentioned (chapter two) even though specialised anticorruption bodies are required by international treaties against corruption,[101] there is no strong evidence that their existence always help to reduce corruption.[102] For this reason, anticorruption bodies (ACBs) should be provided with specific competences to scrutinise legislation and regulation describing the way in which they have contributed to corruption.

Therefore, advocacy powers in anticorruption can represent a powerful tool for the regulatory approach to corruption, operating on the side of the regulatory stock (while the parallel tool, on the side of the regulatory flow, is anticorruption assessment of legislation). Advocacy on legislation is articulated in three connected but different moments.[103]

First, detecting and identifying possible rules and provisions which have operated as incentives to infringe and corrupt, thanks to indicators and methodologies developed also in the framework of anticorruption assessment of regulation (see later in this chapter, section 4.1) and in corruptibility assessment (chapter five), for instance legislation which establishes a subsidies programme.

Second, reporting information to regulators (parliament, government, other regulators and so on) in order to specifically describe the effects produced by the legislation/regulation, for instance, analysing evidence of increasing corruption incidents related to the subsidies programme, due to ineffective controls.

Third, addressing recommendations to competent institutions (parliaments, governments, agencies and so) about the best way to solve problems, also by indicating specific measures to counter-act distortions and possible solution in order to reduce opportunities for corruption in regulation and legislation, eg proposing to limit/eliminate the subsidies programme or (alternatively) by strengthening the system of controls.

Providing anticorruption bodies with structured advocacy powers constitutes an important aspect of regulatory anticorruption, also because at the moment ACBs are not focused on legislation or regulation as drivers of corruption but on administrative activities, following the logic of conventional anticorruption.

---

[101] See OECD, *Specialised Anticorruption Institutions. Review of Models* (OECD, 2008), 5. On the topic of special anticorruption bodies, see also Claes Sandgren, 'Combating Corruption: The Misunderstood Role of Law' (2005) 39(3) *International Lawyer* 729–30.

[102] Ibid, 6. On this point, see Kaila Crider and Jeffrey Milyo, 'Do State Ethics Commissions Reduce Political Corruption? An Exploratory Investigation' (2013 3 *UC Irvine Law Review* 717.

[103] On this point, see the case of the Italian Competition Authority (*Autorità Garante della Concorrenza e del Mercato*-Agcm): 'The Antitrust Authority may officially inform the Government, Parliament, the Regions and Local Authorities whenever pre-existing or emergent legislative and administrative measures promise to create restrictions on competition', www.agcm.it/en/reports/scope-of-activities.html.

104 *Anticorruption: Rules*

In 2008 the OECD reviewed models for ACBs,[104] '[analysing] the main tasks involved in preventing and combating corruption, and presents practical solutions to ensure independence and specialisation of resources for – anticorruption bodies', referring to the international standards and models of anticorruption institutions. The report was updated in 2013.[105]

Preventive anticorruption bodies (art 6, United Nations Convention against Corruption) have been distinguished by the OECD (see chapter two): bodies that prevent corruption and bodies or persons specialised in combating corruption through law enforcement. In order to be effective, these anticorruption institutions should be characterised by independence, specialisation and adequate resources and powers. The comparative overview of different models of specialised institutions highlighted three models: multi-purpose agencies with law enforcement powers and preventive functions; law enforcement agencies, departments and/or units; preventive, policy development and coordination institutions.

In the framework of preventive functions, some have been mentioned: 'research and analysis, policy development and coordination, training and advising various bodies on risk of corruption and available solutions, and other functions'.[106]

The 2013 updated version of the report developed the issue by mentioning the presence of 'dedicated anticorruption policy and corruption-prevention bodies'[107] and 'prevention of corruption by other public institutions'.

Even though ACBs seem not to be focused on advocacy, the idea is drafted in substance, especially when they are in charge of the power to advice 'on risks of corruption and recommending improvements', which should not only be limited to specific anticorruption legislation but rather to 'all initiatives by the legislative and executive branches of government that have a [corruption] component'.[108]

This means that anticorruption bodies should participate 'in the rulemaking and implementation functions of a regulatory body',[109] in a manner similar to that of Competition Authorities. To give an example, the Italian anticorruption legislation (Law no 190/2012, art 1.2, c), conferred advisory powers on the Italian Anticorruption Authority (*Autorità Nazionale Anticorruzione* – Anac) including powers to report and recommend to parliament and the government on the basis of the public procurement code.[110] Moreover, as already mentioned, the

---

[104] OECD, Anticorruption Network for Eastern Europe and Central Asia, *Specialised Anticorruption Institutions Review of models* (OECD, 2008).

[105] OECD, Anticorruption Network for Eastern Europe and Central Asia, *Specialised Anticorruption Institutions Review of models*, 2nd edn (OECD, 2013).

[106] Ibid, 12.

[107] Ibid, 14.

[108] The original word is 'competition', John Clark, *Competition Advocacy: challenges for developing countries* 74.

[109] Ibid, 76.

[110] Art 6.7, e) and f), Legislative Decree no 163/2006, now art 213.3, c) and d), Legislative Decree no 50/2016, where the power to report warnings and to recommend the Government and the Parliament is established even though not focused on opportunities for corruption in legislation ('l'Autorità ... (c) segnala al Governo e al Parlamento, con apposito atto, fenomeni particolarmente gravi di inosservanza o

Italian National Recovery and Resilience Plan, among other 'enabling reforms', has required the repeal and revision of rules that fuel corruption.

The path is, in some sense, unavoidable, especially considering the ineffectiveness of past and current anticorruption performance[111] and the expense of such agencies (ACBs).[112] The regulatory approach deserves attention not least because 'advocacy is also less costly compared to the process of law enforcement'.[113]

3.4. Regulatory Flow

3.4.1. Anticorruption Assessment of Legislation

Over the last 30 years, better regulation tools have been considered indispensable drivers in increasing the quality of regulation,[114] by national, European and international institutions, with specific reference to impact assessment, to consultation and to ex post evaluation.[115]

In the present context, one could reasonably imagine that the problem should be addressed starting from the quality of anticorruption regulation. However, long before it, the problem regards good regulation as a general question: in fact, regulation which is good quality and capable of making rules effective, of ensuring enforcement and increasing compliance,[116] is capable also of bringing corruption under control, to the extent possible. However, in order to strengthen this preventive effect, alongside already mentioned consolidated better regulation tools, in some legal systems a specific and more focused anticorruption assessment of legislation has been introduced.

---

di applicazione distorta della normativa di settore; d) formula al Governo proposte in ordine a modifiche occorrenti in relazione alla normativa vigente di settore').

[111] John R Heilbrunn, *Anticorruption Commissions: Panacea or Real Medicine to Fight Corruption?* (World Bank, 2004) 2: 'it is hardly surprising that anticorruption commissions have compiled a dismal record of effectiveness'.

[112] Ibid, 14.

[113] Irina Knyazeva, 'Competition Advocacy: Soft Power in Competitive Policy', 286. This is the reason why 'some developing countries might more usefully deploy their resources on this issue [advocacy] rather than adopting their own [anticorruption] rules' (the term was 'competition'), Richard Whish and David Bailey, *Competition Law*, 25; see also AE Rodriguez and Malcom B Coate, 'Competition Policy in Transition Economies: the Role of Competition Advocacy' (1997) 23 *Brooklyn Journal of International Law* 365.

[114] On this topic, a first analysis has been developed in Maria De Benedetto, Mario Martelli and Nicoletta Rangone, *La qualità delle regole* (Il Mulino, 2011), and later Maria De Benedetto, 'Good regulation: Organizational and Procedural Tools' (2013) 2 *Italian Journal of Public Law* 235.

[115] See Interinstitutional agreement between the European Parliament, the Council of the EU and the European Commission of 13 April 2016 on *Better Law-Making*.

[116] In general on this point, Gary S Becker and George J Stigler, 'Law Enforcement, Malfeasance, and Compensation of Enforcers' (1974) III *Journal of Legal Studies* 1.

3.4.1.1. A First Step: Good Quality Regulation Per Se

The OECD[117] as well as the European Union (starting from the notion of 'smart regulation'[118] to the idea of 'fit for purpose' regulation[119]) have contributed to describing the wide question of better regulation in terms of a 'good' regulatory regime,[120] strictly connected to compliance with and enforcement of rules.[121] In other words, the issue under discussion is that regulation 'seeks to change behaviour in order to produce desired outcomes'[122] and that consequently it is important to avoid (or, at least, to limit and take under control) non-compliance and creative compliance by effective enforcement.

Furthermore, quality of legislation should be considered as a problem of making legislation clear and accessible but also of making it as 'easy to comply with as possible'.[123] In other words, the 'symbiotic relationship between the formulation of regulatory rules and their application'[124] makes evident the need for specific procedural tools which operate during the law-making (as well as the regulatory) process as an aid for the decision by evaluating in a prognostic way possible impacts of adopting rules. Corruption requires strong and effective (as far as possible) 'anticipatory diagnosis'[125] too.

Good quality regulation is the results of good quality regulatory procedures in which both formal and substantive aspects of regulation are taken into account.

In the framework of better regulation policies, the most famous instrument is the already mentioned impact assessment (regulatory impact analysis in the US,

---

[117] 'Better regulation means to adopt regulations that meet concrete quality standards, avoids unnecessary regulatory burdens and effectively meets clear objectives', OECD, *Overcoming Barriers to Administrative Simplification Strategies: Guidance for Policy Makers* (OECD, 2009) 44. See also OECD, *Recommendation on Improving the Quality of Government Regulation* (OECD, 1995), and *The OECD Report on Regulatory Reform; Synthesis* (OECD, 1997).

[118] European Commission, Communication *Smart Regulation in the European Union*, COM/2010/0543 final, p 3: smart regulation means a regulation 'about the whole policy cycle – from the design of a piece of legislation to implementation, enforcement, evaluation and revision'. See also Robert Baldwin, 'Is better regulation smarter regulation?' (2005) *Public Law* 485.

[119] See European Commission, Communication *EU Regulatory fitness*, COM(2012) 746 final, 3: because of 'the current economic situation demands the EU legislation be even more effective and efficient in achieving its public policy objectives ... REFIT will identify burdens, inconsistencies, gaps and ineffective measures'. See also European Commission, Communication *Strengthening the foundations of Smart regulation – improving evaluation* 3.

[120] Robert Baldwin, Martin Cave and Martin Lodge, *Understanding Regulation. Theory, Strategy and Practice*, 38.

[121] OECD, *Reducing the Risk of Policy Failure: Challenges for Regulatory Compliance* (OECD, 2000). See also Wim Voermans, *Motive-based enforcement*, Working Paper Leiden University, 23 March 2013, in Luzius Mader and Sergey Kabyshev (eds), *Regulatory Reform. Implementation and compliance* (Nomos, 2014) 41.

[122] Cary Coglianese, *Measuring Regulatory Performance. Evaluating the impact of regulation and regulatory policy*, OECD Expert Paper No 1, August 2012, 9.

[123] European Commission, Communication *EU Regulatory fitness*, 9. See also OECD, *Better Regulation in Europe: Italy 2012*, revd edn (OECD, 2013) 101.

[124] Anthony Ogus, *Regulation. Legal Form and Economic Theory*, 90. See also Keith Hawkins, John M Thomas, *Enforcing Regulation* (Kluwer-Nijhoff Publishing, 1984) 173.

[125] See Peter Grabosky, *Counterproductive Regulation* 363.

étude d'impact in France, *análisis de impacto regulatorio* in Spain and, finally, *analisi d'impatto della regolazione* in Italy)[126] which has been introduced – at least formally – in almost all legal systems both at national and European level. Sometimes it works as a 'post-hoc rationalisation'.[127] However, IA is considered by academics and institutions to be the most effective tool to help regulators in taking decisions. IA is structured in a complex and articulated report which includes: definition of the base-line; gathering of evidence; objectives and related indicators; consultation of stakeholders; possible impacts of different regulatory options; the choice of a preferred option which (in any case) would be monitored and evaluated via ex-post evaluations in order to avoid regulatory failures and undesirable side-effects.

3.4.1.2. A Second Step: Highly Focused Anticorruption Tools

If infringements and corruption should be considered as possible (unwanted) impacts of rules, then quality of regulation would be sufficient to catalyse anticorruption effects. However, the increasing sensitivity of public opinion to corruption and the need to obtain more and better results, have prompted governments and international organisations to take into account a more specialised quality of regulation tool, a sort of specialised impact assessment, focusing directly on corruption, which may help to identify and remove recurring factors causing corruption in any kind of legislation and regulation,[128] especially when legislation and regulation create rent-seeking opportunities for enterprises, private individuals and public agents.

This specialised impact assessment has been known by different names in different contexts. In the last decade, the institutional debate developed in many reports and documents referred to 'Anticorruption assessment of laws', to 'Corruption impact assessment' and to 'Corruption proofing', by adopting more or less the same perspective.[129]

---

[126] On this point see Claudio M Radaelli, 'The diffusion of regulatory impact analysis. Best practice or lesson-drawing' (2004), *European Journal of Political Research* 723; *How Context Matters: Regulatory Quality in the European Union*, American Political Science Association Annual Meeting, Chicago, 2–5 September 2004; 'Diffusion without Convergence: How Political Context Shapes the Adoption of Regulatory Impact Assessment' (2005) 12(5) *Journal of European Public Policy* 924; *Why, What, and How? Module on Tools to Improve the Flow of Regulations. Regulatory Impact Assessment*, Wbi Module Handbook Effective Regulatory Reform, 2009.

[127] Cary Coglianese, Heather Kilmartin and Evan Mendelson, 'Transparency and Public Participation in the Federal Rulemaking Process: recommendations for the New Administration' (2008) 77 *George Washington Law Review* 933.

[128] See Jeremy Pope, 'Parliament and Anticorruption legislation', in Rick Stapenhurst, Niall Johnston and Riccardo Pelizzo (eds), *The role of Parliament in curbing corruption* (WBI Development Studies, 2006) 66: 'Parliamentarians, in their law-making phase, can play a major part in creating a social as well as a legal environment in which corruption is less likely to occur and detected when it does'.

[129] On this topic see Luca Di Donato, 'The Quality of Regulation in the Service of Preventing Corruption' (2016) 2 *European Journal of Law Reform*, and Luca Di Donato, 'Better regulation to prevent corruption: The Corruption Impact Assessment (CIA)', in Agustí Cerillo-I-Martinez and Juli Ponce (eds), *Preventing Corruption and Promoting Good Government and Public Integrity* (Bruylant, 2017) 101.

108 *Anticorruption: Rules*

In the *anticorruption assessment*,[130] single provisions of a law must be checked for every typical corruption factor,[131] by resorting to: initial (general) assessment of corruption risk; targeted (specific) assessment of whether or not the law promotes corruption; analysis of corrupt practices in the enforcement of the law; other methods for identifying and avoiding provisions that may promote instances of corruption. In order to make the assessment operational, guidelines have sometimes been provided.[132]

Corruption impact assessment (CIA) has been introduced in some legal systems, even if with different approaches and methodologies.[133] On the basis of the experiences of different countries, the World Bank, the OECD and other international and supranational institutions have promoted 'an analytical mechanism designed to identify and remove corruption risk factors from new and existing legislation'.[134] In other words, CIA has begun to be considered an indispensable tool for supporting decision-makers in identifying and eliminating corruption risk factors in legislation and regulation. CIA should be used ex ante, in order to evaluate 'the risk that, in the case that the legislative act is adopted, it will increase the intensity or scope of corruption behaviour in the regulated area of human activity';[135] it should also be used ex post for evaluating corruption on the basis of concrete incidents (and, in this perspective, could be considered relevant also for advocacy powers, see in this chapter section 3.3.2). To this end, CIA has been based on checklists which focus on three factors: ease of compliance, propriety of discretion and transparency of administrative procedure.[136]

Finally, *corruption proofing* is targeted 'at 'regulatory corruption risks', which constitute existing or missing features in a law that can contribute to corruption regardless of whether the risk was intended or not'.[137] In the framework

---

[130] On this topic, see EV Talapina, VN Yuzhakov, *Guidelines for Initial Assessment of Laws for Corruption Risks*, edited by VN Yuzhakov (Moscow Center for Strategic Development, 2007), http://ecsocman.hse.ru/data/2011/11/28/1270193403/209-213_Abstracts.pdf.

[131] Ibid, 30.

[132] Ibid, 23.

[133] On South Korea, see Arsema Tamyalew, *A Review of the Effectiveness of the Anticorruption and Civil Rights Commission of the Republic of Korea* (The World Bank, 2014).

[134] OECD, *Anticorruption initiatives for Asia and the Pacific Strategies for Business, Government and Civil Society to Fight Corruption in Asia and the Pacific* (OECD, 2009) 187.

[135] Jana Chvalkovska, Petr Jansky, Michal Mejstrik, 'Identifying Corruption in Legislation using Risk Analysis Methods' (2012) 6 *World Academy of Science, Engineering and Technology* 7.

[136] See Tilman Hoppe, *Anticorruption Assessment of Laws (Corruption Proofing). Comparative Study and Methodology* (Regional Cooperation Council, 2014) 175 et seq. Each one of these factors could be described by different criteria: the ease of compliance refers to the adequacy of the burden of compliance, to the adequacy of the level of sanctions and to the possibility of preferential treatment; the propriety of discretion deals with the concreteness and objectiveness of discretionary regulations, appropriateness of consignment/entrustment standards and clarity of financial support standards; the transparency of administrative procedure is connected to accessibility and openness, predictability and the possibility of conflicts of interest.

[137] Ibid, 10.

of corruption proofing, 'every draft law should be corruption-proofed'.[138] All factors and criteria indicated contribute to structure checklists in order to evaluate a specific legislation or regulation from the perspective of possible corruption and to develop a specific report on adopting legislation/regulation.

However, despite being a relevant tool, anticorruption impact assessment may be too limited and inconclusive from the perspective of controlling other infringements which prepare the ground for corruption. As already mentioned (chapter one, section 1.5.3), corruption 'include[s] the active (or passive) collusion of an agent of the state'[139] but there are many cases in which simple infringements express the same illicit rent-seeking activity of corruption[140] and are characterised by the same secrecy, even though we cannot define them as corruption in a strict sense. This kind of infringement will probably create the need to corrupt tomorrow in order to hold onto the illicit extra income.

In the regulatory approach, effective anticorruption should take into account all kinds of infringements. In the same logic (as mentioned above in chapter one, section 1.5.3), we should not only pay attention to the transactions between the Agent and the Client, since they happen at the very end of the process, when corruption occurs and when only repression is needed, whereas a preventive approach necessitates 'very early detection'.[141] All kinds of illicit behaviour and (moreover) all kinds of rent-seeking opportunities should be identified within the scope of regulation in order to prevent infringements and corruption.

For these reasons, it is important to consider comprehensive tools (mechanisms which take into account the risk of infringements more generally) and crime alongside strict corruption, such as the *risk of crime assessment*.[142] Due to the fact that each single infringement may be relevant for corruption during checks and inspections (see chapter one, section 1.7.2), crime proofing of legislation (and not only corruption) should be at the core of anticorruption, as 'a particular form of crime risk assessment and management that measures existing (crime proofing ex post) or future (crime proofing ex ante) opportunities for crime due to legislation, and highlights related interventions aimed at proofing it against crime'.[143]

---

[138] Jeremy Pope, *Parliament and Anticorruption legislation* 65.

[139] Mark Robinson (ed), *Corruption and Development* (Routledge, 2004) 110. See also Roger Bowles, 'Corruption', in Boudewijn Bouckaert and Gerrit De Geest (eds), *Encyclopedia of Law and Economics*, Vol V, The Economics of Crime and Litigation (Edward Elgar, 2000) 476.

[140] See Johann Graf Lambsdorff, 'Corruption and Rent-seeking' (2002) 113 *Public Choice* 97.

[141] Tom Vander Beken, *A Multidisciplinary Approach for detection and Investigation of Corruption* 275.

[142] Developed in the framework of the MARC Project (Mechanism for Assessing the Risk of Crime) due to legislation and products in order to proof them against crime at EU level. MARC Project was financed by the EU Commission under the Sixth European Union Framework Programme.

[143] Ernesto U Savona, *The Crime Risk Assessment Mechanism (CRAM) for proofing EU and National legislation against crime*, Final Report of Project MARC – Developing Mechanisms for Assessing the Risk of Crime due to legislation and products in order to proof them against crime at an EU level, June 2006, Università Cattolica del Sacro Cuore and Transcrime 5.

Table 3.1 Rules Under Scrutiny I – Which (Sensitive) Rules Should Be Monitored

RULES TO BE MONITORED: rules which establish (or have impact on)	EXAMPLES	PATH OF CORRUPTION
Costs	Fee Obligation Tax	INDIRECT (infringement first, in order to avoid the cost; corruption later, during controls)
Benefits	Grant Subsidy Exemption Schemes which provide benefits	DIRECT (if a public agent has discretion over the provision of benefits, corruption: to achieve a benefit which is not due; to achieve benefit in a shorter time or in a greater size)
Prohibitions	of goods and services	INDIRECT (infringement first; corruption later, during controls)
Restrictions	of goods and services	DIRECT (if a public agent has discretion or powers over restrictions) INDIRECT (infringement first; corruption later, during controls)
Regulatory Powers	Connected with the already mentioned elements (pay attention to numbers!)	DIRECT
Enforcement Capacity	Rules which establish, eliminate or reduce law enforcement capacity (ie funding, human resources-staffing and expertise, and so on)	INDIRECT (decreasing controls or reducing the risk of controls incentivises direct non-compliance and infringements; corruption later, during possible controls)

On the basis of relevant risk indicators[144] it should contribute to identify risks of non-compliance and side-effects in sectorial regulation.[145]

In conclusion, to the purpose of regulatory anticorruption, rules which provide costs or benefits, establish prohibition or restrictions, allocate regulatory powers or have impact on law enforcement capacity are 'sensitive' rules. This means that they make possible rent-seeking and might work as tools for profit, contributing to corrupt transactions directly (because a public agent is part of the rent seeking scheme, ie is in charge of providing the desired licence or subsidy) or indirectly (because the rent seeking scheme requires only simple non-compliance with the rule, but a public agent during inspection can put in danger illicit extra income).

Alongside their own specific objective, these kinds of rules create – often as an unintended side-effect – a market of corruption and, for this reason, should be monitored.

3.4.2. Tracing Interests

Interests in the legislative/regulatory process are neither good nor bad in themselves: it depends on concrete evaluations regarding their fair acquisition, their full representation as well as their adequate consideration and due accommodation[146] in the final decision.

From the point of view of anticorruption policies, interests pose a great problem because often they not only compete (understandably) but may result in corrupt practices to unfairly achieve favourable rules: in any case and independently of the criminal relevance of such practices, they express an attempt to distort the previously mentioned fairness in the acquisition, complete representation as well as adequate consideration and due accommodation of other significant interests in the final decision.

---

[144] Elaborated by Jill Dando Institute and Transcrime. Among them: '1) Legislation that introduces product disposal regulations or any other new or more burdensome fee or obligation; 2) Legislation that introduces a concession on a tax or a concession on any other fee or obligation; 3) Legislation that introduces a grant, subsidy, or compensation scheme or any other scheme that provides a benefit; 4) Legislation that introduces or increases the tax on legal goods or in any other way increases the costs of legal goods; 5) Legislation that prohibits or restricts a demanded product or service or in any other way decreases the availability of demanded goods or services; 6) Legislation that introduces or removes a law enforcement capacity, increases or decreases funding for enforcement activity or in any other way impacts the intensity of law enforcement activity; 7) Legislation that provides officials with regulatory power'.
[145] On this topic, see also Tom Vander Beken and Annelies Balcaen, 'Crime Opportunities Provided by Legislation in Market Sectors: Mobile Phones, Waste Disposal, Banking, Pharmaceuticals' (2006) 12(3-4) *European Journal on Criminal Policy and Research* 299.
[146] See Richard B Stewart, 'The Reformation of American Administrative Law' (1965) *Harvard Law Review* 1757.

It is not simple to solve the problem, because (as always) good and bad come together.[147]

3.4.2.1. Lobbying and Consultation

In order to increase the positive contribution of interests in the legislative/regulatory process and to limit possible side-effects (such as corruption),[148] regulators have faced the problem from the perspective of *lobbying* and from the perspective of *consultation*.

Lobbying – fully regulated in some legal systems, such as the US, Canada, Australia and the EU – is a process which moves from the representatives of interest groups and which is directed at regulators in order to gain favourable rules.[149] The starting point is a private interest, in the most part of cases an economic interest: simply because, in the logic of 'collective action',[150] economic interests are more capable of organising themselves and of defining common strategies to achieve advantageous results.[151]

---

[147] See European Commission for Democracy Through Law (Venice Commission), *Report on the role of extra-institutional actors in the democratic system*, adopted by the Venice Commission, Venice, 8–9 March 2013, 11, sec C, where 'opportunities and risks of lobbying for democracy' are analysed.

[148] It is not a fluke that the US Administrative Procedure Act – the most famous, iconic regulation on rule-making (and consultation) – was adopted in 1946, the same year of the Federal Regulation of Lobbying Act.

[149] On this point see OECD, *Recommendation of the Council on Principles for Transparency and Integrity in Lobbying*, 18 Feb 2010 – C(2010)16, where lobbying is defined as: 'the oral or written communication with a public official to influence legislation, policy or administrative decisions, often focuses on the legislative branch at the national and sub-national levels. However, it also takes place in the executive branch, for example, to influence the adoption of regulations or the design of projects and contracts. Consequently, the term public officials include civil and public servants, employees and holders of public office in the executive and legislative branches, whether elected or appointed'. See also European Parliament, Directorate-General for Research, Working Paper, *Lobbying in the European Union: current rules and practices*, 2003, p iii, where the objective of lobbying is described as 'to maintain a favourable regulatory environment for their organizations, members or clients'. See finally the comparative Report of the Ireland Institute of Public Administration (IPA), MM Malone, *Regulation of Lobbyists in Developed Countries. Current Rules and Practices* (2004). On the topic, in general, see Arthur F Bentley, *The process of government: a study of social pressures* (University of Chicago Press, 1908); Rob Baggot, *Pressure Groups Today* (Manchester University Press, 1995); David Coen and Alexander Katsaitis, *Institutional and Constitutional Aspects of Special Interest Representation* (European Parliament, 2015); Darren R Halpin, *The Organization of Political Interest Groups: Designing Advocacy* (Routledge, 2014); Grégory Houillon, *Le lobbying en droit public* (Bruylant, 2012). On the case of Spain, see Manuel Villoria, *Una evaluacion del lobby en España: análisis y propuestas* (Transparency International España, 2014).

[150] Marcur Olson, *The Logic of Collective Action. Public Goods and the Theory of Group*.

[151] Franziska Zibold, *Lobbying the EU institutions*, in Library Briefing-Library of the European Parliament, 18 July 2013, 4, where it is affirmed that: 'Lobbying "success" or impact is very difficult to measure. Some studies have looked at certain policy areas or specific group types, but there is not much general empirical evidence. A study by Bunea [Adriana Bunea, 'Issues, Preferences and Ties: determinants of EU interest groups' preference attainment in the environmental policy area' (2013) 20(4) *Journal of European Public Policy* 552] using examples from environmental policy comes to the conclusion that major business groups representing "concentrated interests" were more successful than groups representing "diffuse interests" (environmental NGOs, local authorities)'.

In some countries there is specific legislation and/or registers of lobbyists (both mandatory and voluntary); in others a self-regulation model has been affirmed (code of conducts); in yet others no regulation has been established.[152]

On the other hand, *consultation* is a process which starts from the input of legislators or regulators themselves and is directed towards achieving the point of view of the targets of the legislative/regulatory process[153] with the aim of improving the gathering of evidence for the decision, strengthening its legitimation and reducing possible litigation. Not all legal systems regulate participation and transparency in rulemaking: in some legal systems – like in Italy – there are no general provisions in order to guarantee participation in rulemaking even though specific provisions in regulatory sectors (such as communications or financial markets) have started being adopted at the behest of European Directives and in the context of Regulatory Impact Analysis regulation.

Although there has always been a public interest in consultation,[154] structured participation in rulemaking is considered to be strictly connected with the *interest representation model*[155] of administrative procedures, developed in the US during the 1960s. Administrative procedures have been opened to the interests in the framework of the rights revolution[156] also with the purpose to avoid (as far as possible) regulatory failures.[157] The new procedural model aims to achieve 'an informed, reasoned exercise of agency discretion that is responsive to the concerns of all affected interests'.[158]

---

[152] See Kristina Grosek and Eulalia Claro, *Regulation of lobbying across the EU at a glance* (European Parliament, December 2016).

[153] See European Commission, Communication *Towards a reinforced culture of consultation and dialogue – General principles and minimum standards for consultation of interested parties by the Commission*, 11.12.2002 COM(2002) 704 final.

[154] In the Middle Ages, Italian communes had *statutarii* (or *correctores* or *emendatores*) who were charged with the task of updating, reviewing, correcting and making coherent legislation. They performed their 'delicate activity' – necessary in order to prevent the enormous growth of statutes – sometimes developed in a sort of 'conclave' (without any opportunity to communicate with the external world until the work had been finished), sometimes engaging in real, though rudimentary, consultation processes. On this issue, see Francesco Calasso, *Medioevo del diritto – I. Le fonti* (Giuffrè, 1954) 424. See also Lawrin Armstrong and Julius Kirshner, *The Politics of Law in Late Medieval and Renaissance Italy* (University of Toronto Press, 2011) 79. See finally Maria De Benedetto, 'Maintenance of Rules', in Ulrich Karpen and Helen Xantachi (eds), *Legislation and Legisprudence in Europe. A Comprehensive Guide for scholars and practitioners*.

[155] On this point see Richard B Stewart, 'The reformation of American Administrative Law', 1671, Charles A Reich, 'The new property' (1964) *Yale Law Journal* 733 and Cass R Sunstein, *After the rights revolution. Reconceiving the regulatory State* (Harvard University Press, 1990).

[156] See Robert L Rabin, *Perspectives on the administrative process* (Little, Brown and Company, 1979), esp 7 where 'deficiencies in the traditional approach' are mentioned.

[157] On regulatory failures, see Cass R Sunstein, *After the rights revolution*, 74 et seq; see also Richard B Stewart, 'Administrative law in the twenty-first century' (2003) *New York University Law Review* 4; see also James O Freedman, *Crisis and legitimacy: the administrative process and American government* (Cambridge University Press, 1978) 125: '*modes of procedure other than trial-type hearings are sometimes better suited to the achievement of governmental policies*'.

[158] James O Freedman, *Crisis and legitimacy: the administrative process and American government*.

114 Anticorruption: Rules

From this perspective, participation in the legislative/regulatory process 'helps the decision-maker to have a more complete and balanced view of the facts and the issues relating to the facts';[159] transparency and public participation 'help produce better, more informed policy decisions';[160] procedures can be considered 'another mechanism for inducing compliance'.[161] Participation of all affected interests in the legislative/regulatory process should be, finally considered positively because it 'allows agencies to obtain information that helps them (1) improve the quality of new regulations, (2) increase the probability of compliance, and (3) create a more complete record for judicial review'.[162]

3.4.2.2. Collecting Interests: The Good and the Bad

It is possible that collecting and evaluating interests expresses not only positive effects on legislative and regulatory procedures, but also dysfunctionalities and even corruption.

Some interests, for example, could be underrepresented in the procedure[163] while other interests – particularly aggressive or characterised by particular force – could prevail (by licit or illicit means, such as bribery) and effectively influence the process, thereby achieving advantageous results.[164]

This is the reason why in regulatory processes special attention should be paid to sensible steps in the procedures and why consultations have been considered by academics even as occasion to 'increase the opportunity for corrupt transactions'.[165]

A strong impulse towards standards of consultation has come from the European Commission in order to improve their positive outcomes and to limit improper influence of groups of interest during the law-making process:

> creating a culture of consultation [can] be achieved by legal rules which [create] a code of conduct that sets minimum standards, focusing on what to consult on, when, whom and how to consult. Those standards will reduce the risk of the policy-makers just

---

[159] See Denis J Galligan, *Due process and fair procedures. A study of administrative procedures* (Clarendon Press, 1996) 131. See also Giacinto della Cananea, *Due Process of Law beyond the State* (Oxford University Press, 2016).

[160] Cary Coglianese, Heather Kilmartin and Evan Mendelson, 'Transparency and public participation in the federal rulemaking process: recommendations for the new administration' (2009) 77 *George Washington Law Review* 927.

[161] Mathew D McCubbins, Roger G. Noll and Barry R. Weingast, 'Administrative Procedures as Instruments of Political Control' (1987) *Journal of Law, Economics and Organization* 244.

[162] Cary Coglianese, Heather Kilmartin and Evan Mendelson, 'Transparency and public participation in the federal rulemaking process: recommendations for the new administration' 946.

[163] See Jerry L Mashaw, 'Structuring a "dense complexity": accountability and the project of administrative law' (2005) *Issues in legal scholarship* 1.

[164] Cass R Sunstein, *After the rights revolution*, 103: 'sometimes regulatory statutes are preceded or followed by the creation of aggressive "public-interest" groups transforming diffuse interests into potent political forces'. On this point see also Richard B Stewart, 'The reformation of American Administrative Law' 1713: 'comparative overrepresentation of regulated or client interests in the process of agency decision results in a persistent policy bias in favour of these interests'.

[165] See Anthony Ogus, 'Corruption and regulatory structures' 341.

listening to one side of the argument or of particular groups getting privileged access on the basis of sectoral interests or nationality, which is a clear weakness with the current method of *ad hoc* consultations. These standards should improve the representativity of civil society organisations and structure their debate with the Institutions.[166]

The European Commission has defined many aspects of consultation: in order 'to be effective' consultations must 'start as early as possible'[167] and must respect minimum standards,[168] such as clear content of the consultation process, consultation target groups, publication, time limits for participation, acknowledgement and feedback. Furthermore, even in impact assessment, a specific consultation stage allows the regulatory options to be refined.[169] Regulators – exercising largely discretionary powers – can consult 'all relevant interests in society'[170] as well as the representative organisations of interests which are substantially affected by the proposed regulation,[171] or statutory bodies, where the proposed regulation relates to its own functions.[172]

Alongside consultation, regulating lobbying seems to have become a priority too.[173] In order to ensure that 'lobbying is done ethically and with the highest standards with a view to conserving and enhancing public confidence and trust in the integrity, objectivity and impartiality of government decision-making',[174] lobbyists' codes of conduct have been adopted. Furthermore, the OECD has set out principles to ensure transparency and integrity in lobbying.[175] The European

---

[166] European Commission, *European Governance: A White Paper*, COM(2001) 428.

[167] European Commission, Communication *Towards a reinforced culture of consultation and dialogue – General principles and minimum standards for consultation of interested parties by the Commission* 18. On this point, US Executive Order 13,563, *Improving Regulation and Regulatory Review*, 18 January 2011, sec 2.

[168] Ibid, 19.

[169] UK Department of Business, Innovation and Skills, *Impact Assessment Guidance* (2010) 9.

[170] European Commission, Communication *Towards a reinforced culture of consultation and dialogue – General principles and minimum standards for consultation of interested parties by the Commission* 5.

[171] UK Legislative and Regulatory Reform Act 2006, s 13.

[172] On this point see Nicoletta Rangone, 'Improving consultation to ensure the EC's democratic legitimacy. From traditional procedural requirements to behavioural insight', forthcoming in *European Law Journal*.

[173] On the topic, in general, Suzanne Mulcahy, *Lobbying in Europe: Hidden Influence, Privileged Access* (Transparency International, 2015); Martin Nettesheim, *Interest representatives' obligation to register in the Transparency Register: EU competences and commitments to fundamental rights* (European Parliament, 2013); Heike Klüwer, *Lobbying in the European Union: interest groups, lobbying coalitions, and policy change* (Oxford University Press, 2013).

[174] Canadian Office of the Commissioner of Lobbying, *Lobbyists' Code of Conduct*, amended version, 2015.

[175] OECD, *Recommendation of the Council on Principles for Transparency and Integrity in Lobbying*, 6: 'Lobbying can provide decision-makers with valuable insights and data, as well as grant stakeholders access to the development and implementation of public policies. However, lobbying can also lead to undue influence, unfair competition and regulatory capture to the detriment of the public interest and effective public policies. A sound framework for transparency in lobbying is therefore crucial to safeguard the integrity of the public decision-making process'. See also OECD, *Lobbyists, government and public trust* (OECD, 2009), Vol 1: *Increasing Transparency through Legislation;* Vol 2 (2012): *Promoting Integrity through Self-regulation;* Vol 3 (2014): *Implementing the OECD Principles for Transparency and Integrity in Lobbying.*

Union established a voluntary Transparency Register for lobbyists, operated jointly by the European Parliament and the EU Commission since June 2011.[176]

3.4.2.3. Regulating Lobbying is not Necessarily the Solution

Despite these efforts, consultation could currently be perceived as a weak form of public participation, not capable of counterbalancing the force of special interest groups which strongly influence legislation and regulation, especially when concerning concentrated benefits and diffuse cost policies:[177] politicians will tend to adopt these kinds of policies,[178] which are highly remunerative from their point of view.[179]

In the same way, it might not be sufficient to resort to lobby regulation:[180] full regulation and registers do not guarantee that the legislative/regulatory process will be preserved from the illicit influence of private interests groups, as in the case for European Parliament 'Cash for law' scandal (2011).[181]

Academics and institutions have started to consider lobbying regulation indispensable for better regulation, in order to ensure transparency, avoid corruption and reduce litigation.[182] Moreover, lobbying has even recently been considered a means for change, especially if understood as a widespread practice of effective citizen-lobbyists, a practice capable of rebalancing the relevance of overrepresented (to be reduced) and underrepresented (to be improved) interests on the policy, regulatory and legislative processes.[183]

---

[176] The 'Transparency Register' has been established by the Agreement between the European Parliament and the European Commission on the establishment of a transparency register for organizations and self-employed individuals engaged in EU policy-making and policy implementation ([2011] OJ L191) and later updated in 2014 ([2014] OJ L277/11). See also the 'Interinstitutional Agreement on a mandatory Transparency Register' COM (2016) 627 final, 28.9.2016 and the Agreement on a Mandatory Transparency Register 15 December 2020. See Juli Ponce Solé, *Negociación de normas y lobbies: por una mejor regulación que favorezca la transparencia, evite la corrupción y reduzca la litigiosidad* (Aranzadi Thomson Reuters, 2015). See also criticisms on the voluntary character of the Register in Anthony Chambers, *The Lobbying of the EU. How to achieve greater transparency*, February 2016, Civitas-Institute for the study of Civil Society, 20 et seq.

[177] Marcur Olson, *The Logic of Collective Action: Public Goods and the Theory of Groups*; see also Gunnar Trumbull, *Strength in numbers: the political power of weak interests* (Harvard University Press, 2012).

[178] On this point see Marcur Olson, *The Logic of Collective Action. Public Goods and the Theory of Group*; Antonio La Spina, *La decisione legislativa. Lineamenti di una teoria* (Giuffrè, 1989) and James Q Wilson (ed), *The Politics of Regulation* (Basic Books, 1980).

[179] On this topic see Alberto Alesina and Guido Tabellini, 'Bureaucrats or Politicians? Part I: A Single Policy Task' (2007) 97 *The American Economic Review* 169 and 'Bureaucrats or Politicians? Part II: Multiple Policy Tasks' (2008) 92 *Journal of Public Economics* 426.

[180] On this point see European Commission for Democracy Through Law (Venice Commission), *Report on the role of extra-institutional actors in the democratic system* 16, where 'types of [lobbying] regulatory systems and their effectiveness' are described.

[181] Bruno Waterfield, 'European Parliament member resigns over "cash for laws" scandal', *The Telegraph*, 20 March 2011.

[182] See Juli Ponce Solé, *Negociación de normas y lobbies: por una mejor regulación que favorezca la transparencia, evite la corrupción y reduzca la litigiosidad*.

[183] See Alberto Alemanno, *Lobbying for Change: Find Your Voice to Create a Better Society* (Icon Books, 2017).

In order to keep lobbying under control and prevent illicit influences, regulation has alternated (and sometimes combined) 'recording subjects' and 'recording objects' approaches.

Alongside traditional lobbyists register arrangements ('recording subjects') – which could require many possible and different sets of information[184] in different legal systems on 'who is lobbying' – lobbying can also be evidenced as a legislative footprint ('recording objects').[185] The legislative footprint is a document that would detail the time, identity and content of a legislator's contact with a stakeholder, in other words, 'when and how lobbying has taken place'. Published as an annex to legislative reports, it would provide insight into who gave input into draft legislation and 'complements the transparency register by allowing insight into who sought to influence what piece of legislation'.[186]

The first way (recording subjects) has revealed weak effectiveness: a survey by the OECD highlighted that the majority of lobbyists support the idea of a mandatory register and also the publication of data (except for financial information):[187] it could be an indication that 'recording subjects' is not considered a problem and that 'the transparency register does not therefore suffice'.[188] The second way (recording objects) has been introduced in the EU Parliament since 2011[189] – though on a voluntary basis – for the purpose of strengthening

---

[184] On this aspect see Justin Greenwood and Joanna Dreger, 'The Transparency Register: a European vanguard of strong lobby regulation?' (2013) 2(2) *Interest Groups & Advocacy* 139.

[185] See Lukas Obholzer, 'A call to members of the European Parliament. Take transparency seriously and enact the "legislative footprint"' (2011) 256 *Ceps Policy Briefs* 1.

[186] Ibid, 3.

[187] See Janina Berg and Daniel Freund, *EU legislative footprint: What's the real influence of lobbying?* (Transparency International, 2016). See also the proposal in European Parliament, Committee on Constitutional Affairs, *Motion for a European Parliament Resolution, Draft Report, Transparency, Accountability and Integrity in the EU institutions*, 2015/2041(INI), 18.11.2015, 3: 'Introducing a legislative footprint, making registration by the lobby as mandatory as possible' and suggesting that 'this legislative footprint should consist of a form annexed to reports, detailing all the lobbyists with whom those in charge of particular file have met in the process of drawing up each report and a second document listing all written input received'. See finally, Sunlight Foundation, *International Lobbying Disclosure Guidelines* (Washington, 2015), in particular part II, which describes 'what data needs to be disclosed', listing: 'Information about organizations that Lobby; Personal and Employment Information of Lobbyists; Lobbying Objectives and Clients; Information about Lobbying Contacts; Lobbying Expenditures'.

[188] See Lukas Obholzer, *A call to members of the European Parliament. Take transparency seriously and enact the 'legislative footprint'*, 2.

[189] See the already mentioned Agreement between the European Parliament and the European Commission on the Establishment of a Transparency Register for Organisations and Self-Employed Individuals Engaged in EU Policy-Making and Policy Implementation 2011 On this point see also *Ley Catalana* 19/2014, de 29 de Diciembre, *De Transparencia, Acceso a la Información Pública y Buen Gobierno* which established at Art 10 that, among other things, must be published and made available: reports and documents in the legislative process, the different texts of the provisions and the relationship and assessment of the documents originated by the procedures of public information and citizen participation and by the intervention of interest groups. See also Art 41 of the Charter of Fundamental Rights (Case T-15/02 *Basf v Commission* (2006) ECR II-497, para 501) regarding the existence of a duty on the Commission to record the information which it receives during meetings or telephone conversations and the nature and extent of such an obligation depend on the content of that information.

and making control of lobbying more effective. Among any other considerations for possible improvements to these instruments, both the first and the second solutions need costly administration and enforcement; in other words registers, certifications, recording of meeting, regulating access to institutional venues, drafting documents (appendix of legislation), a system of sanctions and so on. Evidence and proof of improper influence could be both very difficult and very expensive.

It could also be useful to explore a third solution, consistently with the regulatory approach to corruption and following the idea of 'recording results', in order to make clear exactly 'which is the sensitive rule' for which lobbyists have worked (see above, Table 3.1).

Starting from a regulatory approach, what is really important is not who lobbies or how the lobbying has happened (elements outside and before the rule) but which rule is the result of the lobbying activity and 'who pays and who benefits' for it (by analysing the rule itself). This is, in a certain way, a post-lobbying vision, to do with making the impact of lobbying on rules really transparent, by revealing specific and nominated provisions which are capable of transferring wealth from the generality of citizens to groups of interest, by 'judging the tree by its fruit'.

In order to reduce the negative effects of lobbying and limit as far as possible opportunities for corruption, it should be important to 'label' legislation in order to make the interests in any given rule clear and traceable, as for a list of ingredients for food products.

In fact, public opinion and non-organised interest groups do not in most cases perceive nor react to rules adopted in order to favour individual interests and financially supported by revenues (the already mentioned concentrated benefits and diffuse costs policies).

In order to make the concept clear and tangible, let us look at an example from the Italian context. A governmental decree (no 1/2012, so-called 'Growth for Italy' decree) introduced a pro-competitive regulation for pharmacies which established a minimum customer base of 3,000 people in order for a pharmacy to be opened. The previous legislation (from 1968) established one pharmacy for every 5,000 people (in cities with populations less than 12,500). In the parliamentary approval of the decree (Law no 27/2012) this minimum number was changed to 1 in 3,300. Little seems to have changed really, but the meaning was relevant and absolutely precise: in the first regulation (1968) the same customer base determined three pharmacies; the second regulation (Decree no 1/2012) would have determined five pharmacies: the final regulation established four pharmacies. These kinds of rules should be labelled: it is not difficult to understand that the amendments advantaged a specific groups of interests (pharmacists) and is destined to be paid by the generalities of citizens as a restrictive regulation. In this light, it is completely irrelevant who lobbied and how, if lobbying is right or wrong. In fact, lobbying is not an illicit activity in principle, but an activity which should be transparent in order to make competition between interests effective, to incentivise representation of non-organised interests and in order to prevent inappropriate behaviour, infringements and illicit influences.

However, in most cases the problem is to ensure that competition between interests is fair by making visible clear information and labelling 'sensitive' rules: if during the legislative/regulatory process numbers change, a list gets a bit longer (or shorter), exceptions are inserted, an interest is probably moving.

Parliaments' institutional sites should be designed carefully according to the logic of traceability of interests when it comes to sensitive rules: interests should be 'written in red' and usable in order to achieve full transparency.[190]

Each step in the legislative procedure of such rules should be easily accessible, making available subsequent versions of the original proposal, the amendments and the final text; rules should be established in relation to their original proponents, the amendments or the final version; the name of the proponent should be clickable, making available a list of past and current proposals and amendments, in order to make evident (also using graphics and summary tables) the concrete network of interests inside which they have operated during their mandate.

Along the same lines, both government agency and independent authorities regulation might operate in this way, even when consultations are carried out. The results of consultation processes should be understandable in substance. The final report about a given consultation, starting from the consultation paper or from the draft regulation (in notice and comment procedures), is expected to be transparent in a specific way on specific aspects: which are the sensitive rules (written in red), who pays for and who benefits from each of them, how have the rules changed from the original formulation to the final text and who proposed modifications.

This way (recording results) implies predominantly effective selection and effective framing[191] of really informative relevant data for each sensitive rule: in fact, information should be 'framed to be salient and eye-catching'[192] and 'what

---

[190] On this point see Office of Management and Budget, Office of Information and Regulatory Affairs, Memorandum for the Heads of Executive Departments and Agencies, *Disclosure and Simplification as Regulatory Tools*, 18 June 2010: 'well-designed disclosure policies attempt to convey information clearly and at the time when it is needed ... disclosed information should be as accessible as possible. For that reason, the Internet should ordinarily be used as a means of disclosing information, to the extent feasible and consistent with law ... disclosed information should be as usable as possible. For that reason, information should usually be released in an electronic format that does not require specialized software.'

[191] Nicoletta Rangone, 'A behavioural approach to administrative corruption prevention' 87: 'How information is presented is another issue. Empirical evidence suggests that framing of information (i.e. the format in which the informative content is given) is also crucial in order to induce the desired behaviour. Special attention must be given to drafting how information is made salient.'

[192] Fabiana Di Porto and Nicoletta Rangone, 'Behavioural Sciences in Practice: Lessons for EU Rulemakers', in Alberto Alemanno and Anne-Lise Sibony (eds), *Nudge and the Law: A European Perspective* (Hart Publishing, 2015) 39.

is also relevant for an informed citizenship is not (or not only) the amount of information but also the manner in which this information is given'.[193] In this way, it could be effective, not so expensive, a simple and a strong means also to make concrete principles for transparency and integrity in lobbying, as proposed by the OECD. In particular, where it is affirmed that

> countries should enable stakeholders – including civil society organisations, businesses, the media and the general public – to scrutinise lobbying activities ... countries should consider using information and communication technologies, such as the Internet, to make information accessible to the public in a cost-effective manner ... A vibrant civil society that includes observers, 'watchdogs', representative citizens groups and independent media is key to ensuring proper scrutiny of lobbying activities. Government should also consider facilitating public scrutiny by indicating who has sought to influence legislative or policy-making processes.[194]

Table 3.2 Rules Under Scrutiny II – Tool-Kit: Summarising the Conceptual Framework

RULES	ANTICORRUPTION TOOLS (GENERAL)	ANTICORRUPTION TOOLS (SPECIFIC)	CURRENT SITUATION	RELEVANT INSTITUTIONS
Regulatory stock	SIMPLIFICATION	Simplification of the Statute book - Codification - Cutting legislation - Revision	Operational (more or less) in the OECD area	Parliaments, governments, other regulators, (including special units, law commissions, etc)
		Administrative simplification - Cutting red tape programmes - Administrative burdens reduction programs	Operational (more or less) in the OECD area	
	ADVOCACY POWERS	- Advise government - Report to the parliament - Scrutinising legislation (Recommendations)	Not fully operational see the Italian National Recovery and Resilience Plan	Anticorruption bodies vs governments, parliaments, other regulators

(continued)

---

[193] Nicoletta Rangone, 'A behavioural approach to administrative corruption prevention', 85.
[194] www.oecd.org/corruption/ethics/Lobbying-Brochure.pdf, 6.

Table 3.2 *(Continued)*

Rules	Anticorruption tools (general)	Anticorruption tools (specific)	Current situation	Relevant institutions
Regulatory flow	Quality of regulation tools	Traditional tools - Impact assessment - Ex post evaluation - Consultation	Operational (more or less) in the OECD area	Governments, parliaments, other regulators *with* anti-corruption bodies
		New tool - Anticorruption Impact assessment	Operational in a limited number of countries	
		New tool Corruptibility assessment (chapter 5)	Not operational	
	Tracing interests	Traditional tools - *Recording subjects* (transparency register) - *Recording objects* (legislative footprint)	Operational in some countries and legal systems	Parliaments, governments, other regulators
		New tool - *Recording results* (traceability of interests)	Not operational	

4

Anticorruption: Controls

(Can Controls Help in Reducing Corruption?)

4.1. Controls from a Theoretical Perspective

Whether controls may really help in combating corruption is far from being as easy a question as it might look at a first glance. In fact, a plausible discourse should be based on a comprehensive theoretical framework regarding the role but also the limits of controls.[1] The question is particularly sensitive in those legal systems which ensure the protection of freedoms and fundamental rights: controlling is a great problem in that situation, because liberty can be defined as 'being free from the control or power of another'.[2] According to what is prescribed or proscribed by rules at a certain time in a certain place, the existence of controls indicates per se that individual freedom may be conducive to undesirable results, as in the case of economic freedom which includes the possibility to set up cartels or other anti-competitive practices or in the case of freedom of movement, which includes the possibility to infringe driving codes. From this perspective, controls constitute the step before coercion to avoid undesirable results.

However, because people are 'neither angels nor brutes',[3] legal systems and institutions exist (among other things) for the purpose of balancing freedoms and rights with other values deserving protection and among themselves by establishing legal regimes and mechanisms, such as licences, controls and consequent sanctions.

As a consequence, liberty is meticulously regimented and regulated via limitations and controls even where it is more protected.[4] On the other hand,

---

[1] Florentin Blanc, *From Chasing Violations to Managing Risks* (Edward Elgar, 2018) 289: 'the effect of inspections is ambiguous and can be positive (on trust, on compliance, and to a somewhat unclear extent on safety and other public welfare outcomes), but also negative (on economic activity, employment, and also on trust and compliance if inspection practices are poor)'.
[2] www.merriam-webster.com/thesaurus/liberty. On this point see Friedrich August von Hayek, *The Constitution of Liberty: The Definitive Edition, The Collected Works of F.A. Hayek*, Vol 17, ed Ronald Hamowy (Routledge, 2011; first published 1960) 206: 'Coercion is the control of the essential data of an individual's action by another'.
[3] Blaise Pascal (1623–62), *Thoughts* (The Harvard Classics, 1909–14), fn 358: 'Man is neither angel nor brute, and the unfortunate thing is that he who would act the angel acts the brute'.
[4] Robert Baldwin and Martin Cave, *Taming the corporation. How to regulate for success* (Oxford University Press, 2021), esp 4.

not every degree of limitation and control is compatible with the protection of fundamental rights: quantity influences quality and even formal constitutional democracies may be perceived as increasingly oppressive due to excessive limitations and controls.[5]

What reasons at the base of the *four eyes principle*?[6] How do we justify the power to order dawn raids[7] or why may investigations be carried out secretly? Why should firms should be subject to permanent monitoring of regulatory bodies? Rules concerning specific aspects of controls (whether external or internal, in private or public organisations) are all based on the idea of limited trust in humans. This limited trust (or relative distrust) can refer to three different aspects: firstly, *bounded rationality*,[8] because humans are characterised by cognitive limitations which can be causes of mistakes; secondly, *bounded morality*,[9] because humans are definitely free to choose evil and also because complex sets of motivations may induce people into infringements and illicit behaviour; and, finally, *bounded capability*, because humans may be not in the condition to do something which is required by law (such as a firm which does not have the organisational or financial means to comply with new and overly costly obligations affecting its manufacturing process)[10] or even to know that they should do something. All of this makes controls necessary or, in other words, controls intended to combat undesirable consequences of human behaviour due to bounded rationality, morality and capability.

Table 4.1 The Role of Controls

LIMITS OF HUMANS	FAILURES	ROLE OF CONTROLS
Bounded rationality	Failures in deciding	Correcting
Bounded morality	Failures in complying	Sanctioning
Bounded capability	Failures in acting	Supporting

---

[5] On this point see Erich Kirchler, Erik Hoelzl and Ingrid Wahl, 'Enforced versus Voluntary Tax Compliance: The "Slippery Slope" Framework', (2008) 29 *Journal of Economic Psychology* 210.

[6] The four eyes principle is defined as 'the requirement that a business transaction be approved by at least two individuals', www.collinsdictionary.com/dictionary/english/four-eyes-principle.

[7] Dawn raids are unannounced inspections carried out early in the morning.

[8] On this point, see George Miller, 'The Magical Number Seven, Plus or Minus Two: Some Limits on Our Capacity for Processing Information' (1956) 101(2) *Psychological Review* 343–52 and Herbert A Simon, *Administrative behaviour. A Study of Decision-Making Processes in Administrative Organization*, 2nd edn (The Free Press, 1957).

[9] For a different meaning of 'bounded morality' see Iva Smit, Wendell Wallach and George E Lasker, *Cognitive, Emotive and Ethical Aspects of Decision Making in Humans and in Artificial Intelligence*, Vol III, 1-6, IIAS, where 'bounded morality' is intended as being 'capable of behaving safely, legally, or morally in regard to those situations encountered that fit within the general constraints anticipated by designers'. See also Gerd Gigerenzer, 'Moral Satisficing: Rethinking Moral Behaviour as Bounded Rationality' (2010) 2(3) *Topics*.

[10] On the capacity to comply see John T Scholz, 'Managing Regulatory Enforcement in the United States', in David H Rosenbloom and Richard D Schwartz (eds), *Handbook of Regulation and*

124 Anticorruption: Controls

However, controls do not have only a single role: sometimes controls may be intended to correct, sometimes to support; if needed, they are the necessary step before sanctioning infringements and non-compliance. Advances in research and knowledge about human and social sciences are strongly influencing the theory and practice of controls, as we will see later.

4.1.1. The Mythology (and Threatening Practice) of Efficient Controls

Theoretical and practical visions of controls have long been focused on techniques for effective controlling. One of the most famous and comprehensive theoretical framework of controls is Bentham's Panopticon.[11]

At the end of the eighteenth century, Bentham proposed the impressive idea of a rational and efficient system of controls, intended to strengthen the administrative capacity to inspect. In fact, the circular structure in which an ideal prison (or any other such building) would be built would allow a single inspector to watch all inmates without them knowing when they are being watched. In short, the building's architecture literally organises controls, by giving the perception of continuous surveillance.

Prisons, hospitals and factories[12] were constructed on this theoretical basis in the nineteenth century; the Panoptic theoretical vision was designed for widespread practical use.

Administrative Law (Marcel Dekker, 1994) 423 et seq and Florentin Blanc, *From Chasing Violations to Managing Risks* 141 where he refers to the 'material side of compliance (technical capacity and feasibility, and cost of compliance)' and 153: 'Capacity to comply is also crucial: financial and physical, as well as (to a lesser extent) legal knowledge – but also cost-benefit analysis. In other words, norms that are realistic given prevailing conditions, well explained and communicated, and economically viable stand the best chance of success (a relatively unsurprising finding)'.

[11] Jeremy Bentham, *Panopticon or the inspection-house* (T Payne, 1791), now in vol 4 of *The works of Jeremy Bentham*, ed John Bowring (Russell and Russell, 1962).

[12] For example the prison in the Santo Stefano island, the Padiglione Conolly in the psychiatric hospital of San Niccolò (Siena), or the Worcester State Hospital. On this point see Karl Polanyi, *The Great Transformation. The Political and Economic origins of Our Time* (1944; Beacon Press, 2001), 111 et seq; see also ibid 147: 'Just as, contrary to expectation, the invention of laborsaving machinery had not diminished but actually increased the uses of human labor, the introduction of free markets, far from doing away with the need for control, regulation, and intervention, enormously increased their range. Administrators had to be constantly on the watch to ensure the free working of the system. Thus, even those who wished most ardently to free the state from all unnecessary duties, and whose whole philosophy demanded the restriction of state activities, could not but entrust the self-same state with the new powers, organs, and instruments required for the establishment of laissez-faire'.

Figure 4.1 The Panopticon

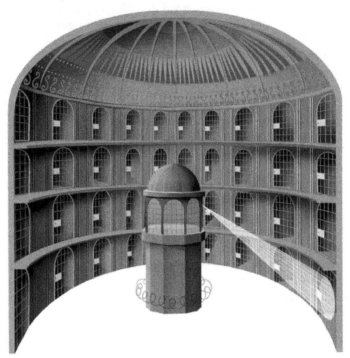

This approach influenced later literature (and practice[13]), such as Orwell's description of Big Brother's 'all-knowledge' in *1984*,[14] Foucault's panoptic theory, as developed in *Surveiller et punir*[15] but also more recently in Chomsky[16] and Bauman.[17]

From the Panopticon onwards, some recurrent elements qualify controls as a system: pervasive, depersonalised and efficient, a system of controls which aims to be capable of ensuring the greatest degree of knowledge with the minimum number of administrative resources.

---

[13] On the paradigm of 'total control' see Florentin Blanc, *From Chasing Violations to Managing Risks* 257 et seq.

[14] George Orwell, *1984* (Secker & Warburg, 1949; reprint Houghton Mifflin Harcourt, 1983) 197: 'Big Brother is infallible and all-powerful … All knowledge'.

[15] On this topic, see Michel Foucault, *Surveiller et punir. Naissance de la prison* (Edition Gallimard, 1975).

[16] See Noam Chomsky, 'A Surveillance State Beyond Imagination Is Being Created in One of the World's Freest Countries', *Alternet* (2 June 2014).

[17] See Zygmunt Bauman and David Lyon, *Liquid surveillance: a conversation* (Polity Press, 2013) esp 52 et seq where liquid surveillance is described as 'post-panoptic'.

However, no system of controls can be considered to be without costs. Such a pervasive vision, in fact, presents limits and side-effects because its administration is hardly compatible with the protection of fundamental rights,[18] as in the case of the individual's privacy and data protection which are structurally threatened. Nowadays, even though the Panopticon model is no longer applicable to people in physical terms (via architecture or building structures), other forms of surveillance are proving to be similar to the Panopticon, being incredibly pervasive, depersonalised and efficient both 'informatically' (via architecture of information systems) and through 'video-monitoring' (via widespread street-level positioning of video-cameras), in so doing conforming a renewed paradigm of the all-knowledge power. Therefore, it should never be forgotten that these costs are material and also considerable, while their relation to benefits is rarely properly evaluated: in fact, more control can lead to a 'slippery slope'[19] of declining compliance in the same way as in the Panopticon, where inmates may come to hate the system so much that they rebel more.

The most recent frontier of efficiency in controls is represented by machine-learning algorithms. Even though 'virtually any decision-making process can be characterized as an algorithm',[20] such algorithms seem to be especially fit to controlling activities and are very useful from an anticorruption perspective. In fact, algorithms make it possible to develop artificial intelligence tools by resorting to indicators of infringements and corruption with the purpose of managing related risks. This tool, implemented via software, greatly helps risk assessment, management of risk and early detection of any kind of infringement. One of the most interesting case in this regard concerns the important sector of public procurement regulation,[21] characterised by high risk of infringements and corruption, where research and studies have been assessed 'the prediction capability of the various indicators using common ML algorithms'.[22] Albeit this promising

---

[18] See Karl Polanyi, *The Great Transformation: The Political and Economic Origins of Our Time* 122: 'His [Bentham's] Industry-Houses were a nightmare of minute utilitarian administration enforced by all the chicanery of scientific management'; see also Michael Perelman, *The Invention of Capitalism: Classical Political Economy and the Secret History of Primitive Accumulation* (Duke University Press, 2000) 21. See finally, Florentin Blanc, 'Moving Away From Total Control in Former Communist Countries – the RRR in Inspections, and Lessons Learned from Reforming them' (2012) *European Journal of Risk Regulation*, 327–41.

[19] See Erich Kirchler, Erik Hoelzl and Ingrid Wahl, 'Enforced versus Voluntary Tax Compliance: The "Slippery Slope" Framework'.

[20] Cary Coglianese, David Lehr, 'Transparency and Algorithmic Governance' (2019) 71(1) *Administrative Law Review* 14.

[21] OECD, Recommendation of the Council on *Public Procurement*, 2015; see also OECD, *Preventing Corruption in Public Procurement*, 2016. Gabriella Margherita Racca, Christopher Yukins (eds), *Integrity and Efficiency in Sustainable Public Contracts. Balancing Corruption Concerns in Public Procurement Internationally* (Bruylant, 2014).

[22] Francesco Decarolis and Cristina Giorgiantonio, 'Corruption red flags in public procurement: new evidence from Italian calls for tenders', *Questioni di Economia e Finanza*, Banca D'Italia, n° 544, February 2020, 6.

application, controls based on artificial intelligence should be used with caution, both from the perspective of their human supervision[23] and from that of 'the risks of non-transparent algorithms'.[24]

4.1.2. Controls in Regulatory Theory

Controls (in the same way as sanctions) are tools for making rules effective, and in this perspective they constitute a real determinant of law. They contribute to the provision to public agencies and officers of information and knowledge about compliance with rules, which is needed to take decisions about possible consequences (ie, negative or positive incentives, it depends on a case by case evaluation). This is the perspective adopted by general theory and philosophy of law, where law is considered as characterised by binding force[25] and where controls are indirectly relevant as the cognitive instruments of enforcement.

Therefore, controls are also *indispensable to the making of effective law*, as argued in fields of research such as public policy[26] and in regulatory studies. From these perspectives, controls *constitute the cognitive element of implementation and regulatory enforcement*, necessary to make each public policy or regulation effective,[27] much beyond the problem of sanctioning. They are directly relevant

---

[23] Cary Coglianese, David Lehr, 'Transparency and Algorithmic Governance' 5, where he mention the 'key distinction between machine-learning applications that support human decisions versus those that substitute for human decisions'.

[24] Gabriella M Racca and Christopher R Yukins, 'Introduction. The Promise and Perils of Innovation in Cross-Border Procurement', in Gabriella M Racca and Christopher R Yukins (eds), *Joint Public Procurement and Innovation Lessons Across Borders* (Bruylant, 2019) 9. On this point see Cary Coglianese, David Lehr, 'Transparency and Algorithmic Governance' 16: 'But these advantages come at a cost to transparency. Machine-learning algorithms are deemed 'black boxes' because it is difficult to put into intuitive language how they function' and 56: 'In the future, a government that makes use of so-called black-box algorithms need not be a black-box government. With responsible practices, government officials can take advantage of machine learning's predictive prowess while remaining faithful to principles of open government. Algorithmic governance can meet the law's demands for transparency while still enhancing efficacy, efficiency, and even legitimacy in government'.

[25] On this point see Alf Ross, *On Law and Justice* (University of California Press, 1959) 38: 'valid law means both an order which is in fact effective and an order which possesses "binding force" derived from a priori principles; law is at the same time something factual in the world of reality and something valid in the world of ideas'. On this aspect see, Santi Romano, *The Legal Order* (transl Mariano Croce, Routledge, 2017). See also Hans Kelsen, *Principles of International Law* (1952; The Lawbook Exchange Ltd, 2003), esp 212 ('the boundaries of the State: the principle of effectiveness') and 414: 'The principle of legitimacy is restricted by the principle of effectiveness'.

[26] On this point, see Jeffrey L Pressman and Aaron Wildavsky, *Implementation: How Great Expectations in Washington Are Dashed in Oakland; Or, Why It's Amazing that Federal Programs Work at All, This Being a Saga of the Economic Development Administration as Told by Two Sympathetic Observers Who Seek to Build Morals on a Foundation*, 3rd edn (University of California Press, 1984) xxiii: 'Implementation, then, is the ability to forge subsequent links in the causal chain so as to obtain the desired results'.

[27] See Maria De Benedetto, 'Effective law from a regulatory and administrative law perspective' (2018), in *European Journal of Risk Reg*ulation 9, esp 406–07.

not only as individual controls but in their being a system.[28] 'Detecting' is, in fact, the first of the 'challenges that regulators encounter in seeking to apply enforcement on the ground' through 'the gaining of information on undesirable and non-compliant behaviour'.[29]

Another relevant point has been[30] featured in the Ayres and Braithwaite pyramid of enforcement[31] in the context of 'responsive regulation' (Figure 4.2).[32]

Figure 4.2 Ayres and Braithwaite's Pyramid of Enforcement

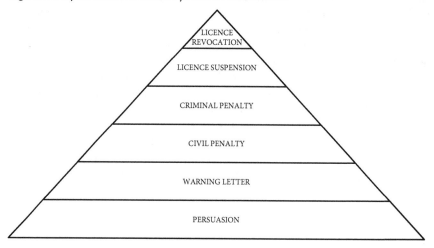

The incredibly influential pyramid[33] expressed the need for enforcement strategies which were more nuanced than in the compliance/deterrence binary model, strategies which should be calibrated by using cooperative methods too.

---

[28] Giandomenico Majone, 'The development of social regulation in the European Community: policy externalities, transaction costs, motivational factors' (1996) *Aussenwirtschaft*, Jahrgang, 27 talks about 'system of control'; see also Keith Hawkins and John M Thomas, 'The Enforcement Process in Regulatory Bureaucracies', in Keith Hawkins and John M Thomas (eds), *Enforcing Regulation* (Kluwer, 1984) 10 where they talk about 'control system'.
[29] Robert Baldwin, Martin Cave and Martin Lodge, *Understanding Regulation. Theory, Strategy and Practice* 227.
[30] On this point see, also, John T Scholz, 'Voluntary Compliance and Regulatory Enforcement' (1984) 6 *Law & Policy* 385.
[31] See Ian Ayres and John Braithwaite, *Responsive Regulation. Transcending the Deregulation Debate* 35. On this point see also www.qld.gov.au/law/laws-regulated-industries-and-accountability/queensland-laws-and-regulations/regulated-industries-and-licensing/fair-trading-enforcement/compliance-program.
[32] On this aspect, see Florentin Blanc, *From Chasing Violations to Managing Risks* 146 where he describes the '*pyramid* of *escalating severity*, and that the regulators need to be *responsive*, i.e., change approaches as business behaviours change'.
[33] On this aspect Peter Mascini, 'Why was the enforcement pyramid so influential? And what price was paid?' (2013) 7(1) *Regulation and Governance*, Special Issue: 'Twenty Years of Responsive Regulation: An Appreciation and Appraisal', 58.

Among other aspects, due to the fact that enforcement includes controls, all this has great influence on the way in which controls are carried out. At the bottom of the pyramid, controls aim to prevent or disincentivise infringements by supporting compliance. Inspectors and enforcement officers in these cases should operate rather as advisors in order to make compliance clearer and simpler and also to reinforce the idea that, in case of non-compliance, enforcement measures are likely.

Higher levels of the pyramid are increasingly reliant on the use of authority, implying that inspections will be accompanied by sanctions, whether they are carried out in workplace, factories, professional offices, even against the will of those inspected. These kinds of sanctions should be reserved for more serious cases, when citizens or firms have demonstrated elements of severe violations.

Among other developments of regulatory theory,[34] 'really responsive regulation'[35] has later suggested that 'regulators need to adapt their strategies to more than the behaviour of regulatees'[36] and that it is necessary 'not only to develop but also to adjust detection techniques to meet new challenges'.[37] This is also necessary to face considerable difficulties in detection which could definitely hinder achievement of regulatory objectives. For instance, 'in some circumstances step by step escalation up the pyramid may not be appropriate. For example, where potentially catastrophic risks are being controlled ... the appropriate reaction may be immediate resort to the higher levels'.[38]

As already mentioned (see above, section, 4.1.1), there is currently much debate at national, European and international level regarding the reform of controls, especially inspections, considered ever more crucial for regulatory effectiveness and a key factor to incentivise compliance.[39] From this perspective the idea of *regulatory delivery*[40] expresses a framework – wider than strict enforcement – in which controls and inspections are 'more compliance-focused, more supportive and risk-based';[41] regulatory delivery (ie 'all activities and tools that can be used

---

[34] Neil Gunningham and Peter Grabosky, *Smart Regulation: Designing Environmental Policy* (Oxford University Press, 1998).

[35] Robert Baldwin and Julia Black, 'Really Responsive Regulation' (2008) 71(1) *Modern Law Review*, 59 and Robert Baldwin and Julia Black, 'Really Responsive Risk-Based Regulation' (2010) 32(2) *Law and Policy* 181.

[36] Robert Baldwin, Martin Cave and Martin Lodge, *Understanding Regulation. Theory, Strategy and Practice* 269.

[37] Ibid, 272.

[38] Robert Baldwin and Julia Black, 'Really Responsive Regulation' 62–63. On this point see Florentin Blanc, *From Chasing Violations to Managing Risks* 146.

[39] OECD, *Regulatory Enforcement and Inspections* (2014) 12: 'enforcement will be taken in its broad meaning, covering all activities of state structures (or structures delegated by the state) aimed at promoting compliance and reaching regulations' outcomes ... These activities may include: information, guidance and prevention; data collection and analysis; inspections; enforcement actions in the narrower sense, ie warnings, improvement notices, fines, prosecutions etc.'

[40] On this point see Graham Russell and Christopher Hodges (eds), *Regulatory Delivery* (Hart, 2019).

[41] Florentin Blanc, *Inspection Reforms: Why, How and with what Results* 7.

to make regulations better implemented and complied with'[42]) considers not only the abstract analysis of rules and their enforcement but 'the regulatory experience' for business as a whole, 'all the interactions between businesses and the various regulatory authorities. It is about day-to-day, ongoing relationships within the framework of rules',[43] including ethical aspects which influence effective relationships between businesses and regulators.[44]

In this context, it still appears convincing that 'the good inspector … has the knack of gaining compliance without stimulating legal contestation'.[45]

4.1.3. Controls and Theory of 'Policing'

As already mentioned, the regulatory perspective can be highly relevant to understand and to prevent infringement and corruption. However, the notion of regulation described above (chapter one, section 1.2.4) is intended to refer not only to regulatory studies 'as such', but also to the different and huge literature in other languages from many fields of research where continental scholars and academics have adopted a different grammar and lexicon to develop the institutional discourse.

In a comprehensive approach, it might be useful to mention the concept of 'police' and the 'role the police played in the modern history of Europe':[46] this concept has been featured starting from the Greek idea of *politeia* (*politia* in Latin) according to which the original meaning of police was all activities regarding the *polis*.[47] As in the early sense of the word, its later use has long continued to express the execution of law or paternalistic government[48] generally,

---

[42] Florentin Blanc, *From Chasing Violations to Managing Risks* 2.

[43] Florentin Blanc, *Inspection Reforms: Why, How and with what Results* 7.

[44] Christopher Hodges, 'Corporate Behaviour: Enforcement, Support or Ethical Culture?' (2015), *Oxford Legal Studies Research Paper* No 19/2015; Christopher Hodges, *Law and Corporate Behaviour* (Hart Publishing, 2015); see finally Christopher Hodges and Ruth Steinholz, *Ethical Business Practice and Regulation. A Behavioural and Values-Based Approach to Compliance and Enforcement* (Hart/Beck, 2018).

[45] Eugene Bardach and Robert A Kagan, *Going by the Book. The Problem of Regulatory Unreasonableness* 128. See also, Florentin Blanc, *Inspection Reforms: Why, How and with what Results* 4 ('Inspection and enforcement procedures').

[46] Hsi-Huey Liang, *The Rise of Modern Police and the European State System from Metternich to the Second World War* (Cambridge University Press, 1992) 1.

[47] Brian Chapman, *Police State* (Macmillan, 1971) 11: 'The Romans took over from the Greeks the term *politeia*, which became latinized as *politia*. It was a derivative from the Greek word for *city*, *polis*, and the English words "politics" and "policy" come from this same root. The term politeia was a comprehensive one, touching on all matters affecting the survival and welfare of the inhabitants of the city.'

[48] Ibid, 28: 'Another important feature of the police in pre-revolutionary France was its paternalism'.

but – during the emergence of modern states in the eighteenth century – it started ever more frequently to indicate also those activities devoted to maintaining internal order.[49]

Since the 1930s, English-speaking literature has focused on the stricter meaning of police ('security police') while the expression 'police state'[50] – literally translated from the German *Polizeistaat* – starts to be understood not in its original sense (as the state ensuring prevention and protection for citizens' welfare, possibly via coercive tools), but as the state characterised by a special authoritarian connotation carried out by a strong system of security police (mostly via coercive tools).[51]

Nevertheless, in France, Italy, Germany, Spain but also in Latin America, alongside the stricter one, a wider use of the term police has long endured,[52] and even today traces of the idea of a general administrative police are present in pieces of legislation regarding regulated sectors.[53]

In short, general administrative policing consists in rules[54] which establish obligations and prohibitions or which regulate private activities (for instance, by requiring licences); it needs supervision (gathering of evidence, enquiries,

---

[49] About the earlier European conception of policing as a comprehensive government of populations see Mark Finnane, 'The Origins of "Modern" Policing', in Paul Knepper and Anja Johansen (eds), *The Oxford Handbook of the History of Crime and Criminal Justice* (Oxford University Press, 2016) 457. See also Lucia Zedner, 'Policing Before and After the Police: The Historical Antecedents of Contemporary Crime Control' (2006) 46(1) *British Journal of Criminology* 78.

[50] Brian Chapman, *Police State* 11: 'The term "police state" has been so misunderstood by English-speaking people that only a plain historical account of its origins will enable the reader properly to understand what follows in later chapters of this study. The misunderstanding has arisen because the word "police" has actually two senses, whereas we normally only use it in one. This misunderstanding became greater when the phrase "police state", a literal translation of the German *Polizeistaat*, entered common English usage in the late 1930s. It then acquired the connotations with which we are familiar, and the real sense of the original was lost.'

[51] See Jennifer Wood and Benoît Dupont (eds) *Democracy, Society and Police* (Cambridge University Press, 2006).

[52] Brian Chapman, *Police State* 14: 'Traces of the word *policie* or *politie* can be found in medieval French, used in the sense of maintaining order in the city, and also in the more general sense of "government"'.

[53] For instance, in Italy competences in matters of administrative policing (*polizia amministrativa*) are established in local government, in public property regulation, and so on. In France, the *Code général des collectivités territoriales*, art L2122-24 states: 'Le maire est chargé, sous le contrôle administratif du représentant de l'Etat dans le département, de l'exercice des pouvoirs de police'. Regarding Latin America, see Corte Constitucional de la República de Colombia, Sentencia No C-024/94: 'encontramos lo que la doctrina ha conocido como la policía administrativa. En términos generales puede ser definida como el conjunto de medidas coercitivas utilizables por la administración para que el particular ajuste su actividad a un fin de utilidad pública y lograr de esa manera la preservación del orden público'. See also, *Policía Administrativa*, in mexico.leyderecho.org, https://mexico.leyderecho.org/policia-administrativa/; see finally, *Policía en Derecho Administrativo*, in leyderecho.org, https://leyderecho.org/policia-en-derecho-administrativo/.

[54] In an historical perspective, see Bernardo Sordi, 'Police/Policey. Linguaggi comuni e difformi sentieri istituzionali nel passaggio dalla polizia di antico regime all'amministrazione moderna' (1997) *Quaderni Fiorentini sulla Storia del Pensiero Giuridico Moderno* 629.

inspections, surveillance);[55] it presupposes, finally, sanctions and coercion,[56] in order to ensure incentives to compliance and thanks to compliance an effect of prevention and protection from risks which (at the end of the day) justifies citizens' submission to administrative power.

The concept of policing[57] would consist in a series of administrative functions (regulating, ordering, controlling, sanctioning),[58] in short it is prescriptions plus (possible) coercion[59] oriented (via controls) to achieve desired effects of prevention and protection in the logic of the effectiveness of legal systems'.[60] This pure and wide concept deserves close attention[61] because with the idea of 'general police' it is possible to jointly conceive of rules regarding their implementation and enforcement (which need controls);[62] moreover, from the perspective of the general police, controls are clearly tools to 'take care' of prevention and protection from risks. All this makes the mechanisms of the general police very close to regulatory enforcement (which refers to regulation, consists mainly in controls and can result in sanctions): albeit different for the historical context which was developed and for its paternalistic approach, the theory of policing seems to converge in some aspects with regulatory theory[63] in the sense that they are both intended to make government as effective as possible and they both consider rules, controls and sanctions.

---

[55] On this point, see Oreste Ranelletti, 'La polizia di sicurezza', in Vittorio Emanuele Orlando (ed), *Primo Trattato completo di diritto amministrativo italiano* (Società Editrice Libraria, IV vol, pt 1, 1904) 313 et seq.

[56] Oreste Ranelletti, 'Concetto della polizia di sicurezza' (1898) LX *Archivio Giuridico* Serafini 432 and LXI, 3 et seq, now in *Scritti scelti* (Jovene 1992) 129, 133 and 147, where he wrote that all rules regarding police, when infringed (thus, possibly) are sanctioned ('tutte le norme di polizia, quando fossero violate, *e quindi eventualmente*, hanno una sanzione coattiva').

[57] Bernardo Sordi, *Police/Policey. Linguaggi comuni e difformi sentieri istituzionali nel passaggio dalla polizia di antico regime all'amministrazione moderna* 628–29, where he analyses police as a term/concept.

[58] Guido Corso, 'Testo unico di p.s., illeciti depenalizzati e competenza: sui limiti costituzionali della potestà di polizia di sicurezza' (1995) *Giurisprudenza Costituzionale* 2166.

[59] See Jean Castagné, *Le controle jurisdictionnel de la légalité des Actes de Police Administrative* (Librairie générale de droit et de jurisprudence, 1964) 20: 'le mot police ... tends alors à être assimilé au mot Droit'.

[60] Paolo Napoli, '"*Police*": la conceptualisation d'un modèle juridico-politique sous l'ancien régime' (II) (1995) 21 *Droits* 155: 'La physionomie spécifique du cas concret impose à l'autorité publique la mesure de sa modulation opérationnelle: c'est par rapport à cette capacité de performance que la règle de police se soustrait au concept de loi'. On this topic, see also Santi Romano, *The Legal Order* (transl Mariano Croce, originally published in 1946; Routledge, 2017). On this aspect (police as orientation to effectiveness), see also Hsi-Huey Liang, *The Rise of Modern Police and the European State System from Metternich to the Second World War* 1.

[61] See Marco Mazzamuto, 'Poteri di polizia e ordine pubblico' (1998) *Diritto Amministrativo* 441, where he observes that 'police' is today studied in different fields of research and could benefit from an interdisciplinary approach ('L'attività della polizia costituisce oggi oggetto di attenzione da parte di nuove discipline ... Si tratta di cogliere l'occasione di questi nuovi interventi per addivenire ad un proficuo intreccio interdisciplinare').

[62] On this point see authors already quoted in chapter one, in particular Hans Kelsen, *General Theory of Law and State* 60 onwards, Karl Olivecrona, *Law as Fact* 130 onwards and Herbert Lionel Adolphus Hart, *The Concept of Law* 97–98.

[63] Oreste Ranelletti, 'Concetto della polizia di sicurezza' 155.

Similarly to regulatory theory, general police surveillance[64] is carried out via good regulation ('*par une sage réglementation*') and via coercion ('*par la coercition*'[65]): in the general administrative police toolbox ('*moyens de la police administrative générale*'[66]), controls represent crucial tools, that are placed at the heart of the process (in the same way as in regulatory enforcement), being indispensable to obtaining information and knowledge about compliance and to legitimise possible decisions about the use of force.

For this reason, and albeit differences, even though 'specialised regulatory enforcement staffs are not usually called "police",[67] regulatory inspectorates and police departments have strong commonalities[68] because 'police and inspectors are both law enforcement officials [and] both are paid to prevent bad things from happening'.[69]

4.1.4. Controlling is Governing, No More and No Less

Is government possible without controlling? In which sense can controlling be considered no more and no less than governing? There is no doubt that government in itself includes controls: due to mistakes, infringements and corruption or due to simple impossibility to comply (see section 4.1) controlling is required to ensure public safety or security, payment of taxes, respect of building or environmental regulation and so on.

Controlling is useful, firstly in a singular logic, in order to check citizens' and firms' compliance with specific obligations (or even in order to support their compliance), both to verify whether they have (or have not) complied and if their compliance has been full, proper and timely. An inspection or other kind of control which discloses non-compliance (or partial, improper or late compliance) is relevant for the decision about possible consequences, such as imposing fines or assigning incentives. For this reason, inspections constitute a sensitive administrative activity of 'fact-finding'[70] which have to be carried out according to normative procedural standards ensuring protection from arbitrary enforcement (ie, prior notice, when necessary; access to files;[71] legal assistance

---

[64] Massimo Severo Giannini, 'Controllo: nozioni e problemi' (1974) *Rivista Trimestrale di Diritto Pubblico* 1269.
[65] Maurice Hauriou, *Précis de droit administratif et de droit public*, 12th edn (Dalloz, 2002) 549.
[66] Ibid, 550.
[67] Robert A Kagan, 'On regulatory inspectorates and police', in Keith Hawkins and John M Thomas (eds), *Enforcing Regulation* (Kluwer-Nijhoff Publishing, 1984) 37.
[68] Ibid, 38.
[69] Ibid, 39.
[70] On this topic, see Carl McFarland, *Judicial Control of the Federal Trade Commission and the Interstate Commerce Commission 1920–1930* (Harvard University Press, 1933) 98; Stephen, G Breyer and Richard B Stewart, *Administrative Law and Regulatory Policy* (Little Brown and Company, 1992) 19.
[71] See Simone White, 'Right of the Defence in Administrative Investigations: Access to the File in EC Investigations' (2009) 2 *Review of European Administrative Law* 55.

during the investigation;[72] verbalisation and so on). From this perspective, achieving information and knowledge (via controls) and taking decisions (after controlling) are and have to be considered as distinct administrative functions, both in administrative theory and practice. The final act of an inspection (a verbal or written report) consists in mere statements, evaluations or judgements on facts, even if it will constitute the basis on which public officers may order or provide further administrative measures.[73]

On the other hand, controlling also expresses a general stance, when focusing on aggregate controls (all controls of a certain type). In this context, controls are real tools of government for two reasons. Firstly, they operate as drivers of the information and knowledge of public bodies, necessary in order to develop, implement and reform public policies. Secondly, controls are needed to achieve deterrence of non-compliance (or support for compliance, depending on the situation) as a general result, looking at the functioning of regulated sectors. In so doing, they help the implementation of regulation as a whole.[74] Deterrence (and support of compliance) in fact, is necessary because administrative operational capacity is finite and it is important – through a small number of controls (monitoring, checks, inspections) – to persuade[75] people about the convenience, opportunity or, in any case, about the preferability of compliance.[76]

For these reasons, the way in which controls (especially inspections) are regulated, planned and implemented – as well as their procedural outcome – is crucial in making each control effective (in a singular logic) and also in making government effective by achieving prevention and protection at which rules aim.

Controls should never be considered as mere administrative technicalities, rather they represent the cornerstone of the more general issue of public powers and their limits. In this vein, even softer forms of government need controlling. Adopting a historical perspective, a very interesting example comes from medieval canon law, which represents one of the roots of modern public law.[77] In canon law, the 'control function' has been carried out for centuries via canonical visitations.[78]

---

[72] Cour de Cassation, Chambre Criminelle, 27 novembre 2013, no 12-86.424, *Car rental*.

[73] See Massimo Severo Giannini, *Corso di diritto amministrativo* (Giuffré, 1967) III, 1, 32.

[74] See Tom R Tyler, *Why people obey the law*; see also John T Scholz, 'Enforcement policy and corporate misconduct: The changing perspective of deterrence theory' (1997) 60(3) *Law and Contemporary Problems* 253.

[75] See Anthony Alcott, 'The effectiveness of law' (1981) 15(2) *Valparaiso University Law Review* 235.

[76] On this point, see Karl Olivecrona, *Law as fact* 140. See also Franklin E Zimring and Gordon J Hawkins, *Deterrence. The Legal Threat in Crime Control* (University of Chicago Press, 1973); see finally, Raymond Paternoster, 'The deterrent effect of the perceived certainty and severity of punishment: a review of the evidence and issues', (1987) *Justice Quarterly* 173.

[77] On this aspect, see Gabriel Le Bras, *Les origines canoniques du droit administratif*, in *L'évolution du droit public: études offertes à Achille Mestre*, (Sirey, 1956) 408: 'Dans le textes anciens, *administratio* désigne tantôt l'exercice s'une function, tantôt la conduite du gouvernement, la gestione d'un patrimoine, la charge entière d'un établissement ou d'un office'.

[78] See Charles Herbermann, 'Canonical Visitation', in *Catholic Encyclopedia* (Robert Appleton Company, 1913) 479, 480 where he wrote that canonical visitation should be 'paternal investigation of diocesan matters'. Guidelines for canonical visitations were adopted in the Middle Ages, in a way

Such controlling was from its beginning characterised by three elements: the 'coming', so that canonical administration has been defined as 'ambulatory';[79] the focus on relations between persons, who are always at the centre, both of the legal system and of the administrative activity;[80] and finally, the cooperative approach because controlling is mainly intended to communicate, to manage problems, to share opinions about solutions as far as possible and only residually to sanction. This more physical, less coercive and more relational contact during controlling has been considered a real paradigm, defined by Foucault as expressing a 'pastoral power'.[81]

In any case, it should be clear that the power to inspect, however it is configured, in terms of lesser or greater coercion, is a way to 'protect' public powers and administrative functions.[82] It represents a tool to ensure full and effective administrative information and knowledge facing citizens' and firms' freedom not to cooperate with, rather facing their freedom even to obstruct it. On the other hand, effective administrative information and knowledge are possible only by considering controls as a whole,[83] ie, in there being a system.

4.2. Controls from a Practical Perspective: Warnings

As already seen, governments and institutions have long looked for effective systems of control intended to detect and prevent, as far as possible, infringements and criminal behaviour. However, when approaching the issue of corruption and controls, we should keep in mind a small number of things, things that might appear evident, even banal: considering these simple warnings and considering globally that the practice of administrative control may contribute to focusing on and in choosing the best possible regulatory strategy to effectively limit infringements and corruption via controls, as far as possible.

---

very similar to current Guidelines for inspections: on this point, see Silvia Di Paolo, 'La centralità della visita nella prassi canonica medievale', in Maria De Benedetto, *Ispezioni e visite canoniche. Un confronto* (Giappichelli, 2019) 61.

[79] Gabriel Le Bras, *Les origines canoniques du droit administratif* 401: 'Un système d'inspections hiérarchiques devait tenir en haleine tous le fonctionnaires. Le nom même de l'évêque signifie son devoir de surveillance ... la visite périodique du diocèse ... sous les Carolingiens, elle l'occasion d'un sorte de gouvernement et l'administration ambulatoire'.

[80] On this point see John J Coughlin, *Law, Person, and Community. Philosophical, Theological, and Comparative Perspectives on Canon Law* (Oxford University Press, 2012).

[81] Michel Foucault, *Security, Territory, Population: Lectures at the Collège de France, 1977–1978* (Palgrave Macmillan, 2007). See on this point Ben Golder, 'Foucault and the Genealogy of Pastoral Power' (2007) 10(2) *Radical Philosophy Review* 157, 162: 'the historical rise of the Christian pastorate as a technology of power'.

[82] More extensively, on this point, Maria De Benedetto, *Istruttoria amministrativa e ordine del mercato* (Giappichelli, 2008) 197 et seq.

[83] Keith Hawkins and John M Thomas, 'The Enforcement Process in Regulatory Bureaucracies', in Keith Hawkins and John M Thomas (eds), *Enforcing Regulation* (Kluwer 1984), 10: 'the control system'.

4.2.1. Controls have a Hybrid Nature

A first point which regulators should take into consideration is that controls present a hybrid nature and controllers are human in the same way as all others. In other words, not only are they tools to combat or prevent corruption but they are also occasions to conclude corrupt transactions. The administrative practice of controlling is dramatically full of cases which confirm this: in fiscal controls, in environmental or food safety inspections, when checking compliance with building permits or with road-safety rules and so on.

Let us consider 'law enforcement officials'[84] when implementing an inspection intended to check if a given public/private activity conforms to established standards. During an inspection (in a matter of fiscality, environment, security) there is a personal contact between the Agent (the inspector) and the Client (the inspected firm or citizen): this contact creates the opportunity for corrupt arrangements and may takes two different forms, depending on the interest which motivates the corruption.

The first is the interest of the Client, who wants (whatever the cost) to hold on to the extra income gained from some illicit activity (for instance, a fiscal evasion) and which is now jeopardised by the inspection.

The second is the interest of the fiscal officer in charge of the inspection, who seeks to take some form of advantage from control by extorting the Client, in order to obtain an illicit extra income through the inspection.

In other words, there is a structural and very typical risk in performing inspections and other kinds of controls. This is indirectly demonstrated by the existence of several ethical codes for inspectors,[85] adopted in many regulatory sectors with the purpose of limiting abuses and illicit behaviours as well as to provide guarantees for citizens and enterprises. This is also demonstrated by anticorruption documents which indicate controls as a key area characterised by high corruption risks.[86]

---

[84] Eugen Bardach, Robert A Kagan, *Going by the Book: The Problem of Regulatory Unreasonableness* 31.

[85] On this point, see Julie Monk, *Reform of Regulatory Enforcement and Inspections in OECD Countries* (OECD, 2012) point 67, 22: 'It is important that inspectors themselves have a code of ethics because it helps regulate individual behaviour to prevent conflicts of interest, regulatory capture, and corruption and protects the interests of those being regulated. It also encourages management to be honest and honourable in their day to day activities and avoids the culture of "anything goes" attitude. When respected, it can help prevent complaints and appeals against inspectors saving valuable time and resources for inspection authorities as these types of cases can take a considerable amount of time and effort to resolve by managers as well as demotivate staff.'

[86] This has been the approach of the Italian Commissione per lo studio e l'elaborazione di proposte in tema di trasparenza e prevenzione della corruzione nella pubblica amministrazione, *La corruzione in Italia. Per una politica di prevenzione. Analisi del fenomeno, profili internazionali e proposte di riforma*, 2012, 171 et seq, where controls have been indicated as a sensible sector; on this point see also Bernardo G Mattarella, *Le regole dell'onestà* (il Mulino, 2009).

Therefore, regulators should know that when they establish a control they are opening a door which could turn the control itself into an opportunity for making illicit profit and even for corruption.[87]

4.2.2. Controlling Includes Administrative Tolerance

When talking about controls, we should also consider non-controls, ie when controls are established but not enforced. Similarly to communication, where it is impossible not to communicate and where all behaviours (including silence) are forms of communication,[88] the same applies to controlling. In fact, since a power of controls is established by rules, lack of such controls becomes meaningful.

Let us consider the huge variety of controls which affect an incredible number of private and public activities in regulated sectors such as fiscality, environment, food security, local police, anti-money laundering, health and safety, state budgets, administrative organisation and so on. In the same regulated sectors, there are an unquantified but definitely enormous quantity of non-controls, defined as 'administrative tolerance' (*tolérance administrative*): when administrations in charge of controls implement them selectively[89] (for instance, only in some periods of the year, because there is a need to make revenue) or when they do not implement controls at all or (finally) when they implement controls without giving them full effect (for instance, by imposing consequent sanctions).[90]

It is very important to accurately analyse and understand reasons which justify administrative tolerance because they can be very different in nature and they can suggest different considerations and responses.

Administrative tolerance may be related, for instance, to organisational inefficiencies or deficiencies, as limits of administrative capacity (too many controls have to be implemented by too few inspectors) (see below, section 4.2.3).

---

[87] See, in this regard, Florentin Blanc, *From Chasing Violations to managing risks* 125: 'Inspections, being one of the main points of contact between regulators and regulated businesses, are a "hotspot" in that respect' and 126 'Inspections, by contrast, offer opportunities for "decentralized" corruption, involving front-line inspectors, small and medium firms, and a variety of "gifts" and favours. In some countries, corruption is essentially the default setting: inspectors go from firm to firm, bribes or gifts are expected, and in their absence enforcement will be ruthless, if needed "making up" violations where there are none'.

[88] On this point, see Paul Watzlawick, Janet Beavin Bavelas and Don D Jackson, *Pragmatics of Human Communication. A Study of Interactional Patterns, Pathologies and Paradoxes* (1st edn 1967; Paperback 2011).

[89] Controls are all selective, on a random basis, when they refer to plans (eg, risk) and even when used corruptly (targeting for the wrong reason). I assume here that public officers may decide when and what controls should be carried out on the basis of their own criteria.

[90] François Rangeon, 'Réflexions sur l'effectivité du droit', in Curapp (ed), *Les usages sociaux du droit*, Colloque, Amiens, 12 May 1989 (Presses Universitaires de France, 1989) Vol 1, 142.

Furthermore, abstention from controlling may also be due to the fear of creating some conflicts with citizens or firms, by suggesting that a given rule need not be enforced at 'street level' (eg economic activities without the required licences): when a regulation has changed and substantive compliance costs are very high or when regulation has become disproportionate or no longer adequate,[91] enforcement officers could decide (even in the absence of any formal decision) to postpone the application, behaving as real 'policy makers'[92] because inspections can often be problematic or even 'explosive'.[93]

Moreover, administrative tolerance may sometimes originate in corrupt agreements. In fact, the magnitude of corruption includes both non-controlling (not controlling something which would have been to the purpose of conferring on someone some kind of illicit advantage) and adulterated controlling (control altered in its content to the purpose of conferring someone some kind of illicit advantage).

Of course, each non-control – independently of its specific motivation – is relevant, because it indicates that an authority cannot or will not enforce the rules.[94]

4.2.3. Controls are a Cost

It is not unusual for regulators to underestimate the almost banal fact that controls produce costs. There are three different typologies of costs related to controls.[95]

Firstly, *administrative costs*. On the one hand, they concern institutions and public bodies in charge of controls, such as the necessary funding for an anticorruption bureau or other kinds of inspectorates:[96] these costs are substantial, as they concern a lot of people. On the other hand, there are also costs created

---

[91] See Anthony Ogus, 'Corruption and regulatory structures' (2004) 26 *Law & Policy* 330–31.

[92] Michael Lipsky, *Street-level Bureaucracy: Dilemmas of the Individual in Public Services* (Russell Sage Foundation, 1980) 13.

[93] On this aspect, it may be of interest that inspections not infrequently are the basis of violent social reactions; for instance an inspection was the occasion to start the Arab Spring revolution, as noted by Florentin Blanc during a Conference in 2012. On this topic see *Arab Spring, pro-democracy protests*, in www.britannica.com: 'The first demonstrations took place in central Tunisia in December 2010, catalyzed by the self-immolation of Mohamed Bouazizi, a 26-year-old street vendor protesting his treatment by local officials.'

[94] On this point, see Tom R Tyler, 'Procedural Justice, Legitimacy, and the Effective Rule of Law' (2003) 30 *Crime and Justice* 311.

[95] On this point see Mervyn J King, *Back Office and Beyond: A Guide to Procedures, Settlements and Risk in Financial Markets* (Harriman House Limited, 2003) 94.

[96] See Robert A Kagan, 'On regulatory inspectorates and police' 60 where he writes: 'Professionalized inspectorates ... would be much more expensive for governments to recruit, train and retain. A staff of lower-paid bureaucrats, programmed to apply checklists by rote, would be much cheaper, and in an era of budgetary restrictions is politically more attractive'.

by anticorruption legislation, which are additional, and which may determine a shifting of resources from other administrative activities and this may produce a 'deflection of attention and organizational competence away from other important matters'.[97] As mentioned, 'practically all corruption controls involve costs and trade-offs'.[98]

Secondly, controls constitute *costs for businesses and citizens*, those involved in an inspection, for instance. This cost may be simply calculated in terms of resources directly devoted to the control and necessary to cooperate and to comply with the inspection; in terms of administrative burdens related to control activities (because businesses and citizens are required to maintain and exhibit records);[99] and also in terms of resources necessary to establish specific internal compliance and anticorruption controls, which may distract from more important administrative activities. Moreover, there could be some other possible costs arising from non-compliance (for example, as a consequence of the violation of a duty of disclosure) or connected with possible reputational damage coming from the control itself.

Finally, there are under-reported *costs of controls*. They may obliquely affect public trust between institutions and citizens/firms. In fact, if controls not only constitute a way to make law effective but also an occasion for corruption, any instance of corruption coming from controls contributes to a destructive effect on the fabric of society, where agents and public officials betrayed the confidence placed in them.[100] In so doing, controls may produce more transaction costs[101] by generating hostility, defiance and by decreasing compliance.[102]

For these reasons, regulating and managing controls is a serious affair, the system of controls should be sustainable and incur as little cost as possible, and it is strongly suggested that regulators reduce the number (and the cost) of controls and that they maximise their effectiveness because the costs of controls indirectly influence the effectiveness of legal systems: when they are not adequately considered in the regulatory process, compliance with rules may be more difficult and enforcement increasingly expensive.

---

[97] Robert Klitgaard, *Controlling Corruption* 27.

[98] James Jacobs, *Dilemmas of Corruption Controls* 292.

[99] See, in this regard, a series of documents, as International Working Group on Administrative Burdens, *The Standard Cost Model: A Framework for Defining and Quantifying Administrative Burdens for Businesses*, 2004; Hampton Report, HM Treasury, *Reducing administrative burdens: effective inspection and enforcement*; SCM Network, *International Standard Cost Model Manual: Measuring and Reducing Administrative Burdens for Businesses*, www.oecd.org/gov/regulatory-policy/34227698.pdf.

[100] Colin Nicholls, Tim Daniel, Martin Polaine and John Hatchard, *Corruption and Misuse of Public Office* (Oxford University Press, 2006) 1.

[101] On this point, see Oliver E Williamson, 'Transaction-Cost Economics: The Governance of Contractual Relations' (1979) 22(2) *Journal of Law and Economics* 242: 'Governance structures which attenuate opportunism and otherwise infuse confidence are evidently needed'.

[102] On this point see Erich Kirchler, Erik Hoelzl and Ingrid Wahl, 'Enforced versus Voluntary Tax Compliance: The "Slippery Slope" Framework'.

4.2.4. Administrative Capacity of Control is Limited

If controls are always expensive,[103] the administrative capacity of controls is always limited. Each inspectorate or administration in charge of controls has, in fact, a given capacity to perform inspections and controls both in terms of quantity (which depends on the number of enforcement officers related to the number of inspections/controls of a mean duration per year) and in terms of available competences (some kind of controls may require specific skills, such as a special accounting expertise or expertise in variety of technical matters).

On the other hand, controlling everything ('total control'[104]) is not only impossible but even undesirable. It is impossible because there would always have to be another level of control, very well expressed by the paradox of 'who guards the guardians?' (see above, chapter one, section 1.8.3). It is undesirable because excessive administrative controlling produces a sequence which risks being endless, while limitations of administrative capacity to control may result in a great opportunity to organise the system of controls in the best possible way.

According to the relevant literature on corruption, 'the optimal level of corruption is not zero'.[105] Rather, as already mentioned (chapter two, section 2.5), there is an 'optimal amount of corruption'[106] (and even an optimal amount of any other kind of infringement in any possible regulatory sectors) which depends directly on the administrative capacity to perform control activity: the point of intersection of the curves which describe the quantity of corruption (or other kind of infringement) and the marginal social cost of reducing corruption (or other kind of infringement) identifies this optimal level, a level which indicates 'the least-cost combination of corrupt activities and efforts to reduce'.[107] However, even though the amount of corruption (or of any other kind of infringement) is featured as 'optimal', capacity of controls in itself is 'suboptimal', in the sense that controls are destined to be (in the most part of cases) inadequate with a view to achieving full regulatory results.

Far from being the end point of the reasoning, this passage represents a crucial step: it not only helps us to focus on the idea that 'corruption is not the only thing

---

[103] On this point, see, in general, Frank Anechiarico, James B Jacobs, *The Pursuit of Absolute Integrity* 193.

[104] See this expression in Florentin Blanc, *From Chasing Violations to managing risks. Origins, Challenges and Evolutions in Regulatory Inspections* 257 and 259: 'Crucially, and by contrast, there is a wide consensus about the way the system *should* work: there should be *effective total control*. Citizens long for it, businesses assume this is how things should work and inspectors are partly pretending, partly genuinely trying to enforce rules (taking bribes is not necessarily in contradiction with trying or pretending to enforce laws). Our argument is that this *objective of total control* is precisely a core element of the problem'.

[105] Robert Klitgaard, *Controlling Corruption* 24.

[106] Ibid, 27.

[107] Ibid, 26.

we care about'[108] but it also helps to prepare effective enforcement strategies and to organise the system of controls in the most effective way. In other words, if administrative capacity of control is limited, this is not necessarily a bad thing, because clear ideas about real capacity of single inspectorates/controllers to perform inspections/controls or (more specifically) about the real capacity of anticorruption bodies to perform anticorruption controls, constitute the necessary baseline to integrate enforcement with other compliance strategies which are 'focused on results'.[109] Careful consideration of the capacity of surveillance oversight bodies, inspectorates, auditors (both in terms of workload and in terms of competences) may contribute to design more realistic compliance and enforcement strategies, to locate the battle against infringements and corruption in the real world and to perform administrative functions in the flesh.

4.2.5. Planning Controls is not a Simple Task

If administrative resources for controls are limited, then administrations should decide how to enforce regulation via limited controls by responding to questions such as: How many controls? Who (and what) should be subject to controls? When should controls be carried out? What frequency of controls can contribute to making controls as effective as possible?

Responding to these questions means planning controls, and implies decisions about their objectives, available resources, methodology, priorities and timing.[110] In order to effectively plan, a risk-based approach provides criteria to prioritise resources on those citizens and firms which present the highest risk.[111]

The UK Hampton Report in 2005 recommended that all regulatory agencies adopt a comprehensive risk-based approach[112] to regulatory enforcement by requiring 'robust risk assessment methodologies to program inspections so that no inspection takes place without a reason'.[113] In 2014 the OECD Report

---

[108] Ibid, 27.
[109] Keith Hawkins, *Law as Last Resort. Prosecution Decision-Making in a Regulatory Agency* (Oxford University Press, 2002) 46.
[110] See, on this point, US Council of the Inspectors General on Integrity and Efficiency, *Quality Standards for Inspection and Evaluation*, January 2012, especially where 'planning' is analysed, 9–10. See also Carolyn Abbot, 'Losing the local? Public participation and legal expertise in planning law' (2020) in *Legal Studies*, 269.
[111] Florentin Blanc, *From Chasing Violations to Managing Risks* 192: 'A *fully risk-based* approach to inspections will include *targeting* based on risk assessment, *focus during visits* and *enforcement decisions* proportional to risk, and *compliance promotion approaches* which are differentiated based on risk (and on compliance drivers analysis)'.
[112] See Julia Black and Robert Baldwin, 'When risk-based regulation aims low: Approaches and challenges' (2012) 6(2) *Regulation & Governance* 131 and Julia Black, 'The emergence of risk-based regulation and the new public risk management in the United Kingdom' (2005) Autumn *Public Law* 512.
[113] Hampton Report, *Reducing administrative burdens: effective inspection and enforcement* 3.

'Regulatory enforcement and inspections' indicated some principles on which 'effective and efficient regulatory enforcement and inspections should be based',[114] particularly relevant for planning inspections and controls. Among others was the principle of *evidence-based enforcement and inspections*, which requires that 'regulatory enforcement and inspections should be evidence-based and measurement-based: deciding what to inspect and how it should be grounded on data and evidence, and results should be evaluated regularly';[115] the principle of *risk-focus and proportionality*, which requires that the 'frequency of inspections and the resources employed should be proportional to the level of risk and enforcement actions should aim at reducing the actual risk posed by infractions'[116] where risk should be intended as 'the combination of the likelihood of an adverse event (hazard, harm) occurring, and of the potential magnitude of the damage caused (itself combining number of people affected, and severity of the damage for each)';[117] the principle of *responsive regulation*[118] which suggests that the 'inspection enforcement actions should be modulated depending on the profile and behaviour of specific businesses';[119] and finally, the principle of *information integration*, which states that 'information and communication technologies should be used to maximize risk-focus, coordination and information-sharing, as well as optimal use of resources'.[120]

However, effective planning depends on the consistency of the whole planning process, which should never be taken for granted. This is articulated at three different levels: the *strategic* (macro) level in which 'policy makers operate at a high level of abstraction and take decisions based on highly "aggregated" risk assessments', where 'analysis such as Regulatory Impact Assessments can take place' and whose output is a 'classification of categories of risk level per type of establishment, and an action programme'; the *operational* (meso) level which is 'concerned with more concrete situations and decisions', where 'the question is not anymore whether to regulate, but what instruments to use' and whose output is the inspections plan; and finally the *targeting and enforcement* (micro) level which 'deals with individual cases (businesses, establishments)', where 'the decision concerns allocation of resources (targeting) and how to respond to a given situation' and whose output is street-level controlling.[121]

---

[114] OECD, *Regulatory Enforcement and Inspections* (OECD, 2014) 9. See also OECD, *Regulatory Enforcement and Inspections Toolkit* (OECD, 2018).
[115] Ibid, 14.
[116] Ibid.
[117] Ibid, 27.
[118] See Ian Ayres, John Braithwaite, *Responsive regulation: Transcending the deregulation debate* (Oxford University Press, 1992) and Robert Baldwin, Julia Black, 'Really responsive regulation' (2008) 71 *Modern Law Review* 59–94.
[119] Ibid, 14
[120] Ibid.
[121] Florentin Blanc, *From Chasing Violations to Managing Risks* 191 where he mention the work of Ferdinand Mertens, *Inspecteeren: Toezicht Door Inspecties* (SDU Uitgevers, 2011).

What is the problem with planning? If the strategic level does not provide a sufficient evidence-based and risk-focused approach (for instance because no regulatory impact analysis (RIA) has been carried out during the law-making process) the whole building will fall. In fact, 'there are only three possibilities in the absence of risk-based planning: "blanket" coverage (every establishment/product is controlled), random inspections, or selection on a basis other than risk'. Without risk-based planning, checks and inspections would be superficial and useless or even casual or (finally) 'based on convenience of inspectors, potential for flattering numbers (of fines, for instance), or rent seeking'.[122]

4.2.6. Sanctions Following Controls Must be Effective in Order to Deter

While administrative capacity to perform controls is limited and controls are costly, it is also important to increase their effectiveness in preventing infringements and corruption. For this purpose, controls as a system should lean strongly towards deterrence by threatening (and effectively imposing) sanctions. However, effective sanctions operate as deterrence against those who infringe and criminals, but they simultaneously send signals to rational calculators and to people who are only barely compliant by reinforcing positive messages to voluntary compliers.

Alongside controls, sanctions of detected non-compliance and infringements constitute the other leg of enforcement. When establishing administrative powers (such as power to investigate and inspect, the power of authorisation, the power to grant subsidies and so on), rules frequently include the possibility to check compliance and to impose penalties and fines, because the fear of sanctions plays its role in the game of effective law.[123] Sanctions, in fact, are economic tools[124] through which law creates an interest in complying with rules.[125]

In the light of the integrated approach to effectiveness, based on the outcomes of rules,[126] the size of sanctions seems to have very little impact,[127] whereas the risk

---

[122] Ibid.
[123] On improving deterrence see John T Scholz, 'Managing Regulatory Enforcement in the United States', in David H Rosenbloom and Richard D Schwartz (eds), *Handbook of Regulation and Administrative Law* (Marcel Dekker, 1994) 426.
[124] On this aspect see Florentin Blanc, *From Chasing Violations to managing risks. Origins, Challenges and Evolutions in Regulatory Inspections* 141–42 where he describes economic incentives as one of the foundations of compliance.
[125] See Carolyn Abbot, *Enforcing Pollution Control Regulation. Strengthening Sanctions and Improving Deterrence* (Hart Publishing, 2009).
[126] Florentin Blanc, *From Chasing Violations to managing risks. Origins, Challenges and Evolutions in Regulatory Inspections* 130.
[127] Ibid 145 and Erich Kirchler, *The Economic Psychology of Tax Behaviour*, (Cambridge University Press, 2007).

with excessive sanctions is that they might backfire. In order to be effective (and to help in making rules effective) sanctions should be well designed by regulation (for example, according to their optimal amount[128]), flexible[129] and adjusted on elasticity of behaviour[130] properly calibrated when in the form of monetary sanctions (because they otherwise operate as a 'price'[131] for non-compliance); sometimes non-monetary sanctions can prove more effective;[132] on the other hand, there are cases in which it would be better to operate via incentives, rewarding enforcement[133] and compliant groups.[134]

According to the most traditional economic view,[135] the individual decision about compliance is a result of an economic reasoning which connects the cost of compliance, the size of the penalty but also the risk of incurring the penalty. From a merely theoretical point of view, increasing the amount of a fine should mean increasing compliance but if the risk of incurring the fine is low (because the system of controls is ineffective or because of recurrent amnesties and pardons which undermine the deterrent effect of the sanctions) then there could be the paradoxical effect that the increase in the fine will produce side-effects, such as an increase in the size of the bribe necessary to corrupt.[136]

The greatest problem in anticorruption policies is, ultimately, making sanctions which are proportionate and certain (as far as possible) and, therefore, an effective deterrent, because despite limits of deterrence strategies 'a deterrence effect exists in certain circumstances, or to a certain degree'.[137] Sanctions should enter into the individual cost-benefit analysis on compliance by making compliance more convenient than corruption.[138] Otherwise, sanctions will operate as a mere indicator for the amount of the bribe without being a deterrent.

---

[128] William M Landes, 'Optimal Sanctions for Antitrust Violations' (1983) 50 *University of Chicago Law Review* 652.

[129] John T Scholz, 'Managing Regulatory Enforcement in the United States' 436.

[130] Lawrence M Friedman, *The legal system. A Social Science Perspective* (Russel Sage, 1975) 71–72.

[131] See Uri Gneezy, Aldo Rustichini, 'A Fine Is a Price' (2000) 29(1) *Journal of Legal Studies* 1.

[132] See Nuno Garoupa, Daniel Klerman, 'Corruption and the Optimal Use of Nonmonetary Sanctions' (2004) 24 *International Review of Law and Economics* 219, 220.

[133] See Gary S Becker, George J Stigler, 'Law enforcement, malfeasance, and compensation of enforcers' (1974) 3(1) *Journal of Legal Studies* 1, 13.

[134] On this point see John A Gardiner and Theodore R Lyman, 'The logic of corruption control', in Arnold J Heidenheimer, Michael Johnston and Victor T Levine (eds), *Political Corruption. A Handbook* (Transaction Publishers, 1993, III ed). 837; Anthony Ogus, 'Corruption and regulatory structures' 337.

[135] Gary S Becker, *Crime and Punishment: An Economic Approach* (1968) in *The Journal of Political Economy*, 76, 169.

[136] See Anthony Ogus, *Corruption and regulatory structures* 336.

[137] Florentin Blanc, *From Chasing Violations to managing risks. Origins, Challenges and Evolutions in Regulatory Inspections* 169, quoting Tom R Tyler, 'What Is Procedural Justice? Criteria Used by Citizens to Assess the Fairness of Legal Procedures' (1988) 22 *Law and Society Review* 103; Christopher Hodges, 'Corporate Behaviour: Enforcement, Support or Ethical Culture?' (2015) Oxford Legal Studies Research Paper No. 19/2015; and Christopher Hodges, *Law and Corporate Behaviour* (Hart Publishing, 2015).

[138] See John A Gardiner and Theodore R Lyman, *The logic of corruption control* 833.

Coming back to the parallel between communication and controlling (above, section 4.2.2), there is another relevant aspect. Not only should sanctions be appropriate, proportionate and calibrated, but be effective and produce deterrence, when necessary. It could be possible to argue that enforcement as a whole (controlling plus sanctioning) works, more or less, as a form of non-verbal communication.[139] If it is true that 'law sends messages',[140] it is nonetheless true that there are two messages:[141] the first comes from the formulation of the rule[142] (which establishes obligations, controls and consequences as sanctions for specific non-compliant behaviours); the second comes from enforcement, and can be consistent or not with the first (for instance, because established controls have/ or have not be implemented, or penalties have/or have not been imposed),[143] influencing the credibility of government.[144]

In this light, deterrence effects related to sanctions may be in danger due to the ineffectiveness of administrative measures following controls, especially in legal systems such as Italy where rates of judicial litigation are very high and unpredictable. In fact, when a fine is imposed (for instance, in a fiscal procedure, such as the assessment of taxes) there is an incentive to litigation. For this reasons, administrations and enforcement officers should contribute to adopt accurate and robust administrative measures (both when controlling and when imposing fines)[145] in order to disincentivise legal actions, to increase sanctions' effectiveness (when necessary) and to make infringements clearly inconvenient.

4.3. Controls from a Practical Perspective: Suggestions

International literature and the most advanced practices in controlling and anticorruption have contributed to identifying factors which may influence effectiveness of controls, such as tools to prevent infringements and corruption.

---

[139] On this point see Albert Mehrabian, *Nonverbal Communication* (Aldine Transaction, 1972).

[140] See Avlana Eisenberg, 'Expressive Enforcement' (2014) *UCLA Law Review* 858. See, finally, Geoffrey P Miller, *An Economic Analysis of Effective Compliance Programs* (New York University Law and Economics Working Papers, Paper 396, 2014) 860. See also Lawrence Lessig 'The Regulation of Social Meaning' (1995) 62 *University of Chicago Law Review* 943.

[141] See Roscoe Pound, 'Law in books and law in action' (1910) 44 *American Law Review* 12.

[142] See William Twining and David Miers, *How to Do Things with Rules* (Cambridge University Press, 2010) 90.

[143] See Arnold J Meltsner, *Policy Analysts in the Bureaucracy* (University of California Press, 1976) 255: 'Effective communication can lead to promotion or demotion, to acceptance or rejection of one's ideas, to success or failure'.

[144] On this point see Robert Nozick, 'Coercion' in Sidney Morgenbesser, Patrick Suppes and Mary White (eds), *Philosophy, Science, and Method. Essays in Honor of Ernest Nagel* (St Martin's Press, 1969) 440.

[145] On this point, John T Scholz, 'Managing Regulatory Enforcement in the United States' 450: 'Compliance officers spend much of their time documenting completed inspections in a manner that justifies their actions according to official guidelines'.

Therefore, with a view to creating effective corruption prevention policies based on controls, these factors must be considered as part of an integrated strategy which gives adequate consideration to information for controls, their accurate design in regulation (also with regard to adequate privacy and data protection standards), planning of controls, enforcement and communication as well as their appropriate reform, when needed. In the following paragraphs these factors will be individually analysed approaching them as being strictly related because they must all be simultaneously considered when designing anticorruption.

4.3.1. Information

Administration needs information – or rather, administrative powers presuppose collecting information in order to adopt well-reasoned administrative decisions which may concretely attain administrative objectives and adequately respond to the public interest.[146] However, information about infringements and corruption is not simple to achieve; in fact, they are secret, carried out 'in the dark' and public officers in charge of controls usually operate with a severe and structural information gap.[147]

At the same time, controls represent the first and stronger tool to bridge the gap by representing not only as regulatory enforcement but also as the real keystone of administrative knowledge. In this regard, while information for controls is needed to implement single inspections, audits and so on (because only information may contribute to 'effectively detecting and investigating incidents of corruption'[148] and other infringements), information which comes from controls constitutes administrative knowledge that is necessary both to carry out further controlling and (in a virtuous circle) to strengthen the gathering of evidence in regulatory processes. On the other hand, mere information may be not conclusive. Rather, because excessive informative burdens may even backfire by decreasing compliance among compliant groups[149] 'businesses should not have to give unnecessary information, nor give the same piece of information twice'.[150]

---

[146] On this point see Maria De Benedetto, 'Competition enforcement: a look at inspections', in Paul Nihoul and Tadeusz Skoczny (eds), *Procedural Fairness in Competition Proceedings* (Edward Elgar, 2015) 145. See also Cary Coglianese, 'Empirical Analysis and Administrative Law' (2002) *University of Illinois Law Review*, 1113. See, in general, on this topic, George J Stigler, 'The Economics of Information' (1961) 69(3) *Journal of Political Economy* 213.

[147] See James Jacobs, *Dilemmas of Corruption Controls* 290: 'it is hard to think of any other crime which so lacks an indicator of prevalence'. On this point see also Alberto Zuliani, 'L'informazione come strumento per contrastare la corruzione', in Marco D'Alberti (ed) *Corruzione e Pubblica Amministrazione* (Jovene, 2017) 483.

[148] Ibid.

[149] Florentin Blanc, *From Chasing Violations to Managing Risks* 196: 'As for those who are inclined to voluntary compliance, burdensome information collection is likely to create resistance and overall lead to a *decrease* in compliance'.

[150] Hampton Report, HM Treasury, *Reducing administrative burdens: effective inspection and enforcement* 7.

Information and knowledge for and from 'state functions' (regulation, administration and controls) are formulated statistically,[151] in the sense that they present an aggregate structure, and they need intelligence.[152]

Regarding their aggregate structure, information for and from controls is ever more channelled into databases and automatised information, while machine learning and artificial intelligence technologies are becoming ever more relevant in administrative decisional processes and in controls.[153] For instance, 'data matching'[154] is an indispensable support of controlling[155] because only intelligent information prepares a risk-based approach to controlling, where 'a strong majority of inspections would be proactive, and data driven, rather than reactive and complaints driven'.[156]

However, criminal data banks rarely reference crimes or infringements in a way which is really useful for preventive administrative tasks, and very often they serve specific goals (such as measuring the number of complaints or police productivity, proceedings pending before judicial offices and so on[157]) while rarely giving information in 'administrative language', ie by indicating relevant regulation or administrative bodies, procedures and agents maybe involved in crimes and infringements. Fiscal data banks in all kinds of legal systems contribute to provisional state budget estimates but also to planning fiscal controls: for instance, they allow the gathering of elements regarding subjective corruptibility, which is relevant because fiscal infringements are considered a good proxy of the tendency to infringe in other sectors. Among others, data banks relating to public procurement and anti-money laundering activities collect important information and may help in understanding how infringements and corruption work, as well as how the

---

[151] On 'statistics and statistical thinking', see Paul Starr, The sociology of official statistics, in William Alonso, Paul Starr (eds), *The Politics of Numbers* (Russel Sage Foundation, 1987) 16; A Desrosières, *La politique des grands nombres. Histoire de la raison statistique*, 3rd edn (La Découverte, 2010); JE Stiglitz, Knowledge as Global Public Good, in I Kaul et al., *Global Public Goods* (Undp, 1999).

[152] In fact, aggregate information, data interpretation and ex-post evaluation represent the way in which public powers may know (before), steer (after) and evaluate (finally) their governing of society and economics. For this reason, official statistics is considered a public good, a matter of common interest which deserves protection, for instance via guarantees of independence for national statistical services, see D Marder, *Independence, an issue of trust*, Unece Conference of European Statisticians, Working Session on Statistical Dissemination and Communication, Geneva, 13–15 May 2008. Economic Secretary to the Treasury, *Statistics, a Matter of Trust. A Consultation Document*, February 1998.

[153] On this aspect see, Cary Coglianese, David Lehr, 'Transparency and Algorithmic Governance' (2019) 71 *Administrative Law Review* 1.

[154] See Daniel J Steinbock, 'Data matching, data mining and due process' (2005) 40(1) *Georgia Law Review* 3–4: '"Data matching" – linking individuals with data about them'.

[155] On this point see Florentin Blanc, *From Chasing Violations to Managing Risks* 176: 'Building effective information management systems to manage such information (including *integrated* systems across several inspectorates) has become far easier (and cheaper) than a few years ago due to technological advances'.

[156] Ibid, 193.

[157] See Constantin Stefanou, Helen Xanthaki (eds), *Towards a European Criminal Record* (Cambridge University Press, 2008).

interests which motivate them operate,[158] in this way increasing the probability of detecting and preventing them, as far as possible.[159] Finally, where available, data banks regarding litigation before any possible kinds of court (civil, criminal, administrative, fiscal and so on) which are opportunely configured and queried may help in focusing on situations deserving of attention, to effectively orient controls.

Due to the risk of information overload,[160] intelligence is needed to make information meaningful and really significant. In this light, risk or anomaly indicators[161] help in identifying relevant situations, steering controls where they are more necessary, and making knowledge from controls usable, even in other fields of administration.

Moreover, in efficient administrations *intelligence* and *controlling at the street-level* (concrete enforcement) are considered distinct functions because they imply very different activities which need to be implemented through specific competences and skills.[162] Let us think of institutions responsible for anti-money laundering tasks, according to international conventions; despite being constituted differently, there are normally financial intelligence units (FIU) in charge of defining anomaly indicators of possible suspicious transactions and of reporting powers while concrete controls are carried out by different agencies and administrations, specifically devoted to checks and inspections. Moreover, fiscal agencies all over the world perform intelligence for tax assessment and about fiscal evasion while fiscal inspections are considered a separate, street-level function.

Among other problems, information may be weakened by technical aspects (such as the material lack of information sharing between public administrations), by legal aspects (such as when this lack of sharing is due to or made more difficult for data protection reasons or other legal motives) and finally by organisational aspects. In this last regard, the central problem is how information is recorded, which also gives an idea as to the scope of its significance. Information about infringements and crimes is very often quite basic with no additional elements (there either is or is not an infringement, there either is or is not a formal complaint, there either is or is not a statement of infringement). Sometimes problems are in the coding; sometimes despite the coding being adequate, the information is not sufficiently exploited.

---

[158] Christoph H Stefes, 'Measuring, Conceptualizing, and Fighting Systemic Corruption: Evidence from Post-Soviet Countries' (2007) 2(1) *Perspectives on Global Issue* 14.

[159] Robert Klitgaard, *Controlling Corruption* 94.

[160] Cass R Sunstein, *Too Much Information. Understanding What You Don't Want to Know* (MIT Press, 2020) 264.

[161] Scott A Fritzen and Shreya Basu, 'From information to indicators: monitoring progress in the fight against corruption in multi-project, multi-stakeholder organizations', in Adam Graycar and Russel G Smith (eds), *Handbook of Global Research and Practice in Corruption* (Edward Elgar, 2011) 285.

[162] Edward L Rubin, 'Bureaucratic Oppression: Its Causes and Cures' (2012) 90(2) *Washington University Law Review* 334: 'To foster an ethos of customer service, control functions should be separated from service functions and assigned to a different unit of the agency'.

In order to improve information and knowledge about infringements and corruption, regulators may also put in place incentives to provide information, by contributing to bridge (at least in part) the information gap between institutions and citizens/firms being controlled. This approach has already been implemented in some sectors, such as in the fight against organised crime and terrorisms but is also used in competition law where leniency programmes[163] have been introduced in order to achieve indispensable 'insider evidence' about the way in which infringements and corruption have been carried out.

This approach is also provided by whistle-blower protection, which has been considered crucial for anticorruption as a way to encourage public officials to report wrongdoing.[164] The idea is that whistle-blower protection deters as well as detects, given the facts that 'employees in both the public and private sectors can access up-to-date information concerning workplace practices and are usually the first to recognise wrongdoing'.[165] On the other hand, whistle-blower protection has been strongly criticised as undermining 'the authority of public-sectors managers ... the morale of a unit or agency without making any significant contribution to reducing corruption'[166] and because 'there are grounds for believing that compensating whistle-blowers may actually induce more corruption'.[167]

Finally, information is not only a contribution to enforcement but also an alternative to it, to avoid both controlling and sanctioning. Let us consider the practice of 'compliance letters' from tax authorities (for instance, in Italy)[168]

---

[163] US Department of Justice: 'The Antitrust Division's Leniency Program is its most important investigative tool for detecting cartel activity. Corporations and individuals who report their cartel activity and cooperate in the Division's investigation of the cartel reported can avoid criminal conviction, fines, and prison sentences if they meet the requirements of the program', www.justice.gov/atr/leniency-program; European Commission: 'In essence, the leniency policy offers companies involved in a cartel – which self-report and hand over evidence – either total immunity from fines or a reduction of fines which the Commission would have otherwise imposed on them. It also benefits the Commission, allowing it not only to pierce the cloak of secrecy in which cartels operate but also to obtain insider evidence of the cartel infringement. The leniency policy also has a very deterrent effect on cartel formation and it destabilises the operation of existing cartels as it seeds distrust and suspicion among cartel members', htps://ec.europa.eu/competition/cartels/leniency/leniency.html.

[164] OECD, *Committing to Effective Whistleblower Protection* (OECD, 2016) 18. The 'definition of whistleblower protection is similar to the 2009 Anti-Bribery Recommendation and is described as legal protection from discriminatory or disciplinary action for employees who disclose to the competent authorities in good faith and on reasonable grounds wrongdoing of whatever kind in the context of their workplace'.

[165] Ibid, 18.

[166] Frank Anechiarico and James B Jacobs, *The Pursuit of Absolute Integrity. How Corruption Control Makes Government Ineffective* 199.

[167] Anthony Ogus, 'Corruption and regulatory structures' 338: 'First, it gives the briber a sanction, should the bribee fail to comply with the agreement, thus overcoming the problem that corruption contracts are not enforceable in the courts. Second, it may encourage gamekeepers to become poachers, by enabling bribers to threaten to frame innocent officials, and thus extort payments from them'. On this topic, see also Nicoletta Rangone, 'A behavioural approach to administrative corruption prevention', in Agustì Cerillo-I-Martinez A and Juli Ponce (eds), *Preventing Corruption and Promoting good Government and Public Integrity* (Bruylant 2017), especially 75 onwards where whistle-blower regulation is analysed.

[168] On this point see Agenzia delle entrate, *L'Agenzia ti scrive: lettere di invito a regolarizzare possibili errori* ('The Revenue Agency writes you: invitation letters to regularise possible mistakes') July 2017,

which intend to share information with taxpayers informing them of possible mistakes or irregularities. This 'I-Know-That-You-Know-That-I-Know'[169] strategy seems to be very effective in inducing compliance before any control has occurred or any administrative measure has been adopted.

As a general assumption, if any kind of data banks may be of interest for control activities, data banks regarding controls may be of interest for other possible types of administrative functions. Let us take into consideration the case of enforcement of social distancing measures via police controls during the COVID-19 pandemic. In many jurisdictions there has been daily evidence and reporting of controls carried out by the police and about the number of breaches of lockdown orders, false declarations, breaches of quarantine for infected persons, and so on. On the basis of this evidence, it would be possible to develop a rough but interesting and promising analysis of compliance regarding social distancing measures. Furthermore, the rate of compliance may express a certain statistical correlation with the flattening of the pandemic curve. In this perspective it could be very important for data to be collected during controls, data treatment and data communication would be oriented to (and ready to be used for) a wide range of administrative purposes, as far as possible.[170]

To summarise, information for and from controls as a tool to combat infringements and corruption has to be developed in the logic of evidence-based policy making.[171] In this general framework, information exchange and intelligence[172] represent new law-enforcement tools, especially where there is an increasing

---

where they refer to sharing of information with the taxpayer ('condivisione delle informazioni con il contribuente').

[169] *Io so che tu sai che io so* is a 1982 Italian movie directed and interpreted by Alberto Sordi.

[170] Florentin Blanc and Maria De Benedetto, 'Enforcing social distancing – assessing what works and what doesn't', in *OECD - On the level*, 12 May 2020: 'A first opportunity to apply such analysis is offered by the Italian case, where the Ministry of the Interior publishes daily data on the results of police controls of citizens and businesses for compliance with the lockdown and social distancing measures. Based on published data, the controls only assess overall compliance (i.e., lumping together both formal non-compliance with self-certification rules, and substantive non-compliance with social distancing), but it remains to be verified whether internal (non-published) data exists with more details. Even if this were not the case, the aggregate levels of compliance/non-compliance can be assessed to consider both whether there are any trends to be observed over time, or between regions, and whether there are any correlations appearing between compliance levels and the evolution of the Covid situation in Italy. At the very least, the aggregate compliance levels could give an indication of what can be achieved with relatively "moderate" levels of control, and compared to outcomes (where available) for other countries with different approaches. Moreover, this study could form the basis for additional recommendations on what kind of data should be recorded in the future by police forces to allow for more meaningful assessment of the situation'.

[171] Sul punto v OECD, *Statistics, Knowledge and Policy: Key Indicators to Inform Decision Making* (OECD, 2005).

[172] See *The Hague Programme: strengthening freedom, security and justice in the European Union* (2005/C 53/01), in particular point 2.6, *Crime prevention*: 'initiative of the Commission to establish European instruments for collecting, analysing and comparing information on crime and victimization and their respective trends in Member States, using national statistics and other sources of information as agreed indicators'. See also *The Stockholm Programme – An open and Secure Europe serving and protecting citizens* (2010/C 115/01).

relevance for the 'application of new technologies to the deterrence and detection of crime'.[173] Information should be managed along an integrated and strategic vision of the data bank network[174] and should circulate among different agencies and administrative bodies in charge of infringements and corruption prevention[175] opportunely incentivised by adequate institutional design,[176] whether they operate in criminal investigations or in administrative controls. In other words, 'information and communication technologies should be used to maximise risk-focus, coordination and information-sharing, as well as optimal use of resources'.[177]

4.3.2. Regulation

As already mentioned, controls and regulation are strictly connected at many levels. In order to make regulation capable (as far as possible) of preventing infringements and corruption, some general remedies have been mentioned and described in chapter three. With respect to regulatory stock, the suggested remedies are simplification and advocacy powers; with respect to regulatory flow, the suggested remedies are anticorruption assessment of regulation and tracing of interests.

However, focusing on the question from the specific perspective of controls, something else can be added to give further clarification of aspects related to causes and effects.[178]

Controls are firstly a question of rules, they exists thanks to regulation.[179] In other words, they depend on regulatory provisions in the same way as any other

---

[173] On this topic, from an historic point of view, see Nicholas de B Katzenbach and Richard W Tome, 'Crime Data Centers: The Use of Computers in Crime Detection and Prevention' (1972) 4 *Columbia Human Rights Law Review* 49–50.
[174] See Constantin Stefanou and Helen Xanthaki (eds), *Towards a European Criminal Record*.
[175] See Adam Graycar and Russel G Smith, *Handbook of Global Research and Practice in Corruption* 290.
[176] Matthew C Stephenson, 'Information Acquisition and Institutional Design' (2011) 124 *Harvard Law Review* 1422.
[177] OECD, *Regulatory enforcement and inspection*: 'Information sharing is essential as it allows inspectorates to have a much more accurate and updated assessment of the risk level of each business, without spending additional resources and enables them to avoid duplication of work. Therefore, common databases should be put in place by governments to be used by different enforcement agencies. Exploiting modern technologies in setting up a joint system for several inspection bodies, rather than procuring separate systems with largely similar specifications, is cost effective and offers considerable benefits in terms of risk-management and coordination. Thus, the OECD recommends that governments support the renewal of information systems for enforcement bodies, aiming at supporting effective risk-management, and give preference to shared systems across several inspectorates whenever possible'.
[178] On regulations, inspections and corruption see Florentin Blanc, *From Chasing Violations to managing risks. Origins, Challenges and Evolutions in Regulatory Inspections* (Edward Elgar, 2018) 125 et seq.
[179] Edward L Rubin, 'Bureaucratic Oppression: Its Causes and Cures' 297: 'It is not surprising that the classic account of bureaucratic oppression, Nikolai Gogol's 'The Overcoat' comes from nineteenth-century Russia, where bureaucracy was used as a means of controlling a vast, under-developed realm, and no mechanisms of democratic supervision were available to moderate its rigors'.

kind of administrative task. In fact, no power of control may be provided until a rule sets out a command, a prohibition or a permission to be controlled; until a rule establishes sanctions to be imposed as a consequence of detected non-compliance; or until a rule identifies and designates a public body, an agency or an inspectorate which will have specific responsibility for checking regulatory compliance via controls.

Furthermore, *effective controls are a question of good rules.* Albeit a difficulty regarding 'the optimal precision of rules',[180] controls are more likely to be effective in preventing infringements and corruption if regulation provides for their accurate design and to evaluate ex ante and ex post assessment regarding their impact. When adopting a regulation, various kinds of controls (inspections, audits, surveys and so on) are established and disciplined as part of the regulatory enforcement system (for instance, in matters of food safety, fiscal law,[181] competition, public procurements and so on). In the same way as sanctions, controls should be accurately considered in the regulatory process (rule design),[182] where their residuality, proportionality and risk-based orientation may be evaluated and where their organisational design is drafted (who controls whom, in which situations, according to what standards, with what consequences and so on). Impact assessment (or impact regulatory analysis) provides this sort of articulated ex ante evaluation and prepares the ex post assessment by including the need for the regulatory intervention, the gathering of evidence, specific regulatory objectives, consultations, indicators and data banks for monitoring, and regulatory options. All these elements contribute to a complex reasoning through which the enforcement system will be more fit to achieve regulatory objectives.[183]

Moreover, *effective regulation is a question of good quality information coming from controls*, because regulation depends on knowledge based on controls. As already mentioned, information and knowledge coming from controls strongly contribute to the gathering of evidence on which regulation is drafted and adopted by describing the real regulatory status quo (number of infringements detected by controls at a certain time, typologies of infringements, their motivations, evidence and criticisms emerged during controls and so on).

---

[180] Colin S Diver, 'The Optimal Precision of Administrative Rules' (1983) 93(1) *Yale Law Journal* 65, where he talks about 'dissatisfaction with the precision of administrative rules, because of either administrative underprecision or excessive regulatory rigidity'; on this aspect, see also Robert Baldwin, *Rules and Government* (Clarendon Press, 1995) 176 et seq.

[181] On this point see, Lennart Wittberg, *Enforcement strategies. How enforcement can improve tax compliance*, Skatteverket Rapport, 14/3/2016.

[182] See Robert Baldwin, *Rules and Government* (Clarendon Press, 1995) 174.

[183] On this point, see the pyramid of enforcement responses, Ian Ayres and John Braithwaite, *Responsive Regulation. Transcending the Deregulation Debate* (Oxford University Press, 1992) 35; see also Valerie Braithwaite and John Braithwaite, 'An Evolving Compliance Model for Tax Enforcement', in Neal Shover and John Paul Wright (eds) *Crimes of privilege. Readings in white-collar crime* (Oxford University Press, 2000) 405 et seq; see finally, Neil Gunningham and Peter Grabosky, *Smart Regulation. Designing Environmental Policy* (Oxford University Press, 1998).

Finally, *effective regulation is a question of effective controls*, because regulatory delivery definitely affects regulatory impact and success.[184] Controls are incredibly relevant for regulatory effectiveness: the better they are capable to detect infringements and corruption, the more they will contribute to deterrence and to incentivise compliance. On the other hand, as mentioned above (chapter one, section 1.7.2) controls may unfortunately give the opportunity for *objective corruption-type controls*, they constitute a 'hotspot':[185] corruption is a special kind of regulatory ineffectiveness and the risk of corruption should be expressly considered during the regulatory process in order to put in place countermeasures to limit corrupt transactions: among other measures, incentives for compliance; staff rotation of inspection's team; transparency of controls; codes of conduct for inspectors; independence of controllers; sufficient guarantees and remuneration for inspectors and so on.

In short, on one side, effective controls are necessary in order to make regulation effective, ie to increase rates of compliance and to reduce infringements and corruption; on the other side, regulation, regulatory enforcement and controls represent elements of a circular system where everything plays a role and mutually influences the effectiveness of law, making it crucial that the regulatory process as the privileged place in which to consider the problem of corruption prevention (among others).

There is no doubt that one of the best ways to prevent corruption during controls via regulation is to limit the need for and the number of controls which may produce the occasion of a direct contact between enforcement officers and citizens/firms by establishing them only when indispensable, only proportionately and only with a strict risk-based orientation.[186]

4.3.3. Privacy and Data Protection

When talking about controls (whether intended to prevent infringements and corruption or not), regulators very often neglect to adequately consider a hidden price which strongly affects people's freedom and, more generally, which has an important influence on the quality of democratic systems: the price of privacy and data protection.

---

[184] On this aspect, see Graham Russell and Christopher Hodges, *Regulatory Delivery* (Hart Publishing, 2019); see also OECD, *Removing administrative barriers, improving regulatory delivery*, 16 September 2020.

[185] Florentin Blanc, *From Chasing Violations to managing risks* 125.

[186] On this point see, Susan Rose-Ackerman, 'Trust, honesty and corruption: reflection on the state-building process' (2001) 42(3) *European Journal of Sociology* 535 where she argues that when monitoring is too difficult and costly 'the solution may be to reduce the human element in administration. One might simply limit the conditions under which trust is needed'.

Advantages related to controls, in fact, are not an absolute. Each typology of control should be justified in terms of utility: balance may be both specific (including the cost/benefit of single controls) and also more general (cost/benefit of the system of controls, also in terms of individual freedoms).[187] Privacy protection and data regulation do not impede controls but they prevent controls from resulting in excessive restrictions of rights by graduating their invasiveness: for instance, some administrations (intelligence services or police) are allowed to carry out more pervasive controls than others, even though in constitutional democracies a minimum amount of privacy protection characterises the activities of even the most intrusive controls.[188]

Figure 4.3 Graduated Invasiveness of Privacy Protection and Data Regulation

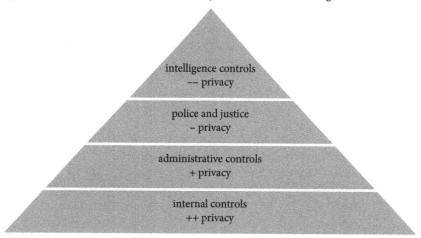

As already mentioned, to prevent infringements and corruption there is a greater need for information quality than for information quantity[189] because the indiscriminate disseminating of large amounts of data is not always useful for controls,

---

[187] See Florentin Blanc, *From Chasing Violations to managing risks* 197: 'Such efforts to achieve more consolidation and sharing of data can be challenged based on privacy concerns (and privacy and data protection legislation, in some cases). There are very different perspectives on what is the appropriate level of privacy and data protection in different countries, and implementing such new systems would be more difficult, eg, in Germany than in the UK from this perspective, even though it is about *corporate* rather than *personal* data'.

[188] On this point, see the table in Giuseppe Busia, 'Privacy, trasparenza e controlli sull'attività pubblica', in Marco D'Alberti, *Corruzione e pubblica amministrazione* 559. Note that Giuseppe Busia was appointed in 2020 as Chair of the Italian Anticorruption Authority.

[189] Art 5 General Data Protection Regulation (GDPR), EU 2016/679, Principles relating to processing of personal data, establishes (among other things) that personal data shall be: 'd. accurate and, where necessary, kept up to date; every reasonable step must be taken to ensure that personal data that are inaccurate, having regard to the purposes for which they are processed, are erased or rectified without delay ("accuracy")'.

rather information overload may reduce data quality, making its analysis more difficult and resulting in late achievement of the objectives of controls and investigation. For this reason, it is necessary to identify valuable and selected information, data which is really useful for regulatory purposes, according to principles expressed by the General Data Protection Regulation, such as lawfulness, fairness and transparency, purpose limitation, data minimisation, accuracy, storage limitation, integrity and confidentiality, and accountability.[190]

What is particularly disputed is the possibility to use big data for controls, information held and used by the so-called Over the Top, especially media over the Internet, even leading to subtle forms of profiling: nowadays the biggest monopolists on the internet definitely manage much more information than public controllers in a framework of reduced guarantees for the freedom of individuals and people's rights.

A system of controls which is privacy oriented aims to avoid the 'privacy rhetoric'[191] and to better organise data bases by allowing a structured comparison between data and situations and by adopting indicators of infringements and corruption in the form of alerts. For these reasons, a series of remedies may be crucial: first, regulating controls in a logic of privacy protection (privacy by design), by setting controls on less intrusive options (privacy by default);[192] second, directing guardians and controllers towards information which is truly meaningful for infringements and corruption, rather than by collecting every piece of information regarding individuals; third, avoiding duplication of public data bases, which increases the risk of mistakes and misalignments by multiplying costs; and finally, avoiding the publication of the same information on sites belonging to different administrations, and concentrating on more relevant information on reference sites, in this way allowing a real benchmark.

---

[190] On this point, see Gloria Gonzales Fuster, *The emergence of Personal Data Protection as a Fundamental Right of the EU* (Springer, 2014) and Daniel J Solove, *Understanding privacy* (Harvard University Press, 2010).

[191] Ruth Gavison, 'Privacy and the Limits of Law' (1980) 89(3) *Yale Law Journal* 420, 421.

[192] Art 25 GRDP (Data protection by design and by default) establishes that: '1. Taking into account the state of the art, the cost of implementation and the nature, scope, context and purposes of processing as well as the risks of varying likelihood and severity for rights and freedoms of natural persons posed by the processing, the controller shall, both at the time of the determination of the means for processing and at the time of the processing itself, implement *appropriate technical and organisational measures*, such as pseudonymisation, which are *designed* to implement data-protection principles, such as data minimisation, in an effective manner and to integrate the necessary safeguards into the processing in order to meet the requirements of this Regulation and protect the rights of data subjects. 2. The controller shall implement appropriate technical and organisational measures for ensuring that, *by default*, only personal data which are necessary for each specific purpose of the processing are processed. That obligation applies to the amount of personal data collected, the extent of their processing, the period of their storage and their accessibility. In particular, such measures shall ensure that by default personal data are not made accessible without the individual's intervention to an indefinite number of natural persons'.

4.3.4. Planning

If administrative capacity to implement controls is limited, then planning is strongly advisable in order to maximise their effectiveness and to make deterrence possible as the effect desired by the rules which establish controls and sanctions.

In many countries,[193] 'state and non-state bodies'[194] have adopted a risk-based approach to regulation[195] which requires adequate planning controls, ie increasing them where necessary, and cutting them in low-risk situations.

Risk-analysis aims to limit the likelihood of socially undesirable phenomena wherever necessary, resorting to risk-based controls in health systems, environmental regulation, financial regulation, food security and so on.[196] It is directed towards more vulnerable areas, where the risk of non-compliance is higher. And finally, it tends to allocate public resources in order to achieve objectives in an optimal way (risk management).

Planning controls are nowadays adopted for all kinds of controls:[197] controls of private activities,[198] controls of administrative activities (both internal[199] and external[200]), and even anticorruption controls.[201] In all cases, planning controls

---

[193] On this point, see Florentin Blanc, *From Chasing Violations to Managing Risks* 106 where he observes 'Some authors have challenged claims of "convergence" and questioned whether risk-based approaches are "universally applicable foundations for improving the quality, efficiency, and rationality of governance across policy domains", as some of their proponents have claimed. In their overview of cases in France and Germany, in counterpoint with the UK, they find (somewhat unsurprisingly) that "the emergence of risk as an organizing concept of governance varies across countries".

[194] Robert Baldwin, Martin Cave and Martin Lodge, *Understanding Regulation. Theories, strategy and practice* 281.

[195] On this aspect, see Christopher Hood, Henry Rothstein and Robert Baldwin, *The Government of Risk. Understanding Risk Regulation Regimes* (Oxford University Press, 2004). See also Livia Lorenzoni, 'Risk-based approach towards corruption prevention', in Agustì Cerillo-I-Martinez A and Juli Ponce (eds), *Preventing Corruption and Promoting good Government and Public Integrity* 111.

[196] Julia Black, 'The role of risk in regulatory processes', in Robert Baldwin, Martin Lodge and Martin Cave, *Oxford Handbook of Regulation* (Oxford University Press, 2010); Robert Baldwin, Julia Black, 'Really responsive regulation' (2009) 71(1) *Modern Law Review* 59; Julia Black, 'Risk Based Regulation: Choices, Practices and Lessons Being Learned', in *Risk and Regulatory Policy: Improving the Governance of Risk* (OECD, 2010); Robert Baldwin and Julia Black, 'Really Responsive Risk Based Regulation' (2010) 32(2) *Law and Policy* 181.

[197] Livia Lorenzoni, 'La pianificazione dei controlli nel contrasto agli illeciti e alla corruzione', in Marco D'Alberti, *Corruzione e pubblica amministrazione* 512 et seq.

[198] Hampton Report, *Reducing Administrative burden: effective inspection and enforcement* (2005); OECD, *Best Practice Principles for Improving Regulatory Enforcement and Inspections* (2014).

[199] On this point, see United States Government Accountability Office, *Standards for Internal Control in the Federal Government* (Green Book), September 2014, 12: 'Management sets objectives before designing an entity's internal control system. Management may include setting objectives as part of the strategic planning process'.

[200] World Bank, *Role of Supreme Audit Institutions (SAIs) in Governments' Response to COVID-19: Emergency and Post Emergency Phases*, June 2020, 3: 'Auditors are expected to be present and visible, assuring their readiness to respond with timely audit products to enhance accountability. At the same time, they should be engaged in assessing risks associated with government programs and responses and planning risk-responsive audit approaches'.

[201] See Australian Government, Department of Industry, Innovation and Science, *Fraud and Corruption Control Plan* 2018-20, www.industry.gov.au/sites/default/files/fraud-and-corruption-control-plan.pdf.

based on risk analysis impose an evidence-based model upon administrative decisions.

However, planning (as a general issue) raises some criticisms, especially when intended to combat infringements and corruption: in fact, planning would require a statistical evaluation of measurable phenomena made more complex by difficulties (and costs) in collecting and managing information about infringements and corruption.

Other criticisms characterise the planning of controls: pervasiveness of corruption, which may result in planning being inadequate to cover the broad spectrum of subjects and procedures involved; model myopia, which tends to perpetuate a historical system of risk indicators by impeding the detection of new forms of corruption;[202] and heterogeneity of sectors and actors involved in controls which may hinder planning effectiveness in a context of fragmented regulatory responsibilities.

Furthermore, despite caveats regarding behavioural and cognitive evidence, when citizens and firms to be controlled understand the rationale of planning, they can quantify the risk of controls and the possible cost of non-compliance (in terms of sanctions): understanding the logic of planning permits cost-benefit calculations connected to violation. Paradoxically, planning may sometimes indirectly facilitate non-compliance.

For these reasons, in planning effective controls, it would be important to turn to:

- centralised systems which collect information about the risk of infringements and corruption in public administrations;
- criteria for the evaluation of risks which consider the pervasiveness and systematic relevance of corruption;
- a certain number of random controls which impede (or at least hinder) any cost-benefit analysis for administrations, citizens and firms.[203]

Finally, when planning controls, two further aspects should matter and be adequately considered: on the one hand, the history of compliance of citizens and firms; on the other side, behavioural and cognitive insights which may contribute to revealing the best way or the best time to control.[204]

---

[202] Robert Baldwin and Julia Black, 'Really Responsive Risk Based Regulation' 206.
[203] Maria De Benedetto, 'Corruption and Controls' 24 et seq.
[204] On this point see Nicoletta Rangone, 'A behavioural approach to administrative corruption prevention', in Agustì Cerillo-I-Martinez A and Juli Ponce (eds), *Preventing Corruption and Promoting good Government and Public Integrity* 88. See also Nicoletta Rangone, 'Making Law Effective: Behavioural Insights into Compliance' (2018) 9(3) *European Journal of Risk Regulation* 483.

4.3.5. Enforcement

As already mentioned, enforcement is an essential aspect of regulation, being part of regulatory delivery[205] which is strictly related to regulatory intended outcomes rather than to mere compliance. Moreover, enforcement and inspections[206] 'appear relevant for economic development, to achieve public welfare goals, and to strengthen the rule of law'. On the other hand, 'inspections and control are absolutely necessary for some, oppressive and hostile for others'[207] and the way in which inspections and controls are concretely implemented may influence their effectiveness and may even determine the increase or decrease in compliance and a corresponding increase or decrease in corruption.

When inspecting, enforcement officers may choose to take different approaches, depending on the situation they have to manage, according to the pyramid of enforcement. At the bottom of the pyramid (where people want to comply or seek to comply), controls would be more cooperative (making compliance as easier as possible and supporting compliance) while at the top they would be ever more stringent and severe, by expressing the best of coercion (by formal controlling and sanctioning).

In a certain way, the idea mirrors the posture of those who are controlled in the enforcement style which changes 'approaches as business behaviours change'.[208]

In this nuanced context, some other considerations may be important in order to make enforcement and controls effective in preventing infringements and corruption.

Adopting the point of view of *administrative procedures*, three factors deserve mention. Firstly, before any inspection, enforcement officers should be adequately informed about the reference framework, both regarding those who are to be inspected and the object of inspection. This knowledge is achieved via database cross-checks to verify convenience and feasibility of tools other than intrusive controls (document requests, questionnaires and so on). Secondly, when it is necessary to gain access to premises (factories, professional offices, commercial establishments and so on), enforcement officers should take care about procedural fairness because the inspection is informed by the right to be heard and they must make sure that the results of inspections will be usable as well as related sanctions will be valid. Thirdly, as far as possible, the results of inspections should be transparent and publicly accessible, with due caution for possible reputational damages.

---

[205] Graham Russell and Christopher Hodges (eds), *Regulatory Delivery*.
[206] On following aspects, see Francesca Di Lascio, 'L'attuazione dei controlli: ispezioni e anticorruzione', in Marco D'Alberti, *Corruzione e pubblica amministrazione* 549–50.
[207] Florentin Blanc, *From Chasing Violations to Managing Risks* 2.
[208] Ibid, 146.

If the point of view of *administrative organisation* were adopted, it would be important to:

- rationalise the design of inspections and increase their coordination;
- strengthen inspection bodies, including reward mechanisms and dedicated training;[209]
- adopt manuals to carry out inspections;[210]
- implement joint inspections; and
- increase the role of inspectors' pools.

4.3.6. Communication

Communication may contribute to the limiting of infringements and corruption; however, anticorruption itself includes communication strategies designed to integrate the role of the media and that of anticorruption agencies in order to make the perception of corruption more realistic and anticorruption more effective.[211]

A first reason why communication is relevant in combating corruption is that it influences compliance as well as the effectiveness of controls, making corruption simply less frequent. At the bottom of the pyramid of enforcement, communication is particularly relevant because 'the bottom of the pyramid corresponds to pure persuasion'.[212] On the other hand, at the top of the pyramid actions will be the best communication strategy.

In fact, communication is considered to be one of the strategies for compliance by operating between institutions (on one side) and citizens and firms (on the other side). Communication supports effective rules and

---

[209] Robert A Kagan, 'On regulatory inspectorates and police' 39.
[210] In some legal systems public officers implement inspections according to Guidelines, Manuals and Handbooks. See, on this point, *School Inspection Handbook*, Handbook for inspecting schools in England under section 5 of the Education Act 2005, December 2017; US Food & Drug Administration, *Inspection Guides* in several sectors (Biotechnology, Devices, Drugs and so on); Food and Agriculture Organization, *Risk-based Food Inspection Manual*, FAO Food and Nutrition Paper 89, 2008.
[211] On this point see Elaine Byrne, Anne-Katrin Arnold, Fumiko Nagano, *Building public support for anti-corruption efforts: why anti-corruption agencies need to communicate and how* (The International Bank for Reconstruction and Development/The World Bank Communication for Governance & Accountability Program 2010), 1: 'when the media supports the anti-corruption agency's work, it is possible to turn the culture of an entire country toward openness and accountability'; see also Heather Marquette, *Communication in anti-corruption work: Articulating messages to structure a communication plan* (OECD, 2014). On this topic, see Giordano Locchi, 'Comunicazioni di massa, Comunicazione pubblica e prevenzione della corruzione', in Marco D'Alberti, *Corruzione e pubblica amministrazione* (Jovene, 2017) 577.
[212] Florentin Blanc, *From Chasing Violations to Managing Risks* 147.

160 Anticorruption: Controls

effective administration[213] and 'is a vital prerequisite to impact':[214] when rules are clear, consistent and characterised by appropriate publicity, their application is facilitated; moreover when rules have been adopted through consultation processes their legitimacy will be stronger and compliance is more likely. However, there is sometimes a problem of consistency in communication, because communication consists not only of good quality verbal messages, nor is it only a one-way process;[215] it implies non-verbal elements and feedback. As already mentioned (section 4.2.6), enforcement works, more or less, as a form of non-verbal communication[216] by confirming (or not) the formulation of the rule[217] and influencing the credibility of government.[218]

However, a second reason why communication can be considered to be an anticorruption tool is that it may also increase the probability of detecting corruption and of making corruption more costly in psychological terms.[219]

Starting from these premises, it could be useful to distinguish journalism – in the more general discourse of media[220] – from public communication activities.

Journalism, especially investigative journalism,[221] can be decisive in a number of cases: for instance, by discouraging any intent to infringe or corrupt when a journalistic investigation is ongoing (pre-emptive response);[222] by encouraging victims (in cases of extortive corruption) to report infringements and corruption to newspapers or journalists (possibly anonymously), in this way allowing the beginning of criminal investigations;[223] and by indirectly influencing compliance

---

[213] Lennart Wittberg, 'Can Communication Activities Improve Compliance?' in Henk Elffers, Wim Huisman and Peter Verboon (eds), *Managing and Maintaining Compliance. Closing the gap between science and practice* (Boom Legal Publishers, 2006) 25.

[214] Lawrence M Friedman, *Impact. How Law Affects Behaviour* (Harvard University Press, 2016) 33.

[215] On feedback see Paul Watzlawick, Janet Beavin Bavelas and Don D Jackson, *Pragmatics of Human Communication. A Study of Interactional Patterns, Pathologies and Paradoxes* (Paperback, 2011) 12.

[216] On this point see Albert Mehrabian, *Nonverbal Communication* (Aldine Transaction, 1972).

[217] See William Twining and David Miers, *How to Do Things with Rules* (Cambridge University Press, 2010) 90.

[218] On this point see Robert Nozick, 'Coercion' in Sidney Morgenbesser, Patrick Suppes and Mary White (eds), *Philosophy, Science, and Method. Essays in Honor of Ernest Nagel* (St Martin's Press, 1969) 440.

[219] Alberto Vannucci, 'Three paradigms for the analysis of corruption' (2015) 1(2) *Labour & Law issues* 11: 'The higher the moral cost for a given agent, the stronger will be his "preference for formal rule-fulfilment", that is, the kind of psychological suffering, discomfort or guilt personally expected in case of infringement, perceived as a betrayal of public trust, independently from its detection'.

[220] See OECD, *The Role of the Media and Investigative Journalism in Combating Corruption* (2018); see also World Bank, *Helping Countries Combat Corruption: The Role of the World Bank* (1997) 44: 'Civil society and the media are crucial to creating and maintaining an atmosphere in public life that discourages fraud and corruption. Indeed, they are arguably the two most important factors in eliminating systemic corruption in public institutions'.

[221] Stephen J Berry, *Watchdog Journalism. The Art of Investigative Reporting* (Oxford University Press, 2009).

[222] See Rick Stapenhurst, *The media's role in curbing corruption* (Working Paper, World Bank Institute, 2000) 8.

[223] See Aymo Brunetti, Beatrice Weder, 'A free press is bad news for corruption' (2003) 87(7-8) *Journal of Public Economics* 1804.

due to the deterrent effects of reputational sanctions connected to the possible spreading of news.

Regarding *public communication*, there is a strong possibility that related activities will:

- increase clarity of obligations, which is indispensable for compliance with rules, in this way strengthening legal certainty and reducing bureaucratic power;[224]
- carry out awareness raising campaigns in order to exploit behaviour which aspires to legality, and by highlighting costs which may be shifted onto society due to the behaviour of those who do not respect rules;[225]
- strengthen the perception of risks associated to controls thanks to communication campaigns;[226] In order for inspectors themselves to be considered good inspectors, they 'must have sufficient knowledge and understanding' but also 'certain personality traits and communications skills'.[227]

In both journalism and public communication the effectiveness of communication as a tool to combat infringements and corruption depends strongly on 'the attitude of the audience toward the communicator',[228] in other words on the credibility of those who communicate.

Moreover, press freedom has been considered as a factor to explain differences in relative degrees of corruption among countries.[229] Nonetheless, nowadays the relationship between the media and the political and economic system is characterised by distortions, pathologies and connections which also determine media capture, sometimes real corruption of journalists, by hindering the 'watchdog role' of information.[230] On the other hand, the journalists' high potential to report and complain about corruption does not always result in lower corruption, while it strongly influences the corruption perception. Furthermore, the role of

---

[224] See on this point, the specific contribution of Haran Ratna, 'The importance of effective communication in healthcare practice' (2019) *Harvard Public Health Review* 23.
[225] See on this topic, Ronald E Rice and Charles K Atkin (eds), 3rd edn, *Public communication campaigns* (Sage, 2001).
[226] See Regina E Lundgren and Andrea H McMakin, *Risk communication: A handbook for communicating environmental, safety, and health risks* 4th edn (Wiley-IEEE Press, 2009).
[227] Eugene Bardach and Robert A Kagan, *Going by the Book: The Problem of Regulatory Unreasonableness* 127.
[228] Carl I Hovland and Walter Weiss, 'The influence of source credibility on communication effectiveness' (1951-52) 15 *Public Opinion Quarterly* 635.
[229] Aymo Brunetti, Beatrice Weder, 'A free press is bad news for corruption' 1802: 'Of the probable controls on bureaucratic corruption a free press is likely to be among the most effective ones'. See also Christine Kalenborn and Christian Lessmann, 'The impact of democracy and press freedom on corruption: Conditionality matters' (2013), in *Journal of Policy Modeling*, 857; Adriana S Cordis and Patrick L Warren, 'Sunshine as disinfectant: The effect of state Freedom of Information Act laws on public corruption' (2014) *Journal of Public Economics* 18.
[230] See Bill Kovach and Tom Rosenstiel, 'Are watchdogs an endangered species?' (2001) *Columbia Journalism Review* 53: 'Rather than a watchdog of powerful institutions, the press is vulnerable to being their tool'.

social networks and of the internet in combating corruption deserves increasing attention.[231]

In this perspective, communication can play an important role in: maintaining effective competition among different kinds of actors who contribute to produce information, especially the journalists; strengthening citizen journalism[232] and in promoting public communication in order to simplify administrative burdens, to reinforce controls and to publicly acknowledge compliant citizens and firms.

4.3.7. Reform

When compliance with rules is low, controls are not so effective; or when the situation so requires, then it could be advisable to reform regulation with special regard to a regime of controls, in order to increase compliance (and the effectiveness of rules) via ever more effective controls.

Indeed, reform of inspections is one relevant aspect in the much wider issue of regulatory reform, which is intended 'to make inspections more risk based … clearly … designed with the same aim: "more effect, less burden", as per the Dutch motto, or "prosperity and protection", as per the English one'.[233]

Adequate reform may positively increase compliance and, in this way, influence the prevention of illicit and corrupt transactions. According to the most relevant document on this topic, the UK Hampton Report, there are 'six areas where reform would be useful, to streamline the regulatory system and reduce the burden of administration on business, without reducing regulatory outcomes'. The areas indicated by the report are 'better Regulatory Impact Assessments to create regulations that are easier to enforce, and easier to understand; consolidation in national regulators to create a simpler, more consistent structure; fewer regulators for individual businesses to deal with, leading to better risk assessment; better coordination of local authority regulatory services; clearer prioritisation of regulatory requirements by Government Departments and national regulators; and better accountability throughout the regulatory system'.[234]

---

[231] See Dana Bekri, Brynne Dunn, Isik Oguzertem, Yan Su, Shivani Upreti, *Harnessing Social Media Tools to Fight Corruption* (LSE Department of International Development, 2011) and Mon-Chi Lio, Meng-Cun Liu and Yu-Pei Ou, 'Can the internet reduce corruption? A cross-country study based on dynamic panel data models' (2011) *Government Information Quarterly* 47. See also Rajeev K Goel, Michael A Nelson and Michael A Naretta, 'The internet as an indicator of corruption Awareness' (2012) *European Journal of Political Economy* 64.

[232] Stephen Quinn and Stephen Lamble, 'Citizen Journalism and Audience-Generated Content', in Stephen Quinn and Stephen Lamble (eds) *Online Newsgathering. Research and Reporting for Journalism* (Focal Press, 2008) 43.

[233] Florentin Blanc, *From Chasing Violations to Managing Risks* 4.

[234] Hampton Report, *Reducing administrative burdens: effective inspection and enforcement* (March, 2005) 55.

According to the OECD,[235] designing and reforming controls should be informed by 'a number of key principles'[236] which are specifically recommended and equally valid in any possible regulatory sector: evidence-based enforcement; selectivity; risk focus and proportionality; responsive regulation; long-term vision; coordination and consolidation; transparent governance; information integration; clear and fair process; compliance promotion; and professionalism.

Starting from this basis, a precondition for adequate designing/reforming of controls requires that regulators provide their exhaustive list by carrying out a detailed survey in each interested regulated sector.[237] Before any reform, in fact, it is always indispensable to obtain a picture of the status quo, in this case with reference to: controllers who are competent in different regulated sectors; typologies of controls (paper checks; site inspections; ex ante or ex post controls, and so on); and the purposes of controls and their results. In some cases, a good practice may include institutional sites where it is possible to consult (for instance) the list of controls for businesses.

Adequate reforms of controls should be simultaneously intended at ensuring three different aspects.

First, reforms require *quality of regulation*, intended as both quality of rules in terms of their clarity and feasibility and as quality of rules about controls.[238] In this perspective, reform may be greatly helped by empirical evidence and from behavioural and cognitive insights, especially in order to facilitate and support compliance[239] as well as to make planning effective and enforcement responsive by ensuring proportionality of controls to the risk of infringements and to the possible harm for general interest (environmental, health, work safety and so on).

Secondly, reforms of controls should be intended to increase *transparency and clarity* regarding both obligations and requirements which will be the object of controls. Moreover, transparency should also characterise the results of controls: in this respect, 'salient' communication has proved to be very effective, as in the case of rating systems and compliance certificates framed in a cognitive-based approach to strengthen their effectiveness via 'imitation'.[240]

---

[235] OECD, Best Practice Principles for Regulatory Policy, *Regulatory Enforcement and Inspections* (2014) 4: 'complements the 2012 Recommendation [of the Council on Regulatory and Policy Governance (OECD, 2012)] and is intended to assist countries in reforming inspections and developing cross-cutting policies on regulatory enforcement'.

[236] Ibid, 9

[237] On this point, see the specific analysis carried out on businesses controls by Nicoletta Rangone, 'Quale *riforma* dei controlli per prevenire la corruzione?' in Marco D'Alberti (ed), *Corruzione e pubblica amministrazione* 597 et seq.

[238] Nicoletta Rangone, 'Quale *riforma* dei controlli per prevenire la corruzione?', 601 et seq.

[239] On this point see Nicoletta Rangone, 'Making Law Effective: Behavioural Insights into Compliance' (2018) 9 *European Journal of Risk Regulation* 483 et seq.

[240] Nicoletta Rangone, 'Quale *riforma* dei controlli per prevenire la corruzione?' 601 and Nicoletta Rangone, 'A behavioural approach to administrative corruption prevention', in Agustí Cerillo-I-Martinez A and Juli Ponce (eds), *Preventing Corruption and Promoting good Government and Public Integrity* 85.

164 *Anticorruption: Controls*

Thirdly, reforming controls should give the greatest consideration to *organisational aspects* which can make the difference, starting from the design of controls, such as:

- clear distribution of competences;[241]
- avoiding overabundance of controls;
- coordination of the activities of controls and data sharing, especially among different controllers in related fields of regulation (for instance, hygiene and food safety, a sector in which several authorities may be competent);
- centralised (or interconnected) data bases in linked areas of controls;
- integrated plans of controls among different administrations (because excessive controls on the same firms are expensive and may discourage compliance[242]); and
- a company dossier with relevant information for enforcement officers.[243]

As a final remark, reforms should help to improve and incentivise controls which meet at the same time procedural expectations and regulatory outcomes because 'the key, in other words, is to have inspectors that are able to spot and help solve *problems* rather than focusing on *violations*'.[244]

Table 4.2 How to Control to Prevent Corruption: Synoptic Table of Remedies

INFORMATION	– strengthening data bases and their networks (starting with criminal ones) to make them useful for anticorruption – strengthening administrative intelligence and distinguishing it from street-level controls – strengthening data bases of administrative litigation making them relevant for anticorruption – strengthening European and international cooperation in administrative information and intelligence – promoting incentives to provide information, such as in antitrust leniency programmes

(continued)

---

[241] On this point, see also Hampton Report, *Reducing administrative burdens: effective inspection and enforcement* 63.
[242] On this point, see Nicoletta Rangone, 'Semplificazione ed effettività dei controlli sulle imprese' (2019) 3 *Rivista Trimestrale di Diritto Pubblico* 883 et seq.
[243] Nicoletta Rangone, 'Quale *riforma* dei controlli per prevenire la corruzione?' 616.
[244] Florentin Blanc, *From Chasing Violations to Managing Risks* 199; Eugene Bardach and Robert A Kagan, *Going by the Book. The Problem of Regulatory Unreasonableness* 79–80: 'Violations vs problems'.

Table 4.2 *(Continued)*

REGULATION	GENERAL REMEDIES (CH 3) *Regulatory stock* simplification advocacy powers *Regulatory flow* corruption impact assessment tracing interests SPECIFIC REMEDIES (CH 4) – incentives for compliance; – staff rotation on inspection teams; – transparency of controls; – codes of conduct for inspectors; – independence of controllers; – sufficient guarantees and remuneration for inspectors
PRIVACY AND DATA PROTECTION	– privacy *by design* (design of controls consistent with privacy protection) and privacy *by default* (less intrusive options of controls) – guardians oriented towards information which is strictly relevant for corruption prevention and not towards any possible information regarding private individuals – focusing controls on discretionary powers – avoiding doubling of public data bases which increase mistakes and misalignments as well as costs – avoiding publicity of same information on sites of different administrations and concentrating more relevant information on reference sites
PLANNING	– centralised systems which collect information about the risk of infringements and corruption in public administrations; – behavioural and cognitive insights as a base for planning controls – criteria for risk evaluation which considers pervasiveness and systematic relevance of corruption; – a certain number of random controls which impede (or hinder) any cost-benefit analysis for administrations, citizens and firms involved in controls
ENFORCEMENT	*From the point of view of administrative procedure*: – before any inspection, there should be adequate knowledge of the reference framework, to be achieved via data base cross-checks to verify convenience and feasibility of tools different from intrusive controls, such as inspections (document requests, questionnaires and so on). – when it is necessary access premises, enforcement officers should ensure fairness of the inspection, informed by the right to be heard, in order to make sure that results of inspections will be usable and sanctions adopted on their basis will be valid.

(continued)

Table 4.2 *(Continued)*

	– as far as possible, inspection results should be transparent and publicly accessible with due caution for possible reputational damages.
	From the point of view of administrative organisation:
	– rationalise institutional inspection design and increase their coordination; – strengthen inspection bodies also via reward mechanisms and dedicated training; – adopt manuals to carry out inspections; – implement joint inspections; – increase the role of inspectors pools.
COMMUNICATION	*As a tool to increase compliance* – promoting public communication to simplify administrative burdens, to reinforce controls, to publicly acknowledge compliant citizens and firms. *As a tool to detect corruption* – maintaining effective competition among different kinds of actors who contribute to producing information, especially journalists; strengthening citizen journalism.
REFORM	– *transparency and clarity* regarding obligations and requirements of rules which will be object of controls (check list); – *transparency* of results of controls; – clear distribution of competences; – avoiding overabundance of controls; – proportionality of controls to risk of infringements, possible danger for general interest (environmental, health, work safety and so on) and impact of violation; – coordination of control activities and data sharing, especially among different controllers in related fields of regulation (for instance, hygiene and food safety, sector in which several authorities are competent); – centralised (or interconnected) data bases in linked areas of controls; – control plans integrated among different administrations.

5

Combating Corruption via Regulation and Controls: Which Formula?

5.1. Corruption (and Anticorruption) from a Regulatory Perspective: A Recap

Combating corruption is strenuous daily work, impossible to manage once and forever because corruption is a chronic disease which manifests itself virulently and persistently in today's over-regulated society. In recent decades, preventing corruption has become an urgent and ever more structural response to increasing dysfunctionalities connected with widespread corruption, at national and international level.

As we have already seen (in chapter two), the strategy for combating corruption greatly depends on the perspective from which the phenomenon is observed.

Current conventional anticorruption policies, for instance, are mainly focused downstream, on several possible typologies and cases of corruption occurring in a number of regulatory sectors (public procurement, financial regulation, granting administration, environmental controls) and on administrative activities of several public agents who may potentially be involved in infringement and corruption. Preventing corruption from such a perspective requires an expensive engagement of a huge number of actors devoted to specialised anticorruption bureaucracy and controls who operate in public administrations, anticorruption bodies but also in firms and companies, as advisors and consultants and so on.

By operating upstream, at a different level, regulatory anticorruption does not require excessive additional bureaucracy, rather it consists of a sort of anticorruption intelligence focusing on a still undervalued 'genetic' factor of corruption: while the goal of political corruption is often to obtain favourable legislation, administrative corruption, in fact, presupposes both the existence and the ineffectiveness of rules or – to put it another way – when rules are effective, there is very limited space for infringements and corruption. This assumption greatly changes the therapy plan: rather than going after mentioned innumerable typologies and cases of corruption or after certain administrative activities, the proposed regulatory anticorruption concentrates on *rules and regulation*. They, in fact, create conditions for rent, both in political corruption (when politicians are bribed to adopt legislation) and in administrative corruption (because rules can create opportunities to obtain gains and avoid losses via compliance, non-compliance or creative compliance). For these reasons, conversely, rules may be regarded carefully in the context of anticorruption policies.

Following the reasoning, three considerations contribute to setting the scene. Firstly, rules are considered *determinants* of any administrative corruption process, insofar as they establish public powers, regulate administrative procedures and confer competences upon public agents with the consequence that without rules there can be no corruption. Secondly, if corruption is a special kind of regulatory side-effect and/or ineffectiveness, rules must be considered across their whole life-cycle, from their proposal to their delivery. Thirdly, the effective functioning of rules (the 'regulatory success'[1]) helps per se to prevent corruption and for this reason regulatory anticorruption requires rules which should be simultaneously clear, consistent, valid, characterised by responsive enforcement and with which compliance is realistic; rules characterised by high rates of compliance and few costs of enforcement; and rules which produce outcomes consistent with regulatory objectives.

All things considered, if administrative corruption corresponds to a side-effect or to a special kind of regulatory ineffectiveness, its specific criminal connotation (ie the distinction between active and passive corruption/extortion or bribery) is not so relevant for our reasoning, given that both parties (one of which is always a public agent) must agree before corruption occurs; they share a rent-seeking activity; they operate in the same context of secrecy, to avoid detection and sanction.

This perspective leads to two consequences. The first regards the notion of corruption, and suggests integrating the famous World Bank definition of corruption (abuse of public power for private benefits): when focusing on administrative corruption it should include the specification 'made possible by bad quality or bad functioning of rules which establishes and regulates such public power'. A second consequence regards anticorruption, which from the regulatory perspective should include the assessment of *corruptibility*, the idea that corruption may be detected early as a measurable risk, which is more likely to occur in certain situations, in the presence of a given regulatory framework, during specific administrative procedures or when people come into contact with certain types of public administrations. Corruptibility is, in fact, related to administrative powers (because the possibility of corruption emerges at the precise moment when administrative competences have been established) and with controls (because any possible kind of audit, inspection or check may not only be a tool to combat corruption, but also a concrete occasion of corrupt transactions).

In this circular reasoning about rules and corruption, controls have to be considered as a key topic, a necessary hub between regulatory enforcement and anticorruption. Controls may regard administrative activities (being external, internal, or anticorruption controls) as well as private activities (with special

---

[1] See Robert Baldwin and Martin Cave, *Taming the corporation. How to regulate for success* (Oxford University Press, 2021).

reference to inspections): in any case, all kinds of controls are significant from an anticorruption perspective because they are all intended to make regulation effective (by protecting interests or preventing risks) and because they all give valuable information to identify and assess the corruptibility of rules at the earliest stage. For this reason they must all be considered as part of the regulatory anticorruption tool-kit.

5.2. Combating Corruption: Why?

Corruption must be controlled because each single corrupt act produces multiple distortions at the same time (as already mentioned in chapter two).

Firstly, corruption produces a *moral distortion*, given the fact that secrecy implies duplicity and impedes integrity (indispensable especially for public officers). Secondly, corruption contributes to a *social distortion* and negatively affects the moral fabric of society by operating as a 'private' and secret trust which hinder general and public confidence. Thirdly, corruption determines a fundamental *distortion in the economic process*, because it changes the value (ie, the result of the economic activity) into mere advantage with the consequence that the economic process in itself is corrupted while transparency in the market is reduced. Fourthly, corruption *distorts regulation*, its objectives and the system of incentives which have been put in place in order to achieve regulatory purposes. Finally, corruption *distorts public administration* because public officers orientation toward the public interest shifts and this impedes trust in institutions.

In summary, corruption simultaneously injures ethics, by offending free, fair and transparent behaviour; it injures society, by weakening relations of confidence, justice and solidarity indispensable to cooperate; it injures economics, by rewarding undeserving people and determining an unjust redistribution of income; it injures law, by hindering regulatory effectiveness; and it injures public administration, by obstructing legitimate, fair and impartial administrative behaviour.

However, administrative corruption cannot be fully understood without considering people's need of (and right to) good administration.[2] Unfortunately, while many cases of corruption occur because citizens and firms collude with

---

[2] Art 41 of the EU Charter of Fundamental Rights: '1. Every person has the right to have his or her affairs handled impartially, fairly and within a reasonable time by the institutions and bodies of the Union. 2. This right includes: the right of every person to be heard, before any individual measure which would affect him or her adversely is taken; the right of every person to have access to his or her file, while respecting the legitimate interests of confidentiality and of professional and business secrecy; the obligation of the administration to give reasons for its decisions'. On this aspect, in general, see Jill Wakefield, *The right to good administration* (Kluwer Law International, 2007). See also The UK Parliamentary and Health Service Ombudsman, *Principles of Good Administration* (2009). On this topic, in general, see Manuel Villoria Mendieta and Agustín Izquierdo Sánchez, *Ética pública y buen gobierno. Valores e instituciones para tiempos de incertidumbre* 2nd edn (Tecnos, 2020) and Agustì Cerillo-I-Martinez A and Juli Ponce (eds), *Preventing Corruption and Promoting good Government and Public Integrity* (Bruylant, 2017).

public agents for illicit results, in many other occasions people and business rightfully need legitimate permits, licences, subsidies and so on. However, these legitimate permits, licences and subsidies do not come, or come too late or are partial with regard to their initial legitimate demands, or are unduly costly by inducing them to moral disengagement in corruption.[3]

5.3. Combating Corruption: How?

Starting from these premises, what is needed to put in place effective anticorruption strategies? What would be the best way to resort to regulation and controls as tools to prevent infringements and corruption?

As previously mentioned (chapter two, section 2.3), regulatory anticorruption is intended to work as an integrated strategy which gives special attention to rules. It is also intended to prevent infringements and corruption long before they can occur, even before they can be conceived, by looking at and working on opportunities for infringement and corruption given by rules, which have been previously adopted or are in the course of adoption, on the one hand and by looking at and working on controls of private as well as of administrative activities, on the other.

Moreover, regulatory anticorruption aims to reduce corruption as well as to increase regulatory effectiveness and good government by accepting insights from conventional anticorruption (CAC) (informed by the traditional deterrence approach, based on incentives and disincentives and on the need for controls) and from behavioural anticorruption (BAC) (focused on real people and intended to exploit the great contribution which comes from behavioural and cognitive sciences in the field of corruption prevention and controls).

Looking for an integrated strategy may help in making the reasoning clearer and simpler.

5.3.1. Regulatory Anticorruption: From Alternative Theoretical Approaches to an Integrated Strategy

The idea of adopting an incentive-disincentive approach, aiming to make compliance more convenient than corruption,[4] has its roots in the model which has

---

[3] Albert Bandura, 'Selective Activation and Disengagement of Moral Control' (1990) 46(1) *Journal of Social Issues* 27, 28: 'Self-sanctions can be disengaged by reconstruing conduct, obscuring causal agency, disregarding or misrepresenting injurious consequences, and blaming and devaluating the victim'; Celia Moore, 'Moral disengagement in processes of organizational corruption' (2008) 80(1) *Journal of Business Ethics* 129–39.

[4] See John A Gardiner and Theodore R Lyman, 'The logic of corruption control', in Arnold J Heidenheimer, Michael Johnston and Victor T Levine (eds), *Political Corruption. A Handbook* 833.

described the individual's decision about compliance as an economic reasoning about its cost, the size of the penalty and also the risk of incurring the penalty.[5] Later compliance models have also considered advances in behavioural sciences, ever more important in policymaking,[6] in order to better understand how people behave and take decisions (in general) and how they decide to engage in corruption (in particular). Relevant insights developed in psychology,[7] in cognitive science and neuroscience,[8] and even cultural and social factors,[9] have all contributed to redefining the importance of rational and economic motives for individual choices and to develop an essential behavioural anticorruption toolkit:[10] behavioural practices,[11] peer effect[12] and intrinsic motivations[13] have lead to greatly improved anticorruption measures.[14]

Both conventional anticorruption (the war machine of anticorruption) and behavioural anticorruption (its continuous updating to advances in compliance theories) share a key point: they place behaviour at the heart of the reasoning despite developing from different starting points, stressing different reasons for compliance and adopting different methodologies.

---

[5] See Gary S Becker, 'Crime and Punishment: An Economic Approach' (1968) 76 *Journal of Political Economy* 169.

[6] Since 2010, the Behavioural Insights Team in the UK Cabinet Office and 2015, the US Social and Behavioural Sciences Team have started to resort to behavioural sciences for public policy. Behavioural change is increasingly becoming key in policymaking, see Pete Lunn, *Regulatory Policy and Behavioural Economics* (OECD, 2014). On this topic, see Memorandum for the Heads of Executives Departments and Agencies, and of Independent Regulatory Agencies, *Behavioural science insight and federal forms*, 15 September 2015.

[7] Jonathan Rusch, 'The Social Psychology of Corruption', www.oecd.org/cleangovbiz/Integrity Forum-16-Jonathan-Rusch.pdf; see also Kendra Dupuy and Siri Neset, 'The Cognitive Psychology of Corruption. Micro-level Explanations for Unethical Behaviour' (2018) U4 Issue. In general, see the work of Daniel Kahneman, *Thinking, Fast and Slow* (Farrar, Straus and Giroux, 2011).

[8] Johann Graf Lambsdorff, 'Behavioural and Experimental Economics as a Guidance to Anticorruption', in Danila Serra and Leonard Wantchekon (eds), *New advances in experimental research on corruption*, Research in Experimental Economics Vol 15, (Emerald Group Publishing, 2012) 279. See also Johann Graf Lambsdorff, 'A Behavioral Science Approach to Preventing Corruption', in *The Global Anticorruption Blog*, https://globalanticorruptionblog.com/2016/02/11/guest-post-a-behavioral-science-approach-topreventing-corruption/.

[9] See Ina Kubbe and Annika Engelbert (eds), *Corruption and Norms. Why Informal Rules Matter* (Palgrave Macmillan, 2018); see also Claudia Baez Camargo 'Can a Behavioural Approach Help Fight Corruption?', Basel Institute on Governance Policy Brief No 1, May 2017, www.baselgovernance.org/sites/collective.l ocalhost/files/publications/170628_policy_brief_ 0.pdf.

[10] Johann Graf Lambsdorff, 'A Behavioral Science Approach to Preventing Corruption'.

[11] Nieves Zúñiga, *Behavioural changes against corruption*, U4 Helpdesk Answer (2018), 2: 'behavioural practices can take several forms, such as information campaigns, collective deliberations, promotion of intrinsic motivation and civic engagement, among others'.

[12] Cosimo Stahl, Saba Kassa, Claudia Baez-Camargo, *Drivers of Petty Corruption and Anticorruption Interventions in Developing Countries – a Semi-Systematic Review* (Basel Institute on Governance, 2017) 12: 'when people assume that everyone else around them is paying bribes and accepting that as a normal state of affairs, then corruption will indeed become normalised'.

[13] See Sander van der Linden, 'Intrinsic Motivation and Pro-Environmental Behaviour' (2015) 5 *Nature Climate Change* 612.

[14] Nieves Zúñiga, *Behavioural changes against corruption*, 8.

In other words, there are no particular reasons why they cannot work together.[15] For example, they may operate in the pattern of reasoning proposed by the conventional approach, despite caveats and necessary clarifications.

In this pattern, the first factor which has been considered to positively influence compliance is *reducing its cost*. In some legal systems where compliance costs are very high or even difficult to pay (such as in Italy) this objective seems even today to be a convincing starting point for any concrete anticorruption policy, especially considering that compliance costs include enormous profits for intermediates and consultants in order to ensure compliance, in order not to comply (also by paying bribes), in order to comply formally or creatively (as in fiscal planning) and in order to manage litigation. In an integrated approach, reducing the cost of compliance may not only influence the individual cost/benefit analysis (as in the early CAC perspective) but also increase the credibility of public institutions and strengthen trust in anticorruption policies.

The second factor which is significant in relation to influencing and promoting compliance is *increasing the risk of controls* (and of related sanctions). If administrative resources for controls are limited, then administrations should decide how to enforce regulation via limited controls[16] by resorting to risk-based planning.[17] In this context, it should be remembered that risk is not always evaluated rationally, rather it strongly depends on perception, and a risk of controls may be characterised by bias as well as being influenceable by *communication* strategies and information campaigns.[18]

The third (and last) factor which has been considered capable of inducing compliance is *sanctioning*. Much progress has been made on this point, making it clear that regulatory incentives (or disincentives) work only if sanctions are effective and well calibrated. In fact, monetary or higher penalties may not always be effective, while sanctions following controls must be effective to deter and prevent infringements and corruption. Further aspects are no less relevant. Literature and practice have confirmed that in order to contribute to effective regulatory delivery, sanctions following controls should be responsive, calibrated and proportional to infringements, and informed by procedural justice. Sometimes positive sanctions are needed, at other times it is better to resort to nuanced incentives/disincentives by rewarding enforcement and compliant groups. On the other hand, while literature in social sciences is contributing to important advancements in this area, political debate seems to be outdated. Even today, when scandals and corruption

---

[15] Ibid, 11.

[16] See Maria De Benedetto, 'Is it possible to prevent corruption via controls?' (2014) 100 *Amicus Curiae* 6.

[17] In general, Robert Baldwin, Martin Cave and Martin Lodge, *Understanding Regulation*, 281.

[18] The Italian Revenue Agency carried out a public information campaign during 2011 and 2012 on the results of unannounced raids in very famous holiday resorts, such as Cortina d'Ampezzo and Portofino, though no evidence about the results of the campaign has been available. On this topic, in general, see Nieves Zúñiga, *Behavioural changes against corruption*, 5.

occur, politicians (at least in Italy) tend to propose criminal responses and an increase in the size of monetary penalties while, according to economic literature and to literature on procedural justice, these solutions are counterproductive and paradoxically conducive to an increase in the size of bribes.[19]

If conventional and behavioural anticorruption may work together in the already described way, regulatory anticorruption moves a step further but is not an alternative to them, by resorting to all available evidence and literature which helps to explain human behaviour, whether rational or beyond rationality. In botanical terms, the regulatory perspective works by 'grafting' conventional and behavioural anticorruption, this graft being necessary for better quality anticorruption to be obtained.

Current conventional anticorruption policies deserve great attention and have the merit of having placed the problem of corruption (at global and national level) at centre stage of the public arena. In the same way, great improvements have come from behavioural anticorruption. Regulatory Anticorruption does not intend to replace them, but moves at another level and focuses on the underestimated contribution which institutions make in preparing the ground for corruption in several ways: by resorting to obsessive regulation which affects the activities of citizens and firms and multiplies administrative powers; by allowing interest groups to influence regulation through lack of transparency; by adopting regulation without adequate gathering of evidence, consultation, ex ante and ex post evaluation and so on; by bad implementation of regulation and ineffective management of public services; by enforcing regulation disproportionately, too rigidly when it would be not necessary or too weakly (administrative tolerance) when strong controls would be suggested. In so doing, institutions (legislators, regulators, enforcement agencies, inspection bodies and so on) increase corruption opportunities. On the other hand, RA focuses on the incredible potential which good regulation and effective regulatory delivery may represent as tools for preventing corruption: by reducing the regulatory stock and unnecessary regulatory burdens and administrative powers; by allowing groups of interest to influence regulation in a really transparent way, making it clear who pays and who benefits for each regulation; by adopting regulation with adequate gathering of evidence, consultation, ex ante and ex post evaluation; by accurately implementing regulation and deliver public services; by enforcing regulation proportionately, more rigidly or cooperatively, depending on the given conditions.

In short, effective regulation (together with its 'sister', good administration) may contribute to reducing the costs and side-effects of rules, revealing themselves to be the cheapest anticorruption tool. In fact, rules which are valid, enforceable and applicable; rules characterised by high rates of compliance and few costs of enforcement; results of rules consistent with regulatory objectives; such rules definitely help to prevent corruption without producing additional bureaucracy.

---

[19] See Susan Rose-Ackerman, *Corruption and Government: Causes, Consequences and Reform*, 54.

5.3.2. Regulatory Anticorruption Toolkit (Corruptibility Assessment)

According to the idea that regulation may (intentionally or otherwise) promote administrative corruption, some legal systems have introduced a corruption impact analysis (chapter three, section 3.4.1) with the purpose of assessing legislation ex ante from an anticorruption perspective and of providing (if required) measures and mechanisms to reduce occasions for corruption, as far as possible.

Alongside developed methodologies for corruption-proofing, there would be a further method to evaluate specific pieces of legislation with the perspective of improving the anticorruption management of the stock of legislation, taken as a whole. This method may be concisely referred to as corruptibility assessment because it focuses on substantive elements related to the probability that both infringements and corruption will follow from certain legislation, in a way that is quite different from (or more general than in) corruption impact assessment, which focuses mainly on strict corruption and on procedural aspects.

Three elements characterise corruptibility assessment: first, incentives/disincentives in regulation/legislation which promote, or give occasion for, or directly contribute to infringements and administrative corruption; second, a protocol to identify and assess corruptibility starting from legal concepts (the Trojan horse of incentives/disincentives in regulation/legislation) and from language indicators, with the objective of automating this kind of screening; third, the need for criminal databases, which 'talk' in administrative language capable of providing valuable information for early administrative preventive anticorruption.

5.3.2.1. Incentives or the Genetics of Corruption

Incentives in regulation have been long studied as an independent topic from an economic point of view, especially during the last 30 years[20] with special reference to commonly used schemes[21] and to differences between incentive regulation and command and control regulation.[22]

---

[20] See for wide and general references on this topic, Jean-Jacques Laffont and Jean Tirole, *A Theory of Incentives in Procurement and Regulation* (MIT Press, 1993). See also, Jean-Jacques Laffont and Jean Tirole, 'The Politics of Government Decision Making: Regulatory Institutions' (1990) 6(1) *Journal of Law, Economics, and Organization* 1 and 'The Politics of Government Decision-Making: A Theory of Regulatory Capture' (1991) 106(4) *Quarterly Journal of Economics* 1089.

[21] *Ibid*, 10–11 where current incentives schemes are analysed on the basis of two dividing lines: 'The first is whether the government is allowed to subsidize (or tax) regulated firms, that is, whether regulated firms can receive public funds and thus not cover all their costs through direct charges to private customers ... The second dividing line is the power of incentives schemes, that is, the link between the firm's transfer from the government and/or the form's prices and its cost or profit performance.'

[22] Incentive regulation has considered as the alternative to control and command regulation, see Tracy Lewis and Chris Garmon, *Fundamentals of Incentive Regulation* (PURC/World Bank International Training Program on Utility Regulation and Strategy, June 1997): 'incentive regulation

In parallel, anticorruption literature has focused on the importance of incentives and disincentives, at different levels. Firstly, by highlighting that corruption is sensitive to incentives, to be understood in a larger meaning, structurally related to rent-seeking and 'considered as one form of rent-seeking'.[23] Secondly, because corruption may affect the official, formal system of incentives by determining 'who obtains the benefits and bears the costs of government action'[24] and may distort 'incentives, undermines institutions, and redistributes wealth and power to the undeserving'.[25] Thirdly, because conversely anticorruption should adopt an incentive/disincentive approach, resorting to rewards as well as to penalties[26] in a mix of 'carrots and sticks'.[27] Finally, because the emerging new kind of behavioural incentives (the 'nudge'[28]) is proven to be particularly fit to anticorruption purposes. In short, reducing incentives for corruption and increasing its costs has been considered 'the first line of attack in an anticorruption campaign'.[29]

However, according to the idea that regulation may be counterproductive, that it may produce side-effects and also that legislative inflation contributes to making opportunities for rent given by combination of rules quite unpredictable, not always do incentives and disincentives operate as if they were intentionally established and managed by regulators. Moreover, in any case, they must be proven in the broader context in which they will applied.

---

is the use of rewards and penalties to induce the utility to achieve desired goals where the utility is afforded some discretion in achieving goals'. See also, Glenn Blackmon, *Incentive Regulation and the Regulation of Incentives* (Kluwer Academic Publishers, 1994) and David EM Sappington, 'Designing Incentive Regulation' (1994) 9(3) *Review of Industrial Organisation* 245.

[23] Johann Graf Lambsdorff, 'Corruption and Rent-seeking' (2002) 113 *Public Choice* 97 esp 104 et seq.

[24] Susan Rose-Ackerman, *Corruption and government: causes, consequences and reform*, 9.

[25] Robert Klitgaard, *Controlling corruption*, 2: 'When corruption undermines property rights, the rule of law, and incentives to invest, economic and political development are crippled'.

[26] Ibid, 77 and John A Gardiner, 'Controlling official corruption and fraud: bureaucratic incentives and disincentives', 33, 42.

[27] Susan Rose-Ackerman, *Corruption and government: causes, consequences and reform*, 78.

[28] Richard H Thaler and Cass R Sunstein, *Nudge. Improving Decisions about Health, Wealth, and Happiness*, revised and expanded edn (Yale University Press, 2008) 6 where nudge is defined: 'any aspect of the choice architecture that alters people's behaviour in a predictable way without forbidding any options or significantly changing their economic incentives. To count as a mere nudge, the intervention must be easy and cheap to avoid'. See also Robert Baldwin, 'From regulation to behaviour change: giving nudge the third degree' (2014) 77(6) *Modern Law Review* 831, 856: 'Classical command and control rules of regulation, and economic incentives, tend to build on the rationality of persons and firms – they issue prescriptions that are overt because they take it that people will use their rationality to react positively to the threats of sanctions or taxes. Enforcement practices tend to work on a rational deterrence basis, and models such as the "responsive regulation" approach, treat regulated persons and firms as cognitively competent responders to overtly issued messages. The implication of these differences is that nudge does not sit wholly happily alongside many other intervention tools'. See, finally, Incentive Research Foundations, *Using Behavioral Economics Insights in Incentives, Rewards, and Recognition: A Nudge Guide* (2017) 6: 'All Nudges Are Incentives but Not All Incentives Are Nudges'.

[29] Susan Rose-Ackerman, *Corruption and government: causes, consequences and reform*, 68.

However, there is large agreement about the opinion that 'corrupt incentives exist because state officials have the power to allocate scarce benefits and impose onerous costs'.[30] As already mentioned (chapter three, section 3.4.1), rules which provide costs or benefits, establish prohibition or restrictions, allocate regulatory powers or have an impact on law enforcement capacity are 'sensitive' rules, from the viewpoint of administrative corruption. In other words, they may encourage detrimental rent-seeking and contribute to corrupt transactions directly (for instance, because a public agent is part of the rent-seeking scheme, in charge of providing the desired licence or subsidy) or indirectly (because in the rent-seeking scheme a public agent is in charge of inspection which can put into danger illicit extra income derived from infringements). Independently of their own specific objectives, these kinds of rules – once approved – contribute to a market of corruption and, for this reason, should be adopted only if necessary while if adopted their effects should be properly designed and monitored.

5.3.2.2. A Protocol to Identify and Assess Corruptibility

How is it possible to monitor these rules in legislation by keeping their corruptibility under control? What aspects in legislation should be monitored? What kind of countermeasures may be adopted in presence of sensitive rules?

Corruption impact assessment (chapter three, section 3.4.1) refers to broad evaluation criteria, such as ease of compliance, propriety of discretion and transparency of administrative procedures,[31] criteria which presuppose an assessment for proposed legislation (but also for legislation in force), focusing mainly on strict corruption and procedural aspects.

However, corruptibility assessment covers a scope wider than that of CIA, because it also includes all possible infringements given the fact that any kind of control (whether fiscal, antitrust, environmental, in matters of work safety, and so on) may result in corruption. Moreover, it considers not only procedural aspects but even the substantive content of rules, by referring to sensitive legal concepts. For instance, frequently cases of corruption are related to administrative authorising powers, established by rules. Licences, authorisations, permits and similar

---

[30] Ibid, 39.

[31] See Tilman Hoppe, *Anticorruption Assessment of Laws (Corruption Proofing). Comparative Study and Methodology* (Regional Cooperation Council, 2014) 175 et seq. Each of these factors could be described by different criteria: the ease of compliance refers to the adequacy of the burden of compliance, to the adequacy of the level of sanctions and to the possibility of preferential treatment; the propriety of discretion deals with the concreteness and objectiveness of discretionary regulations, appropriateness of consignment/entrustment standards and clarity of financial support standards; the transparency of administrative procedure is connected to accessibility and openness, predictability and the possibility of conflicts of interest.

Combating Corruption: How? 177

administrative acts are in fact necessary to engage in and to perform economic and other private activities, for this reason expressing an intrinsic economic value and generating behaviour which may fall into corruption: citizens and firms who do not meet established requirements may infringe law by a false declaration about requirements, or may directly engage in corruption with public agents in charge of issuing licences, authorisations or permits; citizens and firms who meet established requirements, may engage in corruption to obtain a more extensive authorisation, or to obtain authorisation earlier; or they can be extorted by public agents who are obstructing the issue of legitimate licences, authorisations or permits.

Table 5.1 How Authorisations May Contribute to Facilitating Corruption

ENTITLEMENT OF CITIZENS/FIRMS TO AUTHORISATION	ILLICIT BEHAVIOUR	TYPOLOGY OF CORRUPTION
Citizens/firms do not meet established requirements	False declaration about requirements	Infringement. Corruption is possible during controls
	Corrupt agreement to obtain undue authorisation	Corruption
Citizens/firms meet established requirements	Corrupt agreement to obtain a more extensive authorisation or to obtain authorisation earlier	Active or passive corruption, it depends on the initiative
	Public agents obstruct legitimate authorisation	Extortion

In order to establish and regulate such administrative authorising powers, primary legislation, government regulation, even guidelines and manuals are required. Let us focus on primary legislation. It consists in a normative text, formulated in legal language: any established power of authorisation in any possible piece of primary legislation is identifiable thanks to language indicators because legal lexicon – characterised by limited substitutability – is needed both to establish and to regulate such powers.

Text analysis of legislation will reveal the presence of authorisation, intended broadly as the general legal concept which expresses the basic notion of administrative power capable of removing limits for some economic or private activities. Such power may be established by using different words and schemes: authorisation, licence, permit, approval, signature, acceptance, admission, allowance, acceptance, agreement, consent, dispensation, imprimatur, recognition. All of these words should be considered as proxies for the presence of authorising administrative powers in a piece of legislation. In other terms, language may become meaningful (with some caution and precautions[32]) thanks to 'lexical tables'[33] useful for developing more objective indicators for corruptibility assessment (when a certain number of conditions are met) in the framework of preventive anticorruption policies.

Table 5.2 Lexical Table

Sensitive legal concepts	Lexicon
Authorisation (administrative powers capable of removing limits for some economic or private activities).	authorisation, licence, permit, approval, signature, acceptance, admission, allowance, agreement, consent, dispensation, imprimatur, recognition.

The same reasoning works for other legal concepts which operate as further indicators of administrative corruptibility, which have already been mentioned: concessions and subsidies; tax, fees and other obligations; sanctions, fines and other penalties; controls and inspections; subsidies and economic incentives. In other words, those legal concepts and schemes which by rules provide *costs* or *benefits*, establish *prohibition* or *restrictions*, allocate *regulatory powers* or have impact on *law enforcement capacity* (already analysed in chapter three).

The idea at the basis of corruptibility assessment is to identify potential red flags in state (or any other kind of) legislation thanks to which focusing on the risk of administrative corruption incidents produced by single rules, in order to activate necessary countermeasures, ie adequate controls or cutting red tape reforms. Not all possible anticorruption responses are equal: when citizens and firms do not meet established requirements, controls and sanctions are indispensable, but if the number of infringements and corruptions indicates much ineffectiveness, a regulatory response would probably be also necessary (if restrictions are still justified and/or if a different regulation/regulatory enforcement may be more fit to the purpose of keeping infringements and corruption under control); when citizens and firms meet established requirements, and they engage in corruption, for instance to achieve a more extensive authorisation or earlier authorisation, regulatory responses and good administration are needed; when they are extorted and public agents obstruct the issue of authorisation, good and effective administration is the best possible anticorruption response.

---

[32] Lexical tables are a good starting point, even though more sophisticated technical arrangements may be useful to revise results (for instance, NLP natural language processing). In fact, statistical analysis would be the basis on which to develop further evaluations, following artificial intelligence methodologies.

[33] Ludovic Lebart, André Salem and Lisette Berry, *Exploring Textual Data* (Springer, 1998) 45.

Table 5.3 Anticorruption Preventive Responses in Cases of Infringements and Corruption Related to Authorisations

CITIZENS/FIRMS ENTITLEMENT TO AUTHORISATION	ILLICIT BEHAVIOUR	ANTICORRUPTION RESPONSES
Citizens/firms do not meet established requirements	False declaration about requirements	*Controls and sanctions.* When the number of infringements and corruption indicate too large ineffectiveness, it is necessary also a regulatory response (if restrictions are still justified and/or if a different regulation/regulatory enforcement may be more fit to the purpose of taking infringements and corruption under control)
	Corrupt agreement to obtain undue authorisation	
Citizens/firms meet established requirements	Corrupt agreement to obtain a more extensive authorisation or to obtain authorisation earlier	*When corruption regards more extensive authorisation*: regulatory response (if restrictions are still justified). *When corruption regards earlier authorisation*: good and effective administration
	Public agents obstruct legitimate authorisation	Good and effective administration

This basic corruptibility assessment (whose checklist is analysed below) may be useful at more than one level.

From a single perspective, it may be relevant in the context of individual ex ante as well as ex post corruption impact assessment, in order to integrate its methodologies (mainly focused on corruption and on procedural aspects) with reference to substantive aspects and to mentioned sensitive legal concepts. In other words, alongside procedural criteria such as ease of compliance, propriety of discretion and transparency, it would be very useful to highlight whether legislation or regulation present 'anomalies' related to indicators of corruptibility.

From an aggregate perspective, corruptibility assessment constitutes the indispensable tool for the advocacy powers of anticorruption bodies (chapter three, section 3.3.2). The full-scale functioning of corruptibility assessment may produce increasing knowledge about the 'genetics' of corruption by allowing an ever more specific and effective reporting and recommendation powers in matter of anticorruption. They are intended to reduce in the regulatory stock the presence of rules that most frequently constitute or reinforce the risk of corruption incidents or to provide, for these rules, adequate mechanisms for risk reduction (in procedural design or by establishing proper controls). In fact, only ACBs have the expertise and are in an institutional condition to detect and identify possible rules and provisions which have operated as incentives to infringement and corruption; to report information to regulators (parliament, government, other regulators and so on) in order to analytically describe the effects produced by the legislation/regulation; and to address recommendations to competent institutions (parliaments, governments, independent agencies) about the best way to solve problems, also by indicating specific measures to counter-act distortions as well as possible solutions to reduce opportunities for corruption in regulation and legislation. This is exactly the meaning of the measure recently adopted by the Italian Recovery and resilience Plan, by requiring the repeal and revision of rules that fuel corruption.

Moreover, corruptibility assessment is developed thanks to language analysis of legislative texts. This assessment may bring to light not only evidence related to previously established indicators but also other elements, not yet identified, by exploiting the potential of machine learning methodologies and by leading to further possible insights which will contribute to strengthening information and knowledge about normative drivers for corruption.

Finally, corruptibility assessment of legislation may be a great help in responding to the need for more objective indicators of corruption.[34] In fact, as already mentioned, most indices and measurements of corruption are perception-based due to the difficulties in experience-based surveys. Corruptibility assessment refers to objective indicators (related to regulatory stock and regulatory flow) even though different from indicators related to personal experience of corruption. Adopting any opportune and appropriate measures to make possible comparison among legal systems, corruptibility assessment could also contribute to the development of new comparative countries' rankings based on objective indicators.[35]

5.3.2.3. Criminal Databases Should Talk Administrative Language

Research into the 'genetics' of corruption unfortunately proceed in the absence (or only with limited use) of an incredibly relevant area of knowledge, possible in theory but impossible in practice because it is still underestimated: the knowledge which may come from criminal databases (and more generally from databases of any possible kind of litigation). When recording crimes (at every level of criminal

---

[34] On this point see Armando D'Alterio, 'Corruption, a national and global issue', Rome, 27 October 2017, G7 Workshop on Corruption measurement, Diritto penale della globalizzazione, 1 November 2017, www.dirittopenaleglobalizzazione.it/g7-workshop-corruption-measurement-corruption-national-and-global-issue/. The workshop was divided 'into two round tables: the first will focus on defining the dimension and scope within which to measure the phenomenon in a realistic and exhaustive way; the second will address the issue of measuring the risk of corruption in the light of developing anticorruption prevention plans and strategies' (www.esteri.it/mae/en/sala_stampa/archivionotizie/approfondimenti/2017/10/presidenza-italiana-g7-seminario.html).

[35] On this point see Francesco Merloni, *Corruption and Public Administration. The Italian Case in a Comparative Perspective* (Routledge, 2018), esp 138 where 'management by benchmarking', beyond control is analysed.

procedures: policing, prosecution, judicial decision) they are rarely designed to respond directly to administrative queries such as:

- Which specific legislation, statute or regulation has established the administrative power involved in the infringement or in corruption?
- Which public administration/officer is part of the corruption scheme?
- What controls have been established and have not worked?

Table 5.4 Evidence which may come from Queries to Criminal Databases

ELEMENT TO BE RECORDED WHEN DESIGNING A CRIME DATABASE ARCHITECTURE IN MATTER OF CORRUPTION OR INFRINGEMENTS CONNECTED WITH ADMINISTRATIVE ACTIVITIES	POSSIBLE QUALITATIVE/QUANTITATIVE EVIDENCE WHICH MAY COME FROM QUERIES
LEGISLATION: which statute or regulation has established the administrative power involved in the infringement or in corruption?	Some statute or pieces of legislation or regulation may result as occasion of corruption more frequently than others
PUBLIC ADMINISTRATION/OFFICER: which Public administration/officer is part of the corruption scheme	Some sectors of administration or some kind of public officers may be involved in corruption more frequently than others
ADMINISTRATIVE POWER: which administrative power has been used to carry out corruption?	Some administrative powers may result as legal schemes for corruption more frequently than others
CONTROLS: which controls have been established and have not worked?	Some controllers may result as involved in corruption more frequently than others

In other words, a condition to make Regulatory Anticorruption effective (and the Corruptibility Assessment operational, a tool ready-to-go), is to 'translate' into administrative language the information which comes from criminal databases that may be usable for administrative activities.

On the one side, corruption should be analysed statistically[36] while deep statistical representations of corruption should correspond not only to criminal but

---

[36] On 'statistics and statistical thinking', see Paul Starr, 'The sociology of official statistics', in William Alonso and Paul Starr (eds), *The Politics of Numbers* (Russel Sage Foundation, 1987) 16. See also Alain Desrosières, *La politique des grands nombres. Histoire de la raison statistique*, 3rd edn (La Découverte, 2010).

also to administrative categories[37] in order to make knowledge really useful for public policy,[38] because each database has much to say even in fields of administration different from those which justified it at the time of its establishment. Let us consider the incredible importance of fiscal databases.

On the other side, corruptibility must be proven,[39] mainly in terms of statistical methodology (and machine learning): not only should criminal databases talk in administrative language but (more generally) statistical methodologies[40] (and its machine learning improvements) should support administrative intelligence and respond to administrative questions.[41]

5.3.3. Regulatory Anticorruption in Practice

The deep understanding of the relationship between rules and corruption (the already mentioned 'secret of law'[42]) manifests itself as adverse effects (behind an administrative corruption incident there is always an infringed, ineffective rule) but expresses also a great potential because rules may be used for anticorruption purposes by contributing to developing anticorruption tools characterised by greater effectiveness and lower administrative costs.

In chapter three, a first group of regulatory anticorruption tools was analysed and summarised, differentiated according to their classification as tools mainly designed for the application to the regulatory stock or the regulatory flow.

---

[37] Language of statistics has been considered as one of its main limits, William F Ogburn, 'Limitations of Statistics' (1934) 40(1) *American Journal of Sociology* 17: 'a certain amount of explanation is necessary to make the language of coefficients intelligible'.

[38] OECD, *Statistics, Knowledge and Policy: Key Indicators to Inform Decision Making* (OECD, 2005); see also Theodore M Porter, *Trust in Numbers: The Pursuit of Objectivity in Science and Public Life* (Princeton University Press, 1995) and Alain Desrosières, 'Statistics and social critique' (2014) 7(2) *The Open Journal of Sociopolitical Studies* 348.

[39] John L Austin, *How to Do Things with Words* (Clarendon Press, 1962) 4: 'Yet they will succumb to their own timorous fiction, that a statement of the law is a statement of fact'.

[40] In order to assess corruptibility of rules, legal experts should first extract a sample of anomalous rules (rules which have generated episodes of corruption) and a control sample of rules (rules which have not generated episodes of corruption). Secondly, recurring rules in examined cases of corruption should be analysed with regard to indicators such as type of regulatory interventions, public administration interested, established controls, incentives for defensive administration. In particular, the analysis should include the definition of summary indicators which refer to the main characteristics of the sampled rules. Each rule has to be classified according to a battery of qualitative variables (type of costs, benefits, prohibitions, restrictions, etc). The analysis is oriented to the estimation of the effect of synthetic indicators on the probability that a rule will generate corruption. The assessment of the final results will be the basis of guidelines and possible corrective measures for regulators.

[41] Oscar Capdeferro Villagrasa, 'Las herramientas inteligentes anticorrupción: entre la aventura tecnológica y el orden jurídico' (2019) 50 *Revista Geeral de Derecho Administrativo*.

[42] Monique Nuijten and Gehrard Anders (eds), *Corruption and the Secret of law. A Legal Anthropological Perspective* (Ashgate Publishing, 2007).

Regarding the *regulatory stock*, simplification has been indicated as a consolidated, multi-purpose tool which can also be used in the context of anticorruption policies, while advocacy powers represent an emerging anticorruption tool, specifically designed to exploit regulatory anticorruption purposes.

- *Simplification* may involve the statute book (resulting in different activities, such as codification, cutting legislation or simple revision) or may consist in administrative simplification (programmes cutting red tape, administrative burden reduction programmes). Both kinds of simplification are operational (more or less) in the OECD area and involve parliaments, governments, other regulators (including special units, law commissions and other public bodies in charge of simplification and anticorruption).

- *Advocacy powers* consist in reporting to parliaments, governments and other regulators with the purpose of recommending revisions, reforms or countermeasures to limit cases of corruption repeatedly following certain pieces of legislation/regulation. They are not fully operational even though their potential expresses a promising activity for anticorruption bodies in their advisory role to parliaments, governments and other regulators, as in the case of the Italian National Recovery and Resilience Plan (chapter 3, section 3.3.2.2).

Regarding the *regulatory flow*, quality of regulation has been indicated as the unitary framework for consolidated and widespread activities (already developed in many legal systems) intended to promote regulatory effectiveness and anticorruption measures while tracing interests represents an emergent anticorruption practice intended to generate real transparency in the legislative/regulatory process.

- *Quality of regulation* includes ex-ante and ex-post evaluation in the legislative/regulatory process, with specific regard to impact assessment methodologies and to consultation, activities intended to help create good quality and effective legislation/regulation, well known in countries of the OECD area and elsewhere, despite not always being properly used everywhere. Moreover, in a limited number of countries, a new tool – corruption impact assessment – has been introduced with the specific purpose of assessing legislation/regulation from an anticorruption perspective. The responsibility to resort to quality of regulation tools (in general) is shared between parliaments, governments and other regulators while corruption impact assessment calls into question even anticorruption bodies expertise and competences.

- *Tracing interests* is an emerging opportunity to bring about greater transparency in the legislative process with regard to the influence of interest groups, but also with the intention to strengthen corruption prevention. While in some legal systems transparency registers for lobby groups or forms of legislative footprint have been adopted, traceability of interests aims to make clear the creation of rent, the roots and the impact of 'sensitive' rules by labelling them, as is the case for food (see chapter three). Tracing interests would seek to answer the questions: Who first proposed the rule or rules in question? Who proposed amendments? What changed from one version of legislation to another? What were the consequences in terms of costs/benefits distribution? And so on. In short, the aim of tracing interests is to make clear (as far as possible) who pays and who benefits for each piece of legislation not focusing to what has happened before rules or around rules but directly inside rules, looking at what rules establish, resorting to regulatory diagnostic tools and methodologies.

Let us now analyse the functioning of corruptibility assessment, a process which summarises regulatory anticorruption insights, starting from a piece (for instance) of primary legislation ('rules under scrutiny', chapter three). The assessment works in a very simple way, resorting to a checklist, even though the questions provided by the checklist may not be so simple to answer and would imply strong specialist regulatory expertise in sectors under assessment.

The first question in the checklist, in brief, is: *Has this legislation ever been occasion of or has it ever been involved in some way with cases of infringements or corruption*? If the response is NO, legislation may be confirmed from a strict anticorruption perspective, without prejudice for any other possible evaluation regarding the effectiveness of legislation. If the response is YES, the assessment should accurately verify if such legislation is still essential today, due to the existence of normative constraints (for instance, a European Directive which requires national regulation), market failures (for instance, the need of disclosure requirements), other kinds of social purposes (for instance, the need to provide public education or public health care) and so on.

If the response to the second question – *Is this legislation still necessary?* – is NO, the legislation may be repealed, according to established principles and procedures (Actuality, Necessity and Proportionality test, see chapter two, section 2.5). If the response is YES, the following step is checking possible alternatives to such legislation also in terms of regulatory options (for instance, self-regulation or simplification or other public policy tools, such as a communication campaign). If the response to the question *Is there an alternative to such legislation?* is NO, legislation should be maintained and assessed from an anticorruption perspective (for instance by establishing controls or by requiring staff rotation, by reforming sanctions, by resorting to positive incentives, it depends on the content and on the responsiveness of regulation). If the response is YES, regulatory alternatives must be identified and assessed for the purpose of reducing their corruptibility. In any case, the process impose an accurate monitoring of corruption cases related to such legislation and to its delivery at the administrative level. If this monitoring – possible thanks to criminal databases and to available databases in matters of controls and litigation – makes evident any persistent corruption, the corruptibility assessment starts again.

Figure 5.1 Corruptibility Assessment: Assessing a Piece of Primary Corruptible Legislation

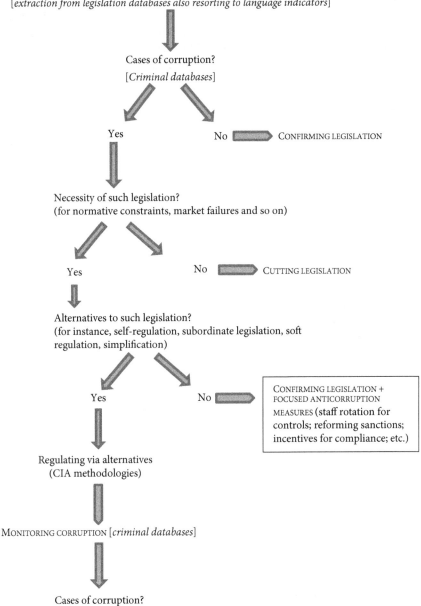

186 Combating Corruption via Regulation and Controls: Which Formula?

To sum up, in order to prevent corruption, an integrated regulatory anticorruption strategy is needed. The strategy should be based on criminal evidence translated in administrative language; focused on opportunities for rent-seeking, infringements and corruption offered by legislation at the administrative level; developed in corruption but also in corruptibility assessment of legislation; and oriented to monitor the presence and the persistence of corruption on the basis of objective indicators, by focusing on the regulatory stock and flow of countries.

Figure 5.2 Corruptibility Assessment in short

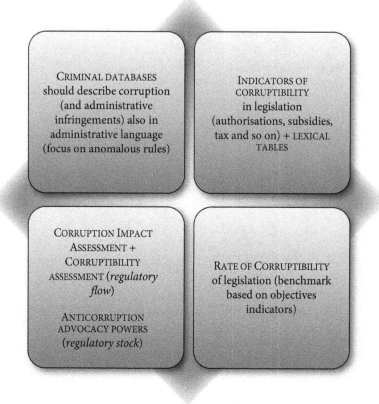

It goes without saying that the outcome of regulatory anticorruption may result from any activity which is carried out by parliaments, governments, public administrations, independent agencies or by any individual public agent intended to contribute to making legislation and regulation effective.

5.4. Combating Corruption: Who?

Corruption may be analysed, studied and understood; anticorruption may be accurately designed, implemented and provided with resources. In any case, both corruption and anticorruption revolve around a human element, which is very difficult to steer and to predict, even in the presence of ever more sophisticated behavioural insights. Corruption and anticorruption, in fact, are not impersonally conducted by 'the business' or 'the citizen', by 'the state' or by 'the public administration' but by humans,[43] each playing their own role in the institutional game.

This is especially true when talking about 'who' has to combat corruption. In particular, who has the responsibility to start the process of anticorruption? What resources, training and incentives have to be arranged to this purpose? By means of which powers and in which institutional network they should operate? Among any other possible actors on stage, legislators and regulators, public agencies (and officers) as well as anticorruption bodies are responsible for implementing convincing and trustworthy anticorruption policies, before and more than any other actors on scene (citizens, companies, advisors and consultants, lobbies, the media and so on). On the other hand, the broader legal and institutional context may be characterised by criminalisation and liability for public officers: never forget that this matters and that defensive bureaucracy must be carefully considered.

5.4.1. Legislators and Regulators

Legislators and regulators seem to be placed right in the front line of the regulatory battle against corruption. To be more precise, legislators and regulators are placed in a position from which (intentionally or unintentionally, it matters little) they have long contributed to creating rent, not only via political/legislative corruption (by favouring interest groups) but via the production of corruptible rules, in other words by increasing the risk of administrative corruption due to poor-quality lawmaking and rule-making and to lack of adequate consideration of legislative and regulatory delivery.

Even though government and other regulators (such as independent authorities) have become ever more relevant than in the past when it comes to producing rules, even today parliaments remain at the centre of the legislative function.[44]

---

[43] Karl Popper, *The Open Society and its Enemies* (Princeton University Press, 2020; 1st edn 1945) 120–21: 'There is another distinction within the field of political problems corresponding to that between persons and institutions. It is the one between the problems of the day and the problems of the future. While the problems of the day are largely personal, the building of the future must necessarily be institutional.'

[44] On this point see many contributions in the book by Maria De Benedetto, Nicola Lupo and Nicoletta Rangone (eds), *The crisis of confidence in legislation* (Nomos/Hart, 2020).

For this reason, the parliament may be considered as the access point to the expert system of legislation[45] and it is symbolically relevant for the reliability of any restoration of confidence in legislation policy, such as anticorruption policies. In this regard, not only is specific anticorruption legislation relevant but each 'sensitive' piece of legislation which provides costs or benefits, establishes prohibitions or restrictions, allocates regulatory powers or has an impact on law enforcement capacity. In all these cases, parliaments should take corruptibility of legislation seriously and carry out any possible efforts in the law-making process to assess, limit and take it under control.

Adopting the point of view of parliaments, two aspects deserve attention, both considered in the context of the regulatory anticorruption toolkit: interests and quality of legislation. Regarding *interests*,[46] the distribution of costs following a piece of legislation is highly significant for political consensus-building and in order to make concrete transparency in the legislative process, in this way affecting trust, credibility and reliability of anticorruption policies. Regarding *quality of legislation*, parliamentary legislation despite difficulties is expected to be good quality and adopted in a transparent way; provided through impact assessment and consultations; followed by monitoring and ex post evaluation in order to make sure that legislative objectives have been achieved. Similar comments can be made for governments and other regulators (such as independent authorities), being applicable in any kind of rule-making processes.

5.4.2. Public Agents and Enforcement Officers (in General)

From a regulatory anticorruption perspective, working for effective regulation is the principal and the cheapest administrative anticorruption strategy. However, effectiveness greatly depends on regulatory delivery which summarises a number of administrative tasks (ie implementation, controls and inspections, sanctioning and so on). Poor implementation and improper enforcement (not infrequently

---

[45] Anthony Giddens *The Consequence of Modernity* (Polity Press, 1990) 27–28: 'Let us now look at the nature of expert systems. By expert systems I mean systems of technical accomplishment or professional expertise that organise large areas of the material and social environments in which we live today. Most laypersons consult "professionals" – lawyers, architects, doctors, and so forth – only in a periodic or irregular fashion. But the systems in which the knowledge of experts is integrated influence many aspects of what we do in a continuous way. I know very little about the codes of knowledge used by the architect and the builder in the design and construction of the home, but I nonetheless have "faith" in what they have done. My "faith" is not so much in them, although I have to trust their competence, as in the authenticity of the expert knowledge which they apply, something which I cannot usually check exhaustively myself.'

[46] Mancur Olson, *The Logic of Collective Action: Public Goods and the Theory of Groups* (Harvard University Press, 1971); see also Gunnar Trumbull, *Strength in numbers: the political power of weak interests* (Harvard University Press, 2012).

due to poor-quality rules) are often the basis of regulatory failures and also the occasion for corrupt agreements.

In other words, public agents and enforcement officers (such as inspectors) are unavoidably placed at the centre of the discourse about corruption and anticorruption:[47] if their involvement is indispensable in order to qualify an infringement as corruption (no public agent, no corruption), they are absolutely decisive when anticorruption policies aim to reverse the course by seeking to refocus public agents and enforcement officers on regulatory objectives entrusted to their care.

Some general caveats may help to outline a remarkably simple reasoning, with no claim of completeness.

Firstly, when developing anticorruption strategies, public administration should no longer be considered as an abstract entity.[48] Due to the fact that institutions live thanks to humans, human motivations matter, behaviour and needs have to be seriously considered in the regulatory game.

Secondly, humans are not monads; rather they live within relations, they need trust and social recognition, even when they play a role in institutions. The relationship between the state (principal) and its public agents[49] is very significant and should be fiduciary, with clear objectives and mandates, well defined outcomes[50] and stable procedural expectations,[51] in order to make any evaluation of administrative performances possible.

Thirdly, in order to play their institutional role, public agents and enforcement officers should be in the condition to do so: they should have proper skills and adequate training; they may refer to a network of colleagues with whom to share experiences and problems as well as to strengthen the self-perception of their institutional function; they should respond to a system of incentives consistent with their administrative function. Moreover, they should be in the condition to actively contribute to the process and this will be possible only by 'creating a constructive approach to *failure* and encouraging *voice* [in this way helping] significantly in lowering the impact of defensive decision making in an organization'.[52]

---

[47] On this point, see Eugene Bardach and Robert A Kagan, *Going by the Book: The Problem of Regulatory Unreasonableness* (Transaction Publishers, 2010; originally published 1982 by Temple University Press).

[48] In general, on this point, see Michael W Bauer, 'Public Administration and Political Science', in Eduardo Ongaro and Sandra van Thiel, (eds), *The Palgrave Handbook of Public Administration and Management in Europe*, Vol 2 (Palgrave Macmillan, 2018) 1054 where he describes the interaction between institutions, instruments and individuals.

[49] FE Dowrick, 'The Relationship of Principal and Agent' (1954) 17(1) *Modern Law Review* 24.

[50] Frédérique E Six, 'Building Interpersonal Trust Within Organizations: A Relational Signaling Perspective' (2007) 11 (3) *Journal of Management of Governance* 285, 292.

[51] Robert Baldwin and Martin Cave, *Taming the corporation. How to regulate for success*, 15.

[52] See Florian Artinger, Sabrina Artinger and Gerd Gigerenzer, 'C. Y. A.: frequency and causes of defensive decisions in public administration' (2019) 12(9) *Business Research* 22.

5.4.3. Anticorruption Bodies (in Particular)

Anticorruption bodies are a relatively new kind of beast in the administrative zoo. They belong to the broad family of external controllers of administrative activity, being in charge of different tasks and competences (as already mentioned in chapter two). They have been introduced only recently, according to recommendations and directives mainly coming from international organisations to the purpose of developing anticorruption preventive systems at national level.

On the other hand, while the presence of these institutions has developed an increasing number of additional administrative burdens, they have been not considered to express relevant anticorruption results. However, what do anticorruption bodies have to do in order to be effective in preventing such an insidious phenomenon? How should they operate to support administration without oppressing it with unnecessary burdens? Which are the peculiarities of their preventive administrative anticorruption when dealing with criminal prosecution of corruption cases?

Responding to these questions from a regulatory anticorruption perspective (first of all) involves a shifting of the focus, from administrative activities and innumerable cases of corruption (downstream), to rules and regulation as opportunities for rent-seeking, infringements and corruption (upstream).

A first type of competences should be understood by administrative *intelligence*, continuous and accurate classification of rent-seeking and incentive system, by developing indicators for carrying out an anticorruption diagnosis in the regulatory stock, applicable also to the purpose of preventive evaluation in the regulatory flow.

A second type of competences should also be understood by the wide emerging function of *anticorruption advocacy* (report, opinions, reporting powers and recommendations), already developed in the field of competition law, in order to identify the opportunities for infringements and corruption present in legislation/regulation and to indicate to majoritarian and non-majoritarian institutions in charge of legislation and regulation interventions which aim at reducing the presence of types of rules that most frequently constitute or reinforce the risk of corruption incidents or at providing for these rules adequate mechanisms to reduce risk (in procedural design, with the provision of controls and the definition of more effective procedures for their performance, of collective decisions instead of single-person decisions, etc).

Only anticorruption bodies may do this job, not only because only they have the expertise to materially carry out this particular assessment but also because they are in charge of the mission 'anticorruption'. This suggests a more explicit mobilisation of ACBs in reviewing legislation and institutional setups by disclosing rent-creation and rent-creators, in so doing counteracting opportunities for rent-extraction, both at political and at administrative level.

5.5. Trust vs Corruption: Governing the Intangible

Adopting a regulatory perspective is a promising path, both to attaining progress in understanding corruption and to improving anticorruption policies. From such a perspective, administrative corruption is not only an infringement involving a public agent, but regulatory ineffectiveness and a serious lack of good administration;[53] rules are determinants of administrative corruption processes and in the same way they may represent an anticorruption tool; controls, far from exclusively being a way to combat infringements and corruption, may often be the occasion for corrupt transactions and for this reason they should be used with caution, according to specific recommendations (chapter four).

This regulatory perspective has focused on an integrated regulatory anticorruption strategy which is informed by effectiveness of regulation (in general) and (in particular) by administrative anticorruption purposes, based mainly on better regulation tools (simplification, impact assessment in general) but also on emerging tools, such as transparency about interests, anticorruption assessment of regulation (corruption impact assessment and corruptibility assessment) and anticorruption management of regulatory stock (anticorruption advocacy powers). Some other tools are important both for regulatory effectiveness and for administrative anticorruption, but in the RA strategy what is also clear is their ambiguity and the risk of backfire, in the case of consultation and controls (which may result in corruption) as well as in the case of communication (which highlights inconsistencies between legislation/regulation and their delivery or which may exacerbate bad news, in this way contributing to a reduction of trust in legislation and compliance).

Table 5.5 Regulatory Anticorruption (a Recap)

TYPE	TOOL	GOAL
Consolidated better regulation tools	*Simplification*	Regulatory effectiveness.
	Impact assessment (and other quality of regulation tools)	
Emerging anticorruption tools	*Tracing interest*	Early anticorruption and transparency. Regulatory effectiveness.
	Corruption impact assessment	
	Corruptibility assessment	
	Anticorruption advocacy powers	
Tools to be used with caution (from an anticorruption perspective)	*Consultation*	Regulatory effectiveness. Anticorruption and transparency (risk of backfire)
	Controls	
	Communication	

---

[53] See on this point, Jill Wakefield, *The right to good administration* (Kluwer, 2007).

Within this framework, regulators should take into the greatest possible consideration also the human, intangible side of regulation: rules, corruption and controls interact with each others as an expression of human liberty; law is a simple attempt to persuade people to adopt socially preferred behaviour; coercion (which always implies bureaucracy) is not always possible, not always effective, not always desirable. All this opens a door on a largely explored 'governance of the intangible'.[54] In fact, even though many causal correlations have still to be studied,[55] the quality of social life, the effectiveness of legal systems, their attractiveness for business, and the prosperity of nations depend largely on intangible factors, among others (and more than any others) trust (chapter one).

Trust is a highly desirable commodity of common life: it presents strong economic relevance,[56] 'helps make governments work better',[57] reduces uncertainty and conflict by increasing cooperation[58] and compliance. On the other hand, trust is resistant to power in the sense that is impossible to coerce, government does not generate trust,[59] trust is not simple to achieve. Trust cannot be bought in a drugstore, be produced in a factory or imposed by decree. When trust in institutions decreases it may only be restored: confidence restoring (or trust repairing) policies are greatly influenced by reciprocity[60] and by comprehensibility of legislation and regulation.[61] From an anticorruption perspective, restoring trust includes an accurate analysis of the reasons which have motivated corruption, as well as an understanding of distrust motivations.[62] In this regard, it suffices to remember that a certain amount of corruption is connected to bad administration.

- *Who has the responsibility for starting the process* of repairing trust in order to increase regulatory effectiveness and to reduce corruption, as far

---

[54] On this aspect, in general, see Stephen MR Covey, *The Speed of Trust. The One Thing That Changes Everything* (Simon & Schuster, 2014). See also Robert C Solomon and Fernando Flores, *Building Trust in Business, Politics, Relationships, and Life* (Oxford University Press, 2001).

[55] Alberto Alesina and Paola Giuliano, 'Culture and institutions' (2015) 53(4) *Journal of Economic Literature* 898.

[56] See, on this point, Partha Dasgupta, 'Trust as a commodity', in Diego Gambetta (ed), *Trust: Making and breaking cooperative relations* (Blackwell, 1988) 65.

[57] Eric M Uslaner, *The Moral Foundations of Trust* (Cambridge University Press, 2002) 8.

[58] Niklas Luhmann, *Trust and Power* (Polity Press, 2017; 1st German edn 1973) 102.

[59] Anthony Pagden, 'The Destruction of Trust and its Economic Consequences in the Case of Eighteenth-century Naples', in Diego Gambetta (ed) *Trust: Making and Breaking Cooperative Relations*, 127. 'no central agency is capable of intentionally creating trust where none previously or independently existed'.

[60] Lawrence C Becker, 'Trust as noncognitive security about motives' (1996) 107(1) *Ethics* 43, where he argues 'for the importance for political philosophy of pursuing an inquiry into the more neglected of the two areas, the noncognitive one. In particular, ... for the importance of what I will call a sense of security about other people's benevolence, conscientiousness, and reciprocity'.

[61] On regulatory comprehensibility see Wendy E Wagner and Will Walker, *Incomprehensible! A Study of How Our Legal System Encourages Incomprehensibility, Why It Matters, and What We Can Do About It* (Cambridge University Press, 2019) and Rachel Augustine Potter, 'Incomprehensibility is a Trust Problem' (31 March 2020) in *The Regulatory Review*: 'Fostering trust in the rulemaking process is a tall order'.

[62] About the importance to develop a theory of distrust, see Eri Bertsou, 'Rethinking political distrust' (2019) 11(2) *European Political Science Review* 213; on this aspect see also Vivien Hart, *Distrust and*

as possible? There is no doubt that *institutions* (and especially parliaments[63]) have to take the first step because they have contributed (no matter if intentionally or unintentionally) to introduce corruptible regulation; because they unavoidably play a special role;[64] because their sort of dominance[65] raises a special responsibility.

- *What might be the benefits of trust repairing policies?* Trust repairing policies move on a level in which freedom is required to activate ethical responses. Freedom constitutes a risk but regulation should accept it, according to its careful assessment of possible harm. Otherwise society will tend to be ever more oppressed by law and a further risk will present itself: trust poverty, a new dramatic pathology which developed countries are experiencing as indicator of decline.

- *What might be the risks of trust repairing policies?* Politicians, regulators and public administration must not mess with trust repairing policies because trust is simpler to destroy than to restore. Institutional communication must be based on facts, consistent, respectful and durable. For this reason, trust restoring policies are possible only as part of a bipartisan, institutional agreement which works as a platform and as a limit for raw political competition, by defining a sort of playground. In order to prevent corruption, regulators must move a step behind, leaving space improperly regulated and promoting trust;[66] at the same time they have to move a step ahead, by redeeming all core competences of the administrative state[67] and by orienting them towards positive regulation,[68] in this way promoting trust.

As a concluding remark, corruption should be considered objectively and institutionally, collecting any possible kind of evidence, with presence of mind, capacity

---

Democracy (Cambridge University Press, 1978) and Joseph S Nye, Philip D Zelikow and David C King (eds), *Why People Do Not Trust Government* (Harvard University Press, 1997).

[63] Pedro C Magalhães, 'Confidence in Parliaments: Performance, Representation, and Accountability', in Mariano Torcal and José Ramón Montero, *Political Disaffection in Contemporary Democracies. Social Capital, Institutions and Politics* (Routledge, 2006) 190; see also Tom Van der Meer, 'In what we trust? A multi-level study into trust in parliament as an evaluation of state characteristics' (2010) 76(3) *International Review of Administrative Sciences*, 517.

[64] Regarding the idea that a libertarian paternalism is possible, see Richard Thaler and Cass Sunstein, 'Libertarian Paternalism' (2001) 93 *American Economic Review* 175 and 'Libertarian Paternalism is Not an Oxymoron' (2003) 70(4) *University of Chicago Law Review* 1159.

[65] Regarding dominant position in competition law, see ECJ Case 322/81, *Michelin v Commission* (1983) ECR 3461, para 57: 'A finding that an undertaking has a dominant position is not in itself a recrimination but simply means that, irrespective of the reasons for which it has such a dominant position, the undertaking concerned has a special responsibility not to allow its conduct to impair genuine undistorted competition on the common market.'

[66] Johann Graf Lambsdorff, 'Preventing Corruption by Promoting Trust. Insights from Behavioral Science' Passauer Diskussionspapiere, Volkswirtschaftliche Reihe V-69-15, University of Passau, Faculty of Business and Economics, 2015.

[67] Adrian Vermeule and Cass R Sunstein, *Law and Leviathan. Redeeming the Administrative State* (Harvard University Press, 2020).

[68] See Robert Baldwin and Martin Cave, *Taming the corporation. How to regulate for success.*

of aggregate diagnosis and avoiding any generic moralistic evaluation as well as any inconclusive moralistic solutions. At the end of the day, regulatory anticorruption may be only a proposal of realism in government, an institutional application of the general principle 'whoever is without sin, cast the first stone' associated with a couple of ideas: limiting 'time thieving'[69] bureaucracy as far as possible, and recognising that if each has a part to play, those who have the extremely relevant institutional task of adopting and enforcing rules, must play leading roles in indicating the way forward.

---

[69] See Francesco Barbieri and Giorgio Giavazzi, *I signori del tempo perso. I burocrati che frenano l'Italia e come provare a sconfiggerli* (Longanesi, 2017) who defined bureaucrats as 'the lords of the lost time'.

INDEX

accountability *see* transparency and accountability
actuality, necessity and proportionality (ANP test)   86, 184
administrative advocacy
   ACBs, of   103–4, 179–80, 190
   anticorruption rules, and   102–5
   competition rules, and   101–2
   definition   100–2
   importance of   100–1
   legislative scrutiny   102
   rule-making, and   104–5
administrative capacity   137, 140–1, 143, 156
administrative controls   47, 49–55
   ACBs, role of   52–3
   criticisms and limitations   54–5
   external controls   50–3
   financial controls   51–2
   internal controls   53–4
   judicial review   50
   objective corruption   41–3
   parliamentary controls   50
   policing, theory of   130–3
   Supreme Audit Institutions (SAIs), role of   51–2
administrative corruption
   anticorruption approaches to   64–6
   authorisation powers, role of   176–9
   conflicts of interest, and   37
   controls over (*see* administrative controls)
   corruptibility assessments, and   176–9
   distortive effects of   64–6
   influences on   167–8
   interpretation   34, 36, 42–3
   objective corruption   41–3
   regulatory ineffectiveness, and   167–8, 182
   rent-creation, and   89–90
   value-neutral economic perspective on   63–4
administrative costs   138–9
administrative knowledge   146
administrative tolerance   137–8

advocacy powers
   ACBs, of   103–4, 179–80, 190
   regulatory stock, and   100–5, 183
   anticorruption rules, and   102–5
   competition rules, and   101–2
   legislative scrutiny   102
African Union Convention on Preventing and Combating Corruption 2003   67
algorithms   126–7
anticorruption bodies (ACBs)
   administrative controls   52–3
   advocacy powers   103–4, 179–80, 190
   anticorruption responsibilities of   190
   corruptibility assessments   179–80
   law enforcement   71, 104
   prevention and investigation   70–2, 104
   rule-making   104–5
   Specialised ACBs   71–2, 104
   types of   70–2, 104
anticorruption controls
   effectiveness of
      communication, and   66, 159–62
      enforcement, and   158–9, 165–6
      influences on   145–66
      information, and   146–51, 164
      planning, and   156–7, 165
      privacy and data protection   153–5, 165
      reform, and   162–4, 166
      regulation, and   151–3, 165, 173
   integrated anticorruption strategy   170–1
   limitations of   136
   practical perspective
      administrative capacity, limits of   140–1
      administrative tolerance, and   137–8
      communication, and   137–8, 145, 159–62, 166
      controls, costs of   138–9
      effective sanctions, necessity of   4, 143–5
      enforcement   136–8, 141–3, 158–9, 165–6
      hybridity   136–7
      information   146–51, 164
      personal contact   136

planning approaches 141–3, 156–7, 165
privacy and data protection 153–5, 165
reform 162–4, 166
regulation 151–3, 165
public-private partnership, need for 20–1
purpose of 122–4, 170
sanctions 4, 143–5
theoretical perspective 48–9, 122–4
  algorithms and AI 126–7
  controlling as governing 133–5
  costs of controls 126
  efficiency, of 124–7
  inspections, role of 133–5
  Panopticon model 124–6
  policing, theory of 130–3
  pyramid of enforcement 128–9, 158–9
  regulatory theory 127–30
anticorruption risks
  backfire 79, 143–4, 146
  defensive administration 82–3
  metastatic bureaucracy 81
  perception *vs.* reality 79–80
  recruitment challenges 83–4
  side-effects, generally 77–8, 86
anticorruption rules 4
  challenges for 92, 98–100
  management and maintenance of 92–4
  market and profit of 90–2
  monitoring 110–11
  over-regulation 98–100
  purpose of 87–8
  regulatory flow
    anticorruption tools 107–11
    corruption proofing 108–9
    good quality regulation 106–7, 183
    impact assessments 106–11
    interests in the legislative/ regulatory process 111–20, 183–4
    legislative assessment 105–11
    lobbying and consultation 112–20
    management of 94
    monitoring 110–11
    overview 121
    risk of crime assessments 109–10
  regulatory stock
    administrative advocacy 100–5
    competition law 101–2
    management of 94
    overview 120
    quality 8–9, 96–8, 106–7, 183, 188
    simplification 95–100, 183
  zero-option approach 93

anticorruption strategies
  actuality, necessity and proportionality (ANP test) 86, 184
  administrative connotation 62
  administrative strategies 35
  anticorruption bodies (ACBs), types of 70–1
  behavioural approach 73–6, 78, 171
  bureaucracy, creation of 80
  conventional approach 72–3, 78
  design features 70–1, 93
  development 62
  domestic administrative strategies 70–2
  feasible objectives 84–6
  global/ regional policies 5, 66–9
    conditionality 69
    international conventions 67–9
    state obligations 68–9
  incentive-disincentive approach 170–1, 175
  limitations of 4, 61, 66, 80, 92
  prevention of corruption
    administrative perspective 65–6
    approaches 64–6
    dual truth concept 64
    economic perspective 65
    moral perspective 64
    policy development 62
    private trust arrangements, influences of 64–5
    regulatory perspective 65, 92–4, 191
    social perspective 64–5
    state obligations 68
  purpose of 34–5
  regulatory approach 65, 76–8, 82–3, 86, 173
  risks of
    backfire 79, 143–4, 146
    defensive administration 82–3
    metastatic bureaucracy 81
    perception *vs.* reality 79–80
    recruitment challenges 83–4
    side-effects, generally 77–8, 86
  trust, role of 64–5, 83–4
artificial intelligence 126–7
authorisations 44, 176–9
Ayres, I. 128–9

backfire, risks of 79, 143–4, 146
Banca Romana scandal 61
behavioural approach 73–6, 78, 171, 173, 175
Bentham, J. 124–5
bounded capability 123
bounded morality 123
bounded rationality 123

Index 197

Braithwaite, J. 128–9
building permits, authorisation 42

canon law 135
civil service, anticorruption strategies 68, 84, 87
coercion 6–8, 29–31, 58, 135, 192
  policing, and 131–3
combating corruption
  approaches
    alternative regulation, identification of 184
    behavioural approach 73–6, 78, 171, 173, 175
    conventional approach 72–3, 78, 171–3
    corruptibility assessment 174–82, 184–6
    cost reduction 172
    criminal databases, role of 147, 174, 180–2
    downstream vs. upstream 167–8
    generally 167–71
    identification and assessment protocols 174–82
    incentive-disincentive approach 170–1, 175
    increased risk of control 172
    integrated approach 172–3
    practical applications 182–6
    reasons for 169–70
    regulatory anticorruption strategies (see anticorruption strategies)
    regulatory checklists 184
    regulatory toolkits 174–82
    responsibility for 170
    sanctions 172–3
    trust, role of 189, 191–4
  responsibility for 170, 187–90
    ACBs 190
    legislators and regulators 187–8
    public agents and enforcement officers 188–9
communication
  anticorruption controls, and 137–8, 145
  compliance, influences on 159–60
  effectiveness of 159–62, 166
  journalism, role of 160–2
  public communication 161
competition law 101–2
compliance
  anticorruption measures 21–2
  approaches 18–20
    cooperative 22, 25, 48, 73, 100, 128, 135, 158

behaviour, and
  compliance certification 20–3
  compliance decisions 16–18, 144
  compliance generation 18–20
certification mechanisms 20–3
deterrence, and 19–20
effectiveness of 25–9
enforcement (*see* enforcement)
influences on
  communication 159–60
  cost reduction 172
  increased risk of control 172
  organisational culture 21–3
  penalties and sanctions 172–3
non-compliance
  creative compliance 18
  penalties 58–60
  reasons for 16–20
over-regulation, implications of 18
programmes 21
reasons for 16–20
regulatory compliance concept 20–1
risk, evaluation of 172
sanctions, and 172–3
trust, role of 29–32
compliance letters 149–50
conditionality 69
conflicts of interest
  administrative tolerance, and 138
  corruption, and 36–7
    actuality vs. possibility 37–8
    impartiality 38
    interpretation 38
    morality, and 39
    over-regulation 38–40
    regulation of 37–8
consultation
  interest representation model 113
  lobbying, and 112–20
controls
  administrative activities, over 47, 49–55
    anticorruption agencies, role of 52–3
    criticisms and limitations 54–5
    external controls 50–3
    financial controls 51–2
    internal controls 53–4
    judicial review 50
    objective corruption 41–3
    parliamentary controls 50

public internal controls 53–4
Supreme Audit Institutions (SAIs), role of 51–2
administrative capacity, limits of 137, 140–1, 143, 156
anticorruption perspective 45–7
convergence 46
corruption, and
   capacities of 84–5
   feasible objectives 84–6
   optimal levels of 84–5, 140
   relationship between 44
costs of 126
criticisms and limitations of 47–9, 54–5
culture and corruption 75
culture of control 46
definition 44–5, 47
economic theory perspective 49
effectiveness 47–9
features of 46
freedoms, and 122–3
governance, possibility without 133–5
law, role in 127–8
legal theory perspective 48–9
objective corruption, and 43–4
Panopticon model 124–6
policing, theory of 130–3
Principal-Agent-Client model 47–8
private activities, over 47, 55–60
   administrative approval controls 56
   compliance and enforcement, and 55–6, 59–60
   conformity controls 56
   criticism and limitations 59–60
   desk-based controls 57–8
   economic regulator controls 56
   field-based controls 58–9
   fundamental rights, conflicts with 57, 59
   inspections 58–9
   non-compliance penalties 58–60
   organisational sustainability 59
   outsourced knowledge 57
   purpose of 56–7
   self-generated knowledge 57
   soft regulation, role of 56–7
   types of 56
purpose of 45, 122–4, 127–8, 133–4
pyramid of enforcement 128–9, 158–9
sustainability, need for 139
total control 140

conventional approach 72–3, 78, 171–3
corruptibility 40–4, 168
   actuality vs. probability 40–1
   administrative powers 41–3
   assessments 174–82
      advocacy powers of ACBs 179–80
      alternative regulation, identification of 184
      authorisation powers, role of 176–9
      corruption impact assessments 108–9, 176
      protocols for 176–80, 184–6
      regulatory flow 105–11
      regulatory incentives 174–6
   controls 43–4
   human nature, and 45
   objective corruption 41–4
corruption
   active vs. passive 36
   administrative corruption 34, 36
   classification/ types of 34, 36
   conflicts of interest, and 36–7
      actuality vs. possibility 37–8
      impartiality 38
      interpretation 38
      morality, and 39
      over-regulation 38–40
      regulation of 37–40
   corruptibility, and 40–5, 168
   costs of, increasing 175
   criminal influences 34, 36
   definitions 32–6, 41, 87, 168
   distortive effects of 64–6, 169
   economic issue, as 33
   genetics of 174–5
   institutional issue, as 33–4
   justifications for 63–4
   morality, and 33, 39, 169
   objective corruption 41–4
   opportunities for, role of law in creation of 88–9
   over-regulation, and 38–40
   perception, role of 32–3
   political corruption 34, 36
   Principal-Agent-Client model 35–6
   regulation, relationship with 88–92
   regulatory issue, as 34–6
   rent-creation, and 89–92
   rent-seeking, and 36, 89–92, 175
   rules as causes of 88–92
   social impacts of 169
   social tolerance for 61

subjective corruption 41
taxation, relationship with 65
value-neutral economics, and 63–4
corruption impact assessments (CIA) 108–9, 176
Corruption Perceptions Index (CPI) 67
corruption proofing 108–9
costs
  administrative costs 138–9
  businesses and citizens, for 139
  controls, of 126, 139
  corruption, of 175
  non-compliance, of 139
  reputational costs 139
  transaction costs 139
COVID-19 pandemic 57, 150

data protection
  anticorruption controls, effectiveness of 153–5, 165
  COVID-19 pandemic 57
  invasiveness of 154
  remedies for breach 155
databases
  automation and data matching 147
  criminal databases 147, 174, 180–2
  data banks, role and limitations of 147–8, 150–1, 174, 180–2
  privacy and data protection conflicts 153–5
  statistical analysis 181–2
deterrence
  enforcement model 25
  rule compliance, and 19–20
  sanctions, role of 143–5
  whistle-blower protection 149

economic perspectives 49, 63–5
enforcement *see also* **sanctions**
  administrative capacity, and 137, 140–1, 143, 156
  administrative organisation, and 159, 166
  administrative procedure, and 158, 165–6
  administrative tolerance, and 137–8
  anticorruption controls, effectiveness of 158–9, 165–6
  comprehensive risk-based approach 141–2
  evidence-based approach 141–2
  governance, as form of 133–5
  intelligence, compared with 148, 150–1
  levels of 142
  planning approaches 141–3
  policing, theory of 130–3

pyramid of enforcement 128–9, 158–9
regulatory delivery 129–30
enforcement officials
  administrative tolerance, and 138
  personal contact 136
  responsibility for combating corruption 188–9
  robust procedures, need for 145
  training, adequacy of 189

four eyes principle 123
freedom of the press 161–2

global anticorruption policies 66

Hampton Report (UK) 46, 141, 162
hotspots 153

impact assessments 106–7
  corruption impact assessments (CIA) 108–9, 176
  enforcement planning, and 142
  procedural reform 162
  specialised impact assessments 107–11
information
  anticorruption controls, and
  automation and data matching 147
  backfire, risk of 146
  compliance letters 149–50
  data banks, role and limitations of 147–8, 150–1
  effectiveness of 146–51, 164
  evidence-based policy making, and 150–1
  information exchange 150–1
  information overload, risks of 148, 154
  intelligence *vs.* concrete enforcement 148, 150–1
  privacy and data protection conflicts 153–5
  provision incentives 149
  regulation, influences on 152
inspections
  control and governance, relationship with 133–5
  personal contact, influences of 136
  private activities, controls over 58–9, 136, 138
  procedural reform 162
  proportionality, and 142
Inter-American Convention against Corruption 1996 67

journalism 160–2
judicial review 50

law, generally
  controls, role in 127–8
  corruption opportunities, creation of 88–9
  definition of 6–7
  legislation, relationship with 6–9
  maintenance of 93–4
  responsibilities of 88
legislation, generally
  definition 6–7
  improper/intrusive 8
  law, relationship with 6–9
  legislative inflation 9, 18
  quality of 8–9, 96–8, 106–7, 163, 183, 188
  role of 4, 7–8
  symbolic legislation 8
legislators, anticorruption responsibilities of 187–8, 193
lobbying 111–20
  benefits and limitations of 116–20
  recording objects approach 117–18
  recording results approach 118
  recording subjects approach 117–18
  rule-making, influences on 113–15
  standards 115–16
  transparency and traceability 119–20

morality 33, 39, 64, 123, 169

National Recovery and Resilience Plan 5, 104–5, 180
necessity
  actuality, necessity and proportionality (ANP test) 86, 184

objective corruption 41–4
  administrative powers type corruption 41–3
  control type corruption 43–4
OECD
  anticorruption recommendations 67
  regulatory enforcement and inspections recommendations 141–2
  regulatory reforms 163
  transparency in lobbying recommendations 115–16, 120
over-regulation
  corruption, and conflicts of interest 38–40
  simplification, role of 98–100

Panopticon model 124–6
parliamentary controls 50, 187–8, 193
planning, of anticorruption controls
  behavioural and cognitive influences 157
  criticism of 157
  effectiveness of 156–7, 165
  risk-analysis 156–7
policing, theory of 130–3
political corruption 167–8
prevention of corruption
  administrative perspective 65–6
  combating, approaches to 64–6
  dual truth concept 64
  economic perspective 65
  moral perspective 64
  policy development 62
  private trust arrangements, influences of 64–5
  regulatory perspective 65, 92–4, 191
  responsibilities for 170, 187–90
  social perspective 64–5
  state obligations 68
Principal-Agent-Client model 35–6, 47–8, 72, 74
privacy and data protection
  anticorruption controls, effectiveness of 153–5, 165
  big data, use of 155
  consumer profiling 155
  invasiveness 154
  remedies for breach 155
private activities, controls over 47, 55–60
  administrative approval controls 56
  compliance and enforcement, and 55–6, 59–60
  conformity controls 56
  criticism and limitations 59–60
  desk-based controls 57–8
  economic regulator controls 56
  field-based controls 58–9
  fundamental rights, conflicts with 57, 59
  inspections 58–9
  non-compliance penalties 58–60
  organisational sustainability 59
  outsourced knowledge 57
  purpose 56–7
  self-generated knowledge 57
  soft regulation, role of 56–7
proportionality 91–2
  actuality, necessity and proportionality (ANP test) 86, 184

enforcement approaches, in 142
 sanctions 144
public agents, anticorruption
 responsibilities 188–9
Public Internal Controls (PIC) systems 53–4
public procurement 68, 72–3, 81
pyramid of enforcement 128–9, 158–9

reform of anticorruption controls
 design principles 163–4
 effectiveness of 162–4, 166
 organisational reforms 164
 regulatory quality 163
regulation, generally
 anticorruption controls
  effectiveness of 151–3, 165, 173
  hotspots 153
  information quality, role of 152
 consequences, link with 10–11
 corruption, relationship with 88–92
 counterproductivity of 175
 definition 10–11
 effectiveness of 13–14, 19, 22–7
 European perspectives on 11–15
 good quality 96–8, 106–7, 183
 impact assessments 106–7
  corruption impact assessments
   (CIA) 108–9, 176
  specialised impact assessments 107–11
 legal convergence, implications of 11–12
 linguistic interpretation challenges 12–13
 lobbying 111–20
 logic of 11–12
 over-regulation 18, 98–100
 profit-making tool, as 90–2
 rules, relationship between 10–16, 173
 smart regulation 15, 106
regulators, anticorruption
 responsibilities 187–8, 193
regulatory approach
 anticorruption strategies 65, 78, 173
  defensive administration risks of 82–3
  interdisciplinarity, and 77
  mechanisms, types of 77
  overview 191
  purpose of 76–7, 94
  risks and objectives 86
 management and maintenance of
  rules 92–4
 prevention of corruption, and 65, 92–4, 191
 zero-option approach 93

regulatory delivery 129–30, 158
Regulatory Fitness and Performance
 Programme (REFIT) 97
regulatory flow
 anticorruption rules and controls
  anticorruption tools 107–11
  corruption proofing 108–9
  effectiveness of 151
  good quality regulation 106–7, 183
  impact assessments 106–11
  interests in the legislative/ regulatory
   process 111–20, 183–4
  legislative assessment 105–11
  lobbying and consultation 112–20
 management of 94
 monitoring 110–11
 overview 121
 risk of crime assessments 109–10
regulatory stock
 advocacy powers 100–5, 183
 anticorruption rules, and 102–5
 competition rules, and 101–2
 legislative scrutiny 102
 anticorruption controls, effectiveness of
  151–2, 183
 competition law 101–2
 corruption proofing 108–9
 interests in the legislative/ regulatory
  process 111–20
  interest representation model 113
  lobbying and consultation 114–20
  standards for consultation 114–16
  transparency, benefits of 114
 management and maintenance of
  92–4
 quality of 96–8, 106–7, 163, 183
 simplification 95–100, 183
  administrative strategies 98
  anticorruption rules, relationship
   with 95–6, 98–100
  competitiveness, and 96
  negative impacts of 95–6
  quality of regulation, and 96–8
  statutory consolidation 97–8
regulatory theory
 anticorruption controls, and 127–30
 policing, and 132–3
 pyramid of enforcement 128–9, 158–9
 regulatory delivery 129–30
rent-creation 89–92
rent-seeking 36, 89–92, 175
risk of crime assessments 109–10

rules, generally
  behaviour, and
    compliance certification 20–3
    compliance decisions 16–18, 144
    compliance generation 18–20
    effectiveness of rules, influences on 23–9
  cause of corruption, as 88–92
  command, prohibitions and permissions 24
  compliance with
    anticorruption measures 21–2
    approaches 18–20
    certification mechanisms 20–3
    creative compliance 18
    deterrence 19–20
    organisational culture, and 21–3
    reasons for 16–20, 144
    regulatory compliance, concept development 20–1
    trust, role of 29–32
  definitions 5–6
  effectiveness of 13–14, 19, 22–3
    compliance and enforcement 25–9
    dysfunction, reasons for 27–9
    functioning, influences on 23–9
    outcome/ impact 27, 29
    steps to 25–7
    trust, role of 29–32
  enforcement 25
  functions of 15–16, 23–5
  incentives and sanctions 24–5
  law, relationship with 6–9
  legislation, and
    law, relationship with 6–9
    quality of 8–9, 96–8, 106–7, 163, 183, 188
    role of 4, 7–8
  management and maintenance of 92–4
  medicines, as 27
  optimal rules 15
  profit-making tool, as 90–2
  regulation, relationship between 10–16, 173
  rule-making
    ACBs, role of 104–5
    administrative advocacy powers 104–5
    interests, influences of 188
    legislative quality 8–9, 96–8, 106–7, 163, 183, 188
    legislators and regulators, role of 50, 187–8
    lobbying and consultation, and 112–20
    transparency and accountability 113–14, 119–20

trust, and
  bounded rationality, and 123
  controls, relationship with 31–2, 123
  institutions, importance of 30–1
  role of 29–32
types of rules 24–5

Saint Paul, doctrine of law and sin 88
sanctions
  compliance role 172–3
  deterrence role 143–5, 170–1, 175
  effectiveness of 4, 143–5
  proportionality 144
  pyramid of enforcement, and 128–9, 158–9
  rules, functions as 24–5
  size, relevance of 143–4
self-generated knowledge 57
smart regulation 15, 106
soft law/ regulation 7, 18, 56–7, 66–7, 102
subsidiarity principle 91–2
Supreme Audit Institutions (SAIs) 51–2

taxation 65
tracing interests 111
transparency and accountability
  international law obligations 68–9
  law reform, and 163
  lobbying and consultation, in 119–20
  rule-making, in 113–14, 119–20
Transparency International 67, 102
trust
  combating corruption, role in 189, 191–4
  private trust arrangements, influences of 64–5
  recruitment challenges 83–4
  rules, and
    bounded rationality, and 123
    controls, relationship with 31–2, 123
    institutions, importance of 30–1
    role of 29–32
  trust-reparing policies 193

United Nations Convention against Corruption 2003 (UNCAC) 67–9

value-neutral economics perspective 63–4

whistle-blowers 149
World Bank 69, 80, 168
Worldwide Governance Indicators (WGI) project 80

Printed in the USA
CPSIA information can be obtained
at www.ICGtesting.com
LVHW010248011023
759716LV00003B/250